WASHINGTON DC: POLITICS AND PLACE

WASHINGTON DC: POLITICS AND PLACE

THE HISTORICAL GEOGRAPHY
OF THE DISTRICT OF COLUMBIA

MARK N. OZER

For further information, please contact:
www.politicsandplace.com

To order additional copies of this book, contact:
Xlibris Corporation
1-888-795-4274
www.Xlibris.com
Orders@Xlibris.com
53591

CONTENTS

List of Plates

Dedication

To all for whom Washington has represented the best of the vision of America as the embodiment of the hope of the world.

ACKNOWLEDGMENTS

This book arose out of my long-standing interest in geography wedded to living in this city whose geographical significance has been buried under its connection to history. It is the interaction of one with the other that has interested me. I have felt that the necessarily superficial focus on the marble monuments by the thousands of bored schoolchildren tends to obscure the true, far more interesting story that a visit during adulthood would bring. I am hopeful that my children and grandchildren will be able to use this book to experience the excitement that I have tried to impart to them. I am indebted to the U.S. Capitol Historical Society for giving some focus on the Capitol building to my long-standing interest. There was also the opportunity to give a well-received course to fellow Washingtonians at American University. Donald Kennon of the U.S. Capitol Historical Society has been supportive; Pamela Scott provided some much-needed rigor to the early versions of the manuscript. I have drawn heavily on her (along with Antoinette Lee's) encyclopedic *Buildings of the District of Columbia* as well as James Goode's *Outdoor Sculpture of Washington, D.C.* I am of course responsible for any errors. On a more personal note, I am indebted to my wife, Martha, who has been my support throughout in all aspects of my life.

INTRODUCTION

Architecture. Sculpture and painting . . . provide evidence, often
more striking and direct manner than literature itself, of the
moral temper and intellectual culture [of those] by whom they
have been practiced . . . and thus become the most effective aids
for the proper understanding of history.

—Charles Eliot Norton, 1873

The United States of America is a government unique in history as the
modern world's first successful rebellion against colonialism. The creative
effort that marked the Constitution was followed almost immediately by
the design of a new community to be its "seat of government" to translate
the separate powers described in the Constitution into physical space
with the legislature enshrined on a hill and the executive less prominent
at a distance away. A sense of rationality imposed order with streets
numbered and alphabetized, and avenues named after states, providing
vistas extending into the distance.

The District of Columbia is a place devoted to politics. Thus, it offers a
unique opportunity to explore the interaction of geography and history,
the *place* and the effects of *politics* on that place. This book describes
the impact of the historical developments on the *place* evidenced by
structures and other artifacts that the reader may explore today. Each
era is exemplified by its characteristic design starting with the neoclassic
original public buildings. These developments are crystallized in the
man-made modifications—the streets, the landscapes, the buildings, and
monuments—the changes in space that document the political trends.
At each stage, the book focuses on specific buildings, their sculpture
and other decoration that embody these changes. The political changes
include the evolution of the concept of America from its republican
origins with limited suffrage to people of different religions and races.
Modernization and globalization have occurred while the previous layers

of local and regional identities and earlier political thinking remain. Concurrently what had been a town in the Tidewater region developed into a national capital and then a world capital.

The selection of the site as well as the grandeur of its design was the result of the vision of George Washington. The city of Washington, as designed by L'Enfant in 1790, contains the major government buildings lying on a coastal plain between the Potomac River on the south and west and its Eastern Branch—the Anacostia River. North is an ellipse of low hills of the Piedmont, forming an amphitheater of the roughly triangular coastal plain. The Rock Creek runs into the Potomac from north to south in a rocky glen through this amphitheater. In the course of its growth in importance over the next two hundred years, the city bears the marks of increased grandeur. The city has grown to meet the design projected when it was first planned in 1790 with broad avenues and vistas to be filled with buildings appropriate for a great empire.

Chapter 1 deals with the selection of the site, its design, and the completion of the public buildings—the Capitol and the President's House in a design that is reminiscent of ancient Rome and its republic. It ends in 1830 following the deaths of Adams and Jefferson in 1826 that marks the end of the revolutionary generation and the arrival of Andrew Jackson in 1829.

It was only after the Civil War that Washington began to fulfill its role as a city as well as a national capital. Its symbolism as a site merely for the capital of a *federal republic* limited its development as a city. Chapter 2 deals with the straggling antebellum Federal City, reflecting a government whose funds and powers were limited. The Congress, representing its various local constituencies, consistently withheld the funds necessary to create a national city. The vision of George Washington—the development of the Potomac basin to support a great city—was superseded in the next generation by the states, including most specifically neighboring Maryland, which fostered improvements in transportation to the benefit of its own port city to the detriment of the Federal City. Chapter 2 deals with the limited aspect of the antebellum city as embodied in several of the most important federal buildings and the Capitol extension in a design that is reminiscent of ancient Greece and Renaissance Rome. It ends with the arrival of the Lincoln administration and the outbreak of the Civil War in 1860.

The federal republican characteristics also imposed limitations on the degree to which a place situated within slaveholding states could express democratic principles. It is both a capital city and a local city: separate yet inseparable. Throughout its history, there has been a disjunction between the commitment to "liberty and justice for all" and the reality experienced by the citizens of the District of Columbia. The limitations on home rule, even today, continue to illustrate the incomplete achievement of the spirit of a truly democratic republic. Its rule by Congress modified the existence of the inhabitants of the city, including its African American population. The converse also occurred when the local character of the city has had impact on national and international politics as when the city's race policies were incompatible with the country's international stance.

After the short period of Reconstruction, the politics of Reconciliation and Reunion took hold. Chapter 3 deals with the impact of the Civil War and its aftermath. The place became an embodiment of the Gilded Age and America's coming-of-age in the American Renaissance that sought to be reminiscent of the earlier Italian Renaissance.

Subsequent chapters will deal with the development of the city as the capital of the reunited nation and increasingly an international capital with imperial pretensions translated in its architecture and decoration. Chapter 4 describes the implementation in its second century during the Progressive Era of what became the neoclassic city that now defines its character and confronts the visitor. It ends with the Depression and the end of the Hoover administration.

Washington "was created for a definite purpose and has been developed according to a definite plan . . . . The purpose was to provide a permanent seat of the National Government [but] also the groundwork of a great community which . . . would develop here because the government was here".[1] When this was written during the presidency of Franklin D. Roosevelt, what had been the city of Washington designed by L'Enfant now encompassed the entire District of Columbia and spilled over into the adjacent Maryland and Virginia suburbs. With the absence of large-scale industry, the growth of the city reflected the growth of the national government. When first transferred from Philadelphia in 1800, the civilian staff numbered 130. Even at the close of the Civil War, this total had increased to only 7,000. In 1937, the total was 112,000. The New Deal under Roosevelt had brought a large number of new people from many parts of the country to what had been a much smaller and more distinctly Southern city. The centralizing tendency and proliferation of government to deal with the Depression was amplified in the successive decades described in chapter 5 when the United States became the head of the victorious coalition during World War II.

Then starting in 1960 with the more sophisticated Kennedy administration, as described in chapter 6, the national capital became the capital city of the Free World during the Cold War. The city as well as the capital also changed in response to the demands of a leadership role with desegregation and greater political rights as well as becoming but a part of a regional setting. The dominant design became increasingly an attenuation of the neoclassicism to an international modernism reflective of its international stature in a much more variegated world.

*   *   *

As in guidebooks, each chapter will follow the evolution of the District of Columbia in its use of landscape, buildings, and their decoration. Each chapter deals with a period embodied successively in buildings such as the U.S. Capitol, Patent Office, enlarged Capitol, the State and War Department, the Pension Building, Library of Congress, Union Station, the Lincoln Memorial, enlarged White House and other executive offices, and the war memorials. We will follow its physical evolution from its origins through the wars and their aftermath that have punctuated its history over the past two hundred years.

The selected places described in **boldface** are places that are **still extant** and documented on the contemporary maps appended to each chapter. The maps dealing with chapter 1 thus would include the streets laid out by L'Enfant and the **Capitol** and **President's House** as completed by the end of the founding revolutionary generation. **The Patent Office Building,** for example, is described in chapter 2 when it was built and will be found listed on the map for that chapter. The last of the maps would be of all of the places mentioned throughout—the present-day city.

There are many guidebooks of Washington but relatively few for the educated general reader. There are also many relatively academic books dealing with the Mall, the Capitol, etc. There are also several encyclopedic books dealing with the buildings of the District of Columbia and the outdoor sculpture. This is uniquely a relatively short book that could be carried around easily by a person. It incorporates the historical background of what one can see and the persons associated with its building. By using any one chapter as a guide, the reader walks through the history of that period as one walks among the buildings, streets, and monuments. The book is geared to the educated reader interested in understanding the *contextual* origins of what could now be seen rather than what is offered in books designed either for the casual tourist or for the academic specialist. One could call it an exercise in urban geography or a guide for the thinking visitor. The book answers questions as to who and why, as well as what, where, and when.

CHAPTER 1
THE REVOLUTIONARY GENERATION /
THE SEAT OF GOVERNMENT (1790-1830)

Introduction

The map that defines the federal district and the city of Washington embodies in space the historical context within which these places came to exist. The first decision was for a ten-mile-square seat of government for the new republic to be separate from any city in any state, and thus from an existing political structure. The selection of the actual site was eventually based upon its place in the important Potomac Basin but also within the constraints of the sectional rivalries as defined in the Compromise of 1790. Its racial policies reflected those of the states from which it was derived and was thus slaveholding. Postponed until the Civil War was any even partial resolution of the issue of race; also postponed until that time was whether it was merely a seat of government or a national capital. The differing visions of the republic and its capital from the start still remain.

A site separate from existing centers of population meant a republic rather than a democracy. The evolution during the first century opened the franchise to all white males, and then at least in principle to all males before opening it to females of any color. Only in the latter portion of the second century were its public spaces opened to mass politics. All these issues appeared at the outset and were crafted within the Compromise of 1790. These tensions remain. The playing out of the Compromise of 1790 over the next more than two hundred years is the theme as expressed in its design of space, crystallized in its buildings and ornaments such as public sculpture that are there for us to see today.

This first chapter deals with the political context for the selection of the site and its early design and development. This then includes the building of the major government buildings—the President's House and the Capitol in the neoclassical model endorsed by Jefferson and Washington, all in preparation for the removal of the federal government to its new capital in December 1800. The design of its buildings was self-consciously a replica of the Roman Republic. Jefferson had in his capitol in Richmond built a replica of the Roman temple at Nîmes. Interrupted by the burning of the public buildings by the British, the U.S. Capitol was actually completed by Bulfinch with the central dome only in 1826. The choice of the subjects of the paintings by Trumbull in the newly completed rotunda can be seen to mark the last vestiges of the revolutionary generation. It is also fitting that July 4, 1826, witnessed the death of both Thomas Jefferson and John Adams, the last of the greats of the revolutionary generation; the election of Andrew Jackson in 1829 marked the rise of a new generation.

Establishing a Federal Seat of Government

The enabling Article I, Section 8, Clause 17 of the Constitution states that "the Congress shall have power to exercise exclusive legislation in all cases whatsoever over such District (not exceeding ten miles square) as may, by cession of particular states . . . become the seat of government of the United States." These provisions identify a principle that evolved out of the experience of the Congress during its previous precarious existence. In so doing, a tension was established that has never been totally solved and remains an issue in American politics today where the citizens of the District of Columbia remain disenfranchised from full participation in the federal government.

The requirement that the federal seat of government be a place under the "exclusive jurisdiction of the Congress" reflected the wish to not be under the sovereignty of any state and therefore subject to its whims. This reflects in part the experience of the Congress of the Confederation. Unprotected, the Congress was subject to attack by unhappy veterans while it was meeting in the Philadelphia State House. This was the occasion for its movement from Philadelphia to Princeton in June 1783 and then to Annapolis and Trenton before its move to New York City in 1785. In addition, during the revolution itself, the Congress had been itinerant, shifting between Philadelphia, Baltimore, Lancaster, and York, dependent on the resources of the host community, often uninvited and not always welcome.

This same existential experience may have been responsible for the requirement that the seat of government would be a site up to ten miles square further suggesting that it be a site relatively undeveloped and not part of any already existing city. This would enable it to be free of the urban sites such as Philadelphia or New York for those who viewed cities as inherently corrupting of a vision of pure *republicanism*.[2] Indeed, a motion was widely supported at the Constitutional Convention, apparently without regard to sectional interest, immediately prior to the adoption of the relevant portion of the Constitution. It sought the exclusion of the federal seat of government from being in the same city as the capital of any state.[3] This provision may be thought to be a code to exclude Philadelphia or New York City from consideration. Although this provision was not explicitly incorporated, the sense of this motion was apparently accepted. The urban component of the existing states was small with the states, particularly in the South, mainly devoted to agriculture. The thinking behind this decision brings to mind the character of the many county courthouses in Southern states. Centrally located in otherwise largely rural county, the courthouse and its adjacent buildings were used for governmental purposes for a short time each year with relatively little in the way of amenities. This anti-Federalist strand of thinking based on the ideology of *republicanism* has continued to be expressed throughout the history of the capital.

The understanding expressed in the Federalist Papers no. 43 by James Madison issued prior to the ratification of the Constitution dealt with the rights of citizens of the federal District. It presupposed that "the State [ceding its territory] will no doubt provide in the compact for the rights and consent of the citizens inhabiting it." This assumption was not met in practice. The citizens of the ceded portions were not given the right of consent or dissent, nor did the states provide for the political rights of the ceded potion, nor was a municipal legislature initially established. During the debate leading to the Residence Act of 1790, these questions were not addressed. Not until February 27, 1801, was an *act concerning the District of Columbia* (the Organic Act of 1801) signed into law just prior to the change in administrations on March 4. Federal control by the Congress was supported by the lame-duck Federalists in the Sixth Congress. The issue was whether the federal government would take control rather than persistence of control by the ceding states of Maryland and Virginia, the latter the stance of the still as yet outnumbered Jeffersonians.[4] On the basis of the exclusive jurisdiction clause, the disenfranchisement of the citizens of the District of Columbia in the Congress remains an issue up to the present day.

Selection of a Site

The passage of the Constitution made necessary the selection of a site for the seat of government. The activities of the First Congress were mainly devoted to this issue.[5] The depth of the divisions threatened the very existence of the new country.[6] The struggle over the selection and the nature of the capital reflected the more basic struggle that dominated politics during the early years of the republic and is inherent in our federal political system. There are those who sought a strong federal government supreme over the states and a capital to reflect its glory. Others supported state supremacy and a strictly limited federal government and capital separate from the urban centers and their consequent urbanity.[7] The capital fight also made obvious the differences between the interests of the Northern and Southern states. These differences were to surface even more on the issue of slavery and race relations coupled with that of states' rights. These issues remained even after the Civil War into the second century of the republic and until today.

The Act of Residence passed by extremely narrow margins in both houses by July 9, 1790, and signed by George Washington on July 16 reflected the major compromise to bring about the selection of the valley of the Potomac River based upon its "centrality" both along the line of the existing coastal states and to the potential development of the Ohio River Valley. Significantly affecting its early development was the proviso that no federal funds were appropriated for its construction. The issue of responsibility for building the *city* as well as the government buildings such as the *Capitol* will continue to bedevil the relations between the two. "That a District or territory not exceeding ten miles square, to be located as hereafter directed on the river Potomac, at some space between the mouths of the Eastern Branch and Conococheague [near present-day Hagerstown, Maryland] [to] be . . . accepted for the permanent seat of the government of the United States." To the dismay of New York City, now after only two years and major expenditure, the capital was to leave, to be moved to Philadelphia until December 1800 when the new capital was to be ready.

The Compromise of 1790 that brought about the passage of the Act of Residence marked the first of the three major compromises that occurred every generation to enable the Union to continue until 1860 despite differences between the sections of the country. The struggle between the two segments of the republic was even more basically between different economic interests. Alexander Hamilton, the leader of what became the Federalist Party, proposed a funding by a national bank of the Revolutionary War debts owed by the states as a means of establishing a commercial financial class tied to the federal government. Southern states with an agrarian slave economy opposed the funding of the debt while also arguing that the Constitution did not expressly grant Congress the power to do so. In addition, as agrarian states, they had relatively little debt, having raised fewer soldiers by which debt was incurred.

James Madison, as a Virginian allied with Jefferson while also the leader in Congress of the incipient Democratic-Republican Party, was strongly involved in placing the capital on the Potomac. The North secured Southern acquiescence to both financial capitalism and the constitutional doctrine of "implied powers." In return, the selection of the Potomac site, albeit in the geographic center of the country at the time, carried the implication that slavery was being countenanced since the District would lie between two slaveholding states. Moreover, the Virginia interests of Madison, Jefferson, and particularly Washington favored this site to enable the development of not only a capital but also a commercial center on the Potomac to rival those of the other sections.[8]

The further decision as to the exact site on the Potomac was left to the president by giving him the power to appoint commissioners to actually lay out the territory. After examining other sites, it is hardly surprising that President Washington in January 1791 selected a site at the mouth of the Eastern Branch (of the Potomac) that encompassed the existing towns of Georgetown and Alexandria—so close to his own home at Mount Vernon.

This decision could well be justified on practical grounds. Similar principles had formed the basis for the emergence of London as the great English metropolis. Port towns such as Georgetown and Alexandria had already arisen as transfer points for goods to be placed on ocean-going ships. Like London on the Thames, they were at the head of navigation of the Potomac River. The Eastern Branch (Anacostia) could also accommodate ships as evidenced by the development of a small port at Bladensburg. North of Georgetown, the river narrowed with shoals, an area known as **Great Falls**. This was also the point at which the river fell from the higher elevation of the Piedmont and the foothills of the Blue Ridge Mountains to the Atlantic Coastal Plain (the Fall Line). With the bypassing of these shoals on the Potomac River already beginning under the "Potomack Company" organized by George Washington, the vision was that the ports could tap into the expected growth in commerce to be found via the settlements in the Ohio Valley.

It was this vision that was an important deciding factor. George Washington's entire adult life had been concerned with surveying and land purchasing as well as ensuring British and subsequently American control of the Potomac basin. He thought that the territory west of the Allegheny Mountains could be connected to the eastern seaboard via a short portage from the headwaters of the Ohio River to the Potomac, the river system that penetrated farthest into the west. It was clearly necessary to counteract the option of sending goods from the Ohio Valley down the Mississippi. That option would weaken ties to the existing states on the eastern seaboard and, with foreign ownership of New Orleans, threaten the very existence of the newly formed United States.[9]

The history of the seat of government during its first generation was concerned with the implementation of this idea, ultimately unsuccessful, of establishing a commercial city to sustain that vision. The efforts of the Potomack Company were ultimately unsuccessful in making the Potomac River more fully navigable by building a canal with locks around such obstacles as the Great Falls. The bypasses were, however, usable only for part of the year when the river was full. In 1830, this earlier attempt was abandoned to be replaced by the Chesapeake and Ohio

Canal to be built entirely parallel to the river requiring considerable capital investment by persons in the District of Columbia as well as by the federal government. The C&O Canal never did reach the Ohio but ended at Cumberland in Western Maryland. The Baltimore and Ohio Railroad did succeed in reaching the Ohio at Wheeling, West Virginia, and became the preferred mode of transport, linking the port of Baltimore to the West.

The Design of the Site

As was every aspect until his death in 1799, the mapping of what came to be called the District of *Columbia* and the city of *Washington* was ultimately under George Washington's personal direction.[10] Thomas Jefferson, as secretary of state in Washington's cabinet, had direct supervision. It is the latter who on February 2, 1791, assigned Andrew Ellicott, America's leading surveyor, the task of outlining the boundaries of the district. Jefferson permitted Ellicott to bring along a neighboring farmer and a self-taught astronomer, a free black called Benjamin Banneker, to carry out some of the measurements. Banneker was helpful in working for several months ending probably in April 1791 when he was succeeded by Ellicott's brothers now once more available to help.[11] Banneker then compiled a popular almanac, containing some of his own measurements. His work, highly recommended by Ellicott, caused Jefferson to withdraw his previous claim that no African American had ever produced anything of scientific merit.

Land had already been ceded in December 1788 by the states of Virginia and Maryland. On Ellicott's recommendation, the southwest boundary was moved to include the wharves and the city of Alexandria. This required another act of the First Congress in February 1791. The inclusion of Alexandria in the federal district was apparently traded for the president's approval for the establishment of a national bank in Philadelphia.[12] The one-third Virginian portion was retroceded to that state in 1846 and forms what is now the city of Alexandria and Arlington County. At present, the District of Columbia is no longer ten miles square but limited to the approximately two-thirds portion that was formerly part of Maryland.

In March 1791, Peter L'Enfant was instructed by Jefferson to design the actual ground plan "for the site of the federal town and buildings." As early as September 1789, prior to the passage of the Residence Act in July 1790, L'Enfant had solicited the job, trading on his personal connection with Washington. Born into an artistic family associated with the French court and himself trained in art, he volunteered as an engineer to serve in the Continental Army. Among his other duties was his illustration of the Manual of Arms written by Baron von Steuben. After the war, he was a founding member of the Society of Cincinnati made up of former officers in the Continental Army. L'Enfant designed its emblem with an eagle, the first private use of the new national bird. Washington, its first president-general, was considered by his fellow officers the reincarnation of the Roman general Cincinnatus who returned to his plow after defeating an enemy of the republic.

Furthermore, L'Enfant had designed the conversion of the New York City Hall into Federal Hall, replete with emblematic eagles representing supreme power and authority (of the Congress) as in the Great Seal of the United States.[13] It was the site of the first inauguration and the home of the new Congress. L'Enfant's credentials for the new far more important job included his Federalist vision, shared with his mentor Alexander Hamilton as well as Washington, that the capital was to be a place for a strong central government.[14] Indeed, it was L'Enfant who first consistently used the term capital for the newly born seat of government.[15]

The opportunity to design a capital city *de novo* was an extraordinary one. To what extent would the capital embody the political principles upon which it was established and serve as a physical embodiment of the Constitution that it was to serve? Yet there was not unanimity as to the character of the republic and thus the character of its new capital city. Unlike the Federalists, for Jefferson and his anti-Federalists, the image of the republic was for a country fit for yeomen working the land. His notion of a capital was as a seat of government and not as a true cultural and political center. As an example, it is suggested that although his move of the capital of Virginia to Richmond during the revolution was to a village more defensible and nearly in the center of the state, it was also one without the university and other amenities that had made Williamsburg a center of life.[16]

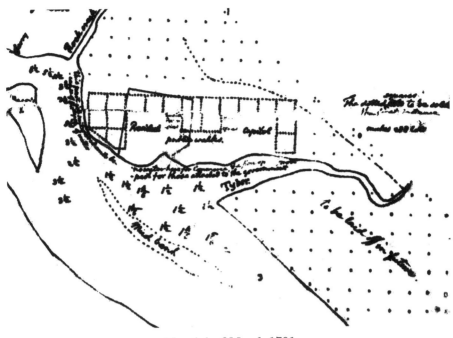

Map 1.1 of March 1791

In March 1791, prior to the start of the work of L'Enfant, Jefferson sketched his ideas as to the site and layout of the capital. (See Map 1.1) It followed the existing plat of Hamburg laid out much earlier and never accomplished, just east of Georgetown and north of where the Tiber Creek enters the Potomac. A modest 273-acre checkerboard grid pattern of streets, there was the President's House to the west and the Congress House to the east with a public walk connecting the two. By the end of March 1791, L'Enfant had developed his much grander vision for the site to encompass the entire area between Georgetown and the Eastern Branch. One aspect focused on the expansion of the existing Ferry Road on a ridge connecting the bodies of water to become a much wider road "proportioned to the greatness which a City the Capitale of a powerful empire ought to manifest".[17] This idea became fixed in his final plan as the present-day **Pennsylvania Avenue** connecting with bridges spanning each river, now the **East Capitol Bridge** on the Anacostia and the **Key Bridge** on the Potomac. The marshy land just south of the original Ferry Road now encompasses the Federal Triangle between Pennsylvania Avenue and the National Mall.

L'Enfant's attention was also drawn to the ridge parallel to the Potomac, now **Capitol Hill**, upon which grand public buildings could be advantageously placed. Most significantly, he also suggested radiating avenues rather than only the standard grid. The attribution of this innovation, the bane of all newcomers to the city, has been contentious. It has been variously traced to L'Enfant's familiarity with the design of Versailles and to his supposed knowledge of Evelyn's baroque design for London after the Great Fire of 1666.[18] These attributions persist despite L'Enfant's claim that this was original and unique and derived from his sense of the topography of the area and the eminences where important buildings might be placed and viewed from a distance.[19]

L'Enfant's grand vision, compatible with the country's "vast empire," accorded with Washington's need to secure the cooperation of the existing landowners. Rather than selecting between those with land near Georgetown (formerly Hamburg) west of Tiber Creek versus those with land south and east of Tiber Creek (formerly Carrollsburg) near the Eastern Branch, happily, the entire site would be encompassed within the Federal City. On that basis, the property owners agreed on March 29, 1791, to cede all their land while retaining ownership of half their lots. Land to be used for streets was free and only the land to be used for public buildings was paid for, at a relatively low cost of $67/acre. The area encompassed approximately six thousand acres or eleven square miles, three miles greater than London at that time and ten miles greater than Philadelphia, then the largest city in the country.[20] Jefferson's early rough sketch now appeared moot. The boundaries include what became the present-day city of Washington, covering the flat area between Georgetown and the Eastern Branch incorporating the ridge known as Jenkins Hill and whose northern boundary would be at the base of the rise from the coastal plain to the Piedmont (now Florida Avenue).

This large-scale city was necessary so that, in the presence of only a small amount of funding by the states of Virginia and Maryland and the absence of any funding by the federal government, the sale of lots could provide sufficient financing for the public buildings. The plan for a land sale to finance the buildings of the capital was commonplace. Starting with the organization of the Northwest territory and Indian lands, sale of federally owned public land was the primary mode for financing governmental expenses in the absence of other sources of revenue.

L'Enfant met with Washington in late June 1791 to outline his preliminary plan and gain his personal approval. It outlined the diagonal avenues to connect each part of the city . . . making the real distance less from place to place and to connect with the major roads entering the city. It was necessary to adapt the street grid, ultimately less than ideally done[21], to the preeminent avenues connecting places identified by their commanding the most extensive prospects.[22] L'Enfant clearly recognized the topography of the site in his planning. The President's Palace would be on a ridge overlooking the Potomac to the west while the congressional building was to be placed in the east at the western end of Jenkins Heights. The axis between the two would be the site of an equestrian statue dedicated to Washington promised by Congress after his victory at Yorktown (later the site of the **Washington Monument**). The base of the triangle formed by connecting the two major components would be a public walk along with a park and gardens. The essentials of the design relating the two major buildings and the public park (the Mall) were now in place. The plan was approved by all those involved on June 28, 1791.

The distance between the two major branches of government should not be "too great . . . but a sort of decorum" be maintained. The great distance (1.5 miles) eventually separating the two has been attributed to the need to appease the two competing groups of proprietors rather than merely exemplifying the constitutional issue of separation of powers.[23] Yet the plan did establish separate areas of influence for the major parts. The executive departments would be situated close to the President's House. It was suggested that the third major part, the Court, would be placed somewhere between the two other powers but not connected directly with either, approximating the present site of Judiciary Square, at Fourth and D streets NW.

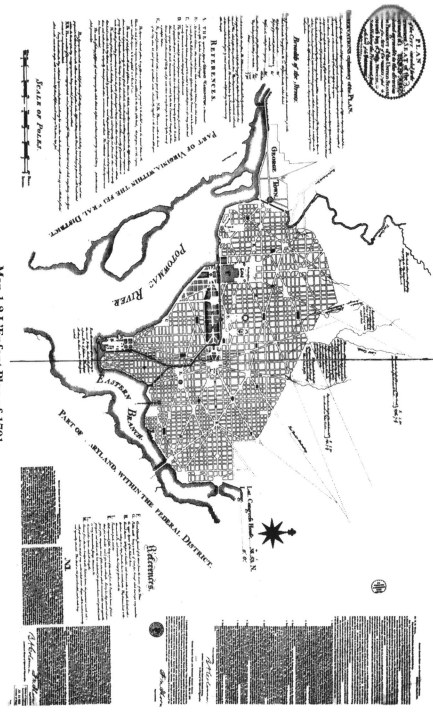

Map 1.2 L'Enfant Plan of 1791

By August 1791, L'Enfant had further defined the relationship of the street grid and the diagonal avenues. It is at that time on or about August 26, 1791, that L'Enfant presented his manuscript plan to President Washington in Philadelphia. The map illustrates the still extant principal elements of his design: the wide diagonals crisscrossing the grid pattern, the relationship of the President's Palace to the Congress House, and the central focus of a monument to Washington. Also illustrated, but to be abandoned, was the planned vista between the two major public buildings united by the major street connecting the two. (See Map 1.2)

In September 1791, the commissioners had decided upon the name of the **City of Washington** in the **Territory of Columbia** as the title to be affixed to the expected map to be used for sale of lots. It is interesting that by this time, the earlier image of Columbus as a greedy Spaniard had been transformed to represent a "far-sighted visionary." *A History of America* published in 1777 was one instance of many that stressed his discovery, fortitude, and perseverance, qualities that would, in the context of the rejection of the English connection by the now-independent Americans, enable him to become the grandfather of the new nation. *Columbia* was used to differentiate from the earlier, now tainted, use of the term *Britannia.*[24]

The centrality of the Capitol was established by the street system just as the city was considered central to the country at that time. The street system is still maintained, although amplified by expansion beyond the original boundaries of the city of Washington. Supposedly recommended by Jefferson analogous to his plan for Richmond, Virginia: "The streets to be named alphabetically one way and numerically the other, the former divided into north and south letters, the latter into east and west numbers, from the Capitol".[25] This principle persists with **East Capitol, North and South Capitol streets (as well as the Mall)**, delineating NE, SE, SW, and NW quadrants despite the asymmetry in the size of these sections created by the expansion beyond the early boundaries.

The major problem faced by Washington was the financing of the public buildings and of the expansive street system over such a large area of wilderness. The prodigal use of land for extraordinarily wide streets was consistent with the land deal engineered by George Washington with the proprietors. Such acreage was freely given. Indeed, it is estimated that more than half of the total acreage were public lands such as streets, circles, and parks.[26] In the absence of major governmental appropriations, the sale of the actual lots ceded by the proprietors was crucial. The attempted sale of lots in October 1791 was not successful, attributed at least partially to the refusal of L'Enfant to permit his still premature plan to be viewed by potential buyers. Still, other personal difficulties arose between L'Enfant and the commissioners to whom he nominally reported. Such differences obscured their even more fundamental concerns about scale and costs. The fact that more than half the land was to be used for public buildings and streets diminished land available to the proprietors for their profit.[27] Washington, caught between these conflicts, instructed Jefferson to dismiss L'Enfant on February 28, 1792, and failed to reinstate him.

Map 1.3 Ellicott Map of 1792

Jefferson assigned Ellicott the task of finishing a plan to be used for the further sale of lots. Although derived almost entirely from L'Enfant, Ellicott's name alone was attached to this engraved plan of February 1792. (See Map 1.3) The Ellicott Plan contained several of the editorial changes in the original L'Enfant manuscript plan penciled in by Jefferson. For example, the Presidential Palace was designated as House and Congress House as the Capitol. Jefferson changed the latter to accord with his experience in Williamsburg and to resonate with the historical roots of the new republic derived from its Roman *Capitoline Hill* prototype. Ellicott also was the first to use the term "mall" to describe the park leading from the Capitol to its west.

This plan also included *avenues* as wide as 160 feet wide named after the thirteen original states, double the width of ordinary streets. The order of names assigned by Ellicott reflects their geographical distribution within the country and their significance at that time. **Pennsylvania,** the state where the Congress had met, was the name to be given to the especially wide avenue connecting the Capitol and the Presidential Mansion. Avenues above it to the north were given names of Northern states with the major avenue traversing the city to be given to **Massachusetts,** the state most active in the revolution. Middle Atlantic states with names such as **New York** were in the center, with that name to be given to the avenue abutting the President's House in recognition of it being the early capital. The names of Southern states were to be assigned to Capitol Hill with a major traversing avenue to be assigned to **Virginia** below to the south, as its most populous and significant. Maryland and New Jersey avenues were to intersect the Capitol Square possibly because the Continental Congress met at towns in those two states when not in Philadelphia. Delaware is to be given precedence near the Capitol since it was the first state to ratify the Constitution.[28] Despite the availability of this more specific map, the second sale of lots on October 9, 1792, was also unsuccessful.

The final official plan was one finished somewhat later noting the depths of water in the channels and along the shores of the rivers, information deemed essential for potential commercial buyers for a city envisaged by Washington as a "riverside town." By this time, although the basic principles had been established by him, to his eternal disappointment, L'Enfant was no longer involved in the undertaking. He remained unrecognized for his contributions until the McMillan Plan renewed interest around 1900; and in 1909, his body was exhumed, placed in the rotunda of the Capitol, and finally entombed on Arlington Heights in front of the Custis-Lee Mansion overlooking his creation.

A Modified Design

The next battle over the design developed by L'Enfant was related to his dismissal but also to the intent of his too grandiose design. He had designed a city worthy of the Federalist idea of a new nation. The final design of the capital city and moreover its implementation further reflects the ambiguous image of the republic it was to serve. The Federalist idea he served was under attack. Republicans opposed the trappings of aristocracy and monarchy such as palaces and grand cities.

L'Enfant had the notion of establishing at least fifteen sites where streets on the grid intersected with the diagonal avenues to form potential squares. In his manuscript plan of 1791, each of the squares to be assigned to the various states were colored yellow. A site was to be assigned to each of the then fifteen existing states (Vermont and Kentucky in addition to the original thirteen) to encourage each state to take a specific interest in its development. This arrangement was an attempt for a basis for coordinated development of the city. The intent was to incorporate the several states to aid in the establishment of a federal seat of government that would also represent the character of the newly enacted Constitution. Failure to implement such a scheme for simultaneous development may have also contributed to the straggling quality that earned the title the City of Magnificent Distances through most of its first century. Many of these sites did remain to be adorned as envisaged by L'Enfant, but by national military heroes in the era after the Civil War.[29]

L'Enfant also designated the use of squares between the President's Mansion and the Capitol for such purposes as a national pantheon (a knoll, later the site of the Patent Office and Post Office) to be patterned after the Pantheon in Paris. The significant albeit slight rise in height between the two focal points of the executive and legislature was to be used for the judiciary (later actually the site of **Judiciary Square** but devoted to the District of Columbia courts) at F and Indiana avenues between Fourth and Fifth streets NW. The envisaged significant commercial street

(**East Capitol Street**), leading to the Zero Milestone, a monument one mile east of the Capitol, is now exemplified only by **Lincoln Park** in which Lincoln's statue as *The Emancipator* now stands. Most important, L'Enfant envisaged that he would be able to determine the design of what he called the Presidential Palace to reflect a far grander building than the eventual President's House. Grand squares in front of the Presidential Palace and the Capitol were later eliminated, as well as many of the sight lines between these two focal buildings thus violating his fundamental principle of "reciprocity of sight."

The design of the particularly important public buildings is the next step that illustrates the difficulties in accomplishing the task under the stringent financial conditions. During the early years, there was always the danger that the fragile coalition supporting the choice on the Potomac would unravel or that partisans for Philadelphia would prevail. It took much of Washington's wisdom and power to keep it afloat.[30] Toward the end of his second term, Congress denied Washington even the right to raise private funds for implementing his other dream to provide the centralizing force of a national university. Limits to presidential power were imposed on George Washington who had expended much of his hard-won stature as a "disinterested man of virtue" in pursuit of his dream of a centralizing federal city on the banks of the Potomac.[31]

The completion of the public buildings was essential to anchor the Federal City permanently on the Potomac site. The Residence Act of 1790 had merely specified that suitable buildings be erected. L'Enfant, in his preliminary plan in June 1791, had laid out the dimensions of the public buildings on a grand scale. For example, the Presidential Palace was to be approximately seven hundred feet east to west and two hundred feet north to south. Excavation of the foundations had started. Even after L'Enfant's dismissal in February 1792, diagonal avenues that remained were envisaged to center upon the building itself that could only be accomplished by a house much larger than was eventually built. For example, five avenues were to radiate north from the façade like rays of the sun. There was retention of these avenues named after Connecticut and Vermont that now radiate only from the vicinity of the President's House and do not provide a "reciprocity of sight." The President's Park to the south was to extend to the planned equestrian statue of George Washington and to the Potomac beyond, a view all the way to Alexandria.

The scope of the design has been attributed to that of the royal château at Marly built by Mansart in the seventeenth century, likely to be well-known to L'Enfant as well as the north-south axis of the Madeleine intersecting at the statue of Louis XV with the east-west axis of the Tuileries in Paris.[32]

The Public Buildings

Although the president and Jefferson were united in the representational value of public architecture expressed in ancient Roman eighteenth-century neoclassicism[33], they differed in the scale they sought. Jefferson, by his European residence, was familiar with the power of the architectural groupings that housed and represented the authority of the oppressive state. In the implementation of the plans of L'Enfant, albeit now much reduced, it was Washington who consistently sought to expand the scale of what was proposed while Jefferson did the contrary. The latter's actions were subtle and oblique so as to not jeopardize the legislative consensus that had brought the site to his Virginia.[34]

The term **President's House** displaced in official usage L'Enfant's President's Palace. Advertisements for a competition were sent out by mid-March 1792. James Hoban, favored by Washington, won the competition for the President's House to be rectangular and of stone, as a place worthy of a "first gentleman." The design was further amplified by Washington for areas for formal entertainment consistent with the role he established for the president. The oval central room later called the **Blue Room** reflected Washington's preference for an oval room, already in place in his residence in Philadelphia, as a setting for his formal presidential receptions. The **East Room,** a large space to entertain crowds, reflected Washington's own addition of a banquet room to Mount Vernon. The north wall was placed where L'Enfant had envisaged the front door but the diminution in north to south as well as east-west dimensions displaced the building from its orientation to the Capitol. Ultimately, the dimensions were 168 feet east to west and eighty-five feet north to south including in the latter the bow window of the Blue Room. To reduce costs, bricks were used, made on the premises from soil there—rich in clay and sand. Sandstone used for the exterior walls was drawn from a quarry in Aquia downriver on the Potomac brought to the site by barge.

The southwest cornerstone was placed on October 13, 1792, under Hoban's continued direction. Born in Ireland and trained in architectural drafting in Dublin, Hoban was familiar with the characteristics of Irish Georgian manor house architecture. He had migrated to the United States sometime after 1785. Settled in Charleston, South Carolina, he had been introduced to Washington on the latter's Southern tour. After the departure of L'Enfant, Washington called upon Hoban on the basis of his work in Charleston. The design of the President's House has been attributed to Leinster House, the Dublin home of the Duke of Leinster, later Ireland's parliament house. There were similarities in plan and façade but several differences indicating modifications such as the oval Blue Room and the lowering of the building to two stories from the original's three. The house represents a Renaissance design with elements of the baroque. Although not as palatial as first planned, it was clearly stately. Rushed to completion, John Adams moved in on December 1, 1800, while plaster was still drying in the East Room. Hoban remained associated with the White House for the rest of his life, responsible for its rebuilding after its destruction in 1814 and its later north portico.

L'Enfant had established the principle of clustering the departments of the executive branch near the President's House. However, it was Washington, cognizant of the needs of the executive, who ensured that those departments would actually be placed there.[35] At the time of the move, actually starting in the summer of 1800, the redbrick buildings adjacent to the President's House for the Department of Treasury on the east and Department of War to the west had not yet been completed to house the some 130 employees of the federal government. Following its destruction by the British, this cluster would be rebuilt following 1816. The State Department joined with the Treasury on the east and the Navy Department joined with the War Department on the west. Eventually in the Jackson administration, the east side became the site for the beginnings of the present-day **Treasury** and, in the Grant administration, on the west side the **State, War, and Navy Departments (now the Old Executive Office Building)**.

The Capitol was the other significant public building to also be made of stone. Its design was also open to a public competition. The home of the legislature, it was both the central building of the new country and of the city that it was to represent. It was essential for it to be ready on the first Monday in December 1800. Once again, the theme was to recollect a classical motif, representing a connection to the ancient past as a legitimating foundation for the new country. The Capitol was the first major building in the United States to be influenced by the eighteenth-century English neoclassical style called the federal style in America.

The exterior was adorned by the lavish Corinthian style order in recognition of the great importance of the building. The winning design by Dr. William Thornton in 1793 was on a larger scale than the President's House. However, at 350 feet, it approached merely half the original scale for L'Enfant's Presidential Palace. An English-educated physician and amateur architect, Thornton revised his exterior design around the domed center reminiscent of the ancient Roman Pantheon with two wings devoted to the two branches of the Congress united by a continuous front. In so doing, the neoclassical building appeared to Washington and Jefferson to represent the principles of the new government; namely "national union, the bicameral legislative bodies it housed, and easy accessibility to all Americans".[36] The use of the Roman model of the Pantheon was very much in Jefferson's mind when he recommended to L'Enfant in 1791 the use of "models of antiquity" and later his own use of the rotunda at the University of Virginia.

The foundations were started in August 1793 to contain the elevation of Thornton but the interior design of Hallett, a French-trained architect who had come in second in the competition. Hallet's suggested elimination of the central ceremonial rotunda conveniently also removed the site for a statue of George Washington and his proposed tomb. The controversial ceremonial rotunda was put off ostensibly in the name of economy.[37] Hallett was eventually discharged by Washington, over disagreements with Thornton who then became one of the commissioners monitoring the entire effort.

However, there would be no entombment of Washington after his death in 1799 in the central shrine of the republic. Later efforts were unsuccessful to make the rotunda contain a mausoleum dedicated to Washington. A bare-chested statue of Washington in a Roman toga by Greenough, commissioned for the rotunda as a substitute for a mausoleum, and placed there for a time, now languishes in the Smithsonian Museum of American History. The spirit of dedication within the rotunda to the founder was accomplished finally only by the painting on the dome of *The Apotheosis of Washington* by Brumidi in the 1860s.

Thornton, identified as a Jeffersonian Democrat, remained in Washington for another thirty-five years, mainly as the director of the Patent Office. He was also responsible for the design of two important buildings that remain extant. The **Octagon House,** actually a hexagon with a circular tower at the entrance, was a solution to the triangular lot produced by the intersection of New York Avenue and Eighteenth Street NW. The first private mansion to be built, it was important in reinforcing the street plan of the city as laid out by L'Enfant. John Tayloe, the owner of Mt. Airy Plantation south of Washington, was reputed to be the richest plantation owner in Virginia. The house was the site where the Treaty of Ghent was signed in 1814, ending the war of 1812, since Tayloe had loaned the house to James and Dolley Madison to use after the destruction of the White House. Also by Thornton is the central circular portion of **Tudor Place** at 1644 Thirty-first Street in Georgetown that replicates some of the character of the Octagon. Designed for the Thomas and Martha Custis Peter, the latter the granddaughter of Martha Washington and a Federalist partisan, it remained a private house until its recent conversion to a museum.

The north wing of the Capitol to contain the Senate was given priority and was ready for occupancy, albeit poorly built, by the expected date in 1800. Like the President's House, it was made of the porous freestone from the Aquia quarry. When the federal government arrived in the city in 1800, 372 houses deemed habitable had also been built, far fewer than necessary to house the legislators as well as others seeking their future in the new town. Although the deadline had been met and a magnificent scheme outlined, the reality was far different. The ambivalence as to the role of a national capital as a vital center would continue to dog its development.[38] The promise of a federal city was in the future, but the commitment to neoclassicism was fixed to a large degree for the present.

Under Jefferson as president and Benjamin Henry Latrobe as surveyor of public buildings and thus architect of the Capitol, the commitment to neoclassicism was strengthened. Jefferson was particularly enamored of models from his stay in France and of Rome; Latrobe of Greek models. The two figures very much acted as a team although clashing frequently with Jefferson taking an active role based on his wishes to provide a museum of ancient models of architecture for the edification of Americans.[39] While living in Richmond, Latrobe completed the exterior of the Virginia State Capitol designed by Jefferson after the Maison Carrée in Nîmes. The temporary south building used by the House of Representatives was replaced by the building of a south wing along with repair of the earlier poorly built north Senate wing into what were the most architecturally sophisticated spaces in America. Latrobe, Irish born and British trained, was heavily influenced by the Greek revival then going on in England. He had been well trained as an architect in England and, as America's first professionally trained architect, can be called the father of that profession in this country.[40] Latrobe was also responsible for the use of very popular capitals on the columns expressive of the "American order" to replace the classical Ionic, Doric, and Corinthian orders. Those of a corncob enclosed by its husk representing agriculture are in the Supreme Court lower vestibule, those of tobacco leaves representing trade in the small rotunda outside the Senate, and those of magnolia, representing the arts, in the Senate upper gallery.

There was renewed agitation to move the seat of government after the destruction of the public buildings by fire in 1814 by the British in the War of 1812. However, there was a recrudescence of national feeling after the war, and Washington remained the national capital. Latrobe was once again employed in the rebuilding of the Capitol in the neoclassical mode. In rebuilding the Senate chamber after its destruction, Latrobe expanded it into a semicircle to accommodate the increased number of senators. By 1821, there were to be twenty-four states with forty-eight senators. He designed a half-domed room with a great arch, framing a marble colonnade in front of which sat the vice president, its presiding officer. The 1824 portrait of an idealized George Washington by Rembrandt Peale, the second son of the artist Charles Willson Peale, is in the Roman tradition entitled *Patriae Pater (Father of his Country)* surrounded by an oaken wreath and surmounted by a mask representing Jupiter. This so-called Porthole Painting is the most famous of the younger Peale's portraits that also include those of John Calhoun and Thomas Jefferson, the latter in the Blue Room of the White House. Rembrandt Peale eventually created multiple versions of his version of Washington "of everlasting memory" reflecting the artist's exposure to neoclassicism in his trip to Paris in 1808 as well as the Houdon bust of Washington done from life. The painting was bought by the Senate in 1832, prompted by the centenary of Washington's birth. It is now once again placed in its original position in the restored Old Senate Chamber.

The much larger semicircular House of Representatives was to contain almost two hundred persons by 1820, filling the entire south wing. As in the Senate chamber, a lantern that is still evident was placed on the roof to provide ventilation. Colonnades were placed at both the half dome and flat sides of the chamber. Above the colonnade at one end, a grouping by the Italian sculptor Enrico Causici portrays in plaster *Genius of the Constitution*. A spread-winged eagle is adjacent to a standing female suggestive of Minerva, the Roman goddess of wisdom, used to exemplify

Plate 1.1
The Car of History

America. Also adjoining is a group of rods (fasces) emblematic of the power of the Roman Senate around which is entwined a serpent holding them together. The latter is reminiscent of Benjamin Franklin's famous cut snake "Join or Die".[41] The most famous of the sculptures is called *The Car of History* by Carlo Franzoni (See Plate 1.1). A chariot with feathered sides rests on a single wheel containing a clock surmounted by the figure of Clio, "the Muse of History," writing in a book on her upraised knee. This room became **Statuary Hall** during the Civil War after the completion of the house chamber in the Capitol extension.

The Supreme Court was never placed in what L'Enfant had projected to be Judiciary Square. The Court, the third of the major parts identified in the Constitution, had the least definition of its powers at the start. Perhaps reflective of this fact, the Court was not assigned a site of its own commensurate with the homes of the executive and the legislature. The Court was first housed in the lower level of the north or Senate wing. Latrobe's original vaulted space has been recently restored after having been used for offices. In this, the first Supreme Court chamber, opposite the bench, there is a plaster relief of a female *Justice* in classical attire, unconventionally without blindfold but holding scales and resting on a sword. *Justice* looks toward a nude-winged *Genius* pointing toward a tablet inscribed "The Constitution of the U.S." The American eagle is also present but with its wings folded guarding law books. Also by Carlo Franzoni, it dates from 1816 and is one of the oldest works of art in the Capitol. In the 1850s, the Court moved to what was the then recently vacated Latrobe-designed Senate chamber in the north wing. It remained there until the Court's own neoclassical building was completed in 1935. In accordance with Jefferson's aim to make the Capitol illustrate the range of classical architecture, Latrobe carried out **Doric order capitals in the Supreme Court chamber, Ionic order in the Senate chamber, and Corinthian in the House chamber**.

The Library of Congress was originally placed in the north wing overlooking the Mall. Following the burning of the Capitol in 1814, it was placed within the western portion of the central building behind the west portico. There it remained, with alterations following recurrent fires, until the completion in 1897 of its own building reminiscent of the Renaissance and baroque eras to the northeast of the Capitol (present-day **Jefferson Building**).

A succession of architects had contributed their ideas to the design of the central portion, including Latrobe, but it was Charles Bulfinch who completed the central portion of the **rotunda** and its dome in 1826 as the Hall of the People. The dome was largely of brick and stone with the outer dome made of wood sheathed in copper but never gilded. Bulfinch resisted enormous congressional pressure to use the space for committee meeting rooms. Wellborn in Boston and Harvard trained, Bulfinch traveled to Paris when Jefferson was minister to learn about architecture. The first American-born architect, he was already famous for his domed Massachusetts State House in Boston. Beneath the rotunda, he built heavy piers and columns that suggest a crypt that could be used for burial of George Washington.

John Trumbull, the son of Jonathan Trumbull, the governor of Connecticut during the revolutionary period, and once an aide-de-camp to Washington, was trained as an artist by Benjamin West in London. Jefferson helped sponsor him in commemorating the revolutionary period in his four life-size history paintings. These are the *Declaration of Independence, Surrender of General Burgoyne at Saratoga, Surrender of Cornwallis at Yorktown,* and *Washington Surrendering his Commission.* The neoclassical setting of the first, Philadelphia's Federal Hall, and the last, a room in the Maryland State House, emphasize the Roman origins of the new republic. The last of the quartet reflected the action of the Roman general Cincinnatus in giving up his power. These paintings establish the rotunda as the ceremonial center of the Capitol and the symbol of national union[42]

Plate 1.2 Declaration of Independence

Plate 1.3 Surrender of General Burgoyne at Saratoga

Plate 1.4 Surrender of Cornwallis at Yorktown

Plate 1.5 Washington Surrendering his Commission

The east portico, now the main entrance, designed by Latrobe with its staircase, eight columns and adjacent pilaster colonnades was also based on input from Jefferson. It was finally completed by Bulfinch in 1826. It was the last portion completed of the original Capitol that was started by George Washington in 1793 in accordance to the design of Thornton. The dimensions of the now completed Capitol were a front of 351 feet, a depth of 131 feet with the dome 145 feet high.[43]

Luigi Persico, a Neopolitan-born artist, had, while living in Lancaster Pennsylvania, become friendly with James Buchanan who remained his patron. Persico completed in 1828 the pediment of the east portico with the rather sparse sculptural group known as *The Genius of America* in tune with the ideology of the revolutionary generation just then ending (See Plate 1.6). The central figure of an armed female *America* holds a spear and a shield inscribed U.S.A. with a pedestal emblazoned with July 4, 1776. Adjoining is an American eagle, considered to be symbolic of the supreme authority of Congress appearing to be the active, even aggressive bird protecting liberty and the Constitution.[44] Facing to the right is the female figure of *Hope* with an anchor, to the left is the female figure of *Justice* with scales and a scroll emblazoned with the word "Constitution" and "17 September 1787," the date of its approval by the Constitutional Convention. The original design was modified by the then-president John Quincy Adams to "represent the American Union founded in the Declaration of Independence and consummated by the organization of the general government under the Federal Constitution, supported by Justice in the past, and relying on Hope in Providence in the future."

Plate 1.6 The Genius of America

The President's House was rebuilt under the direction of Hoban after its destruction in 1814. It was the policy of Madison to emphasize the continuity of the rebuilt building to its original form. However, the entire main floor was now given over to ceremonial use as has continued to be its role. The furnishings destroyed by the British were replaced by those purchased by Monroe during his stay in Paris as ambassador, some of which are still evident in the Blue Room. The president's office moved to the second floor where it remained until the completion of the Oval Office under President Taft. Now clearly painted white, the **Executive Mansion** became at least unofficially **the White House**. Also rebuilt were the east and west one-story dependencies built by Jefferson as service wings analogous to his design of Monticello. With extensive modifications during the administrations of Theodore Roosevelt and then of Franklin Roosevelt, these East and West wings remain part of the present-day White House. The ionic columned **north portico** was completed by 1829 in accordance with the design by Hoban at the start of the Jackson administration.

The public buildings created during this revolutionary generation particularly reflected the influence of Jefferson. It embodied a new style that by its revival of classical motifs is different from the Georgian and the baroque of its British antecedents. Its origin in the spirit of ancient Greece as well as Rome represents also a political stance compatible with the *republican* ideology of the new nation[45] This so-called Greek revival was to develop further in the hands of Robert Mills in the next generation to contribute to the monumental character of the new city. **The map 1.4 shows the completion of the two major public buildings with the President's House moved from its initial location as designed by L'Enfant.**

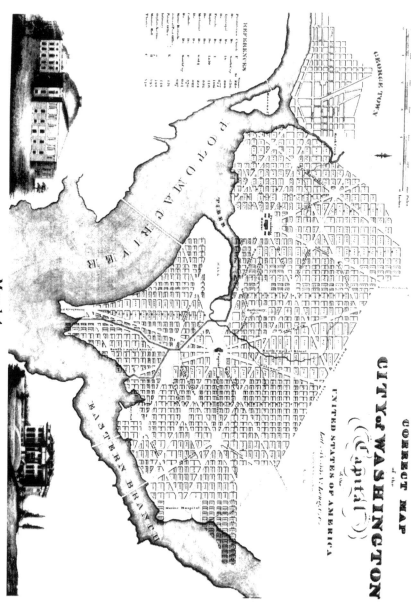

Map 1.4
Map of 1820

CHAPTER 2
THE ANTEBELLUM PERIOD /
THE FEDERAL CITY (1830-1860)

Introduction

Washington's development both a *city* and a *capital* was constrained by the weakness of the national government and the limited resources provided it and, in turn, available to the fledgling Federal City.[1] The additional funds generated by executive departments themselves such as the Post Office and Patent Office (whose previous homes was destroyed by fire) enabled the next great surge of public buildings starting in the 1830s under President Andrew Jackson. The neoclassical Greek revival grandeur of their design by Robert Mills, the heir to Latrobe, set the tone for the further development much later of the monumental capital.

The popularity of Greek motifs in British architecture had arisen in the eighteenth century on the basis of the early archeological findings and by travelers to Greece, culminating in the arrival in London of the Elgin marbles from the Parthenon.[2] When Benjamin Latrobe immigrated to the United States in 1798, he "married English neo-classicism to Jeffersonian neoclassicism [and] . . . from that moment the classical revival in America took on a national form." Even more than its English prototype . . . it possessed political connotations—images of New World democracy—less readily applicable to Britain".[3] By the 1820s, this was coupled also to the popularity of Greece itself. There was widespread sympathy in Western Europe for the struggle the Greek people were undergoing for independence from the Ottomans along with increased recognition of Athenian political history as emblematic of democracy, all particularly resonating in an American republic cognizant of its uniqueness.

However, by the 1850s and the victory of the Mexican War, the United States had expanded into a continental power. *Manifest Destiny* provided an ideology that was particularly documented in decoration of the Senate corridors of the Capitol building extension that also echoed Roman motifs derived from Raphael's work in the Vatican. The common national mission, only partially superceding sectional rivalry, was conquest of the continent by white Anglo-Saxons, building on the foundation of the Spanish conquistadors.[4]

Washington as *Capital*

The Washington Monument

At the start of this era, the Mall did not have any defining features. The era would see the building of the Smithsonian Castle and the beginning of the Washington Monument, still its two most distinctive elements. The centennial of George Washington's birth in 1832 still did not see fulfilled the original idea of his tomb or cenotaph in the **Capitol rotunda**. Horace Greenough's unsatisfactory statue of a Washington as a toga-clad Zeus was eventually installed there, but only for a very short time. After several other sites, it is now inconspicuously ensconced at the **Smithsonian Museum of History on the Mall**. The centennial also led to the development of a plan for a **monument** commemorating Washington. Congress provided the site to be the long-planned centerpiece of L'Enfant's Mall. Robert Mills had designed the earlier obelisk monument to George Washington in Baltimore's Monument Square. His original design for Washington contained a grandiose Pantheon-like temple base surmounted by an obelisk, patterned after the ancient **Mausoleum at Halicarnassus** but with Ionic columns. It thus combined Greek and Egyptian elements.[5]

Started in 1848 by a private group, money for implementing Mills' design ran out soon thereafter. The Egyptian-style obelisk alone was finally completed by the federal government during 1879-1884. Lieutenant Colonel Thomas Lincoln Casey of the U.S. Army Corps of Engineers was instrumental in carrying it out and placing his name atop. Against all proposals to the contrary, he concentrated on building an unadorned shaft.[6] Mills had projected its height to be six hundred feet. This was finally reduced to 555 feet in recognition of its width at the base of fifty-five feet to meet the usual proportions of the ancient Egyptian obelisk of 10:1. It was topped by a tapered aluminum pyramidion, then a relatively uncommon metal. At its completion, it was the tallest structure in the world until superseded by the Eiffel Tower in 1889. The Washington Monument still remains the world's tallest *all-masonry* structure and clearly fulfills the original objective of a massive and sublime pile, as it rises to the clouds.[7]

Robert Mills was an American-born professional architect trained under both James Hoban and Benjamin Henry Latrobe as well as a protégé of Thomas Jefferson. Mills was one of the pioneers of fireproof construction with the use of concrete. He built Greek revival governmental buildings in many settings. Appointed by President Jackson in 1836, he was responsible for carrying out several of the new series of stone "public buildings" for the executive departments that would reinforce the image of Washington as a national capital. The number of employees in the Treasury and Post Office, although still rather few, had increased far beyond any others.[8] There was income from customs duties and the sale of public lands as well as income from postage. In addition, the income generated by the applicants for patents could be used to construct what was needed to be a new fireproof building for that bureau. In line with his mentor, Benjamin Henry Latrobe, in the work on the U.S. Capitol, the trio of buildings by Mills illustrate an Ionic **Treasury,** a Doric **Patent Office**, and a Corinthian **Post Office**.

The Treasury Building

The first of a trio of buildings for which Robert Mills was responsible is the **Treasury Building** adjacent to the west of the President's House. The original building for the Department of the Treasury, designed by Hadfield and rebuilt by Latrobe after the War of 1812, faced Pennsylvania Avenue. Mills designed a great colonnaded east wing of what was eventually to be a massive building. It was developed in stages from 1836 to 1869 by a series of architects while maintaining the original exterior design. The columns with Ionic capitals in the east wing were reminiscent of those of the **Erechtheum on the Acropolis**. Their massiveness is reminiscent of the **Temple of Diana at Ephesus**, one of the wonders of the ancient world. The east wing, built in sandstone, as were the Capitol and President's House, was much later replaced by granite, also used for the subsequent wings. The Ionic colonnade with slight differences in detail was echoed in subsequent buildings such as the Treasury Department annex across Pennsylvania Avenue and in the Chamber of Commerce on nearby Lafayette Square, both designed by Cass Gilbert in the early twentieth-century Beaux-Arts style. Indeed, an Ionic front became iconic for bank buildings everywhere in the United States.

Plate 2.1 South Wing of the U.S. Treasury

The east wing was completed by Thomas Walter by the addition of pedimented pavilions on either end after his selection as architect to the Capitol. Appointed the first supervising architect of the Treasury in 1852, New England born and trained, Ammi B. Young was noted for his use of granite exteriors and cast-iron interiors to create fireproof buildings throughout the United States. In completing the south wing, (See Plate 2.1) he created what was a singular American "order" incorporating the eagle to substitute for the acanthus leaf of the classic Corinthian order. But the south wing also obscured a major component of the L'Enfant Plan to create a "reciprocity of view" between the U.S. Capitol and the President's House. The "bend" in Pennsylvania Avenue remains. Isaiah Rogers was the successor in 1863 who completed the west wing. Born in Massachusetts, Rogers was famous for his hotel buildings including the Tremont House, the premier Boston hotel, the first with indoor plumbing.

Moreover, he was a personal friend of his fellow Cincinnatian, Lincoln's secretary of the treasury Salmon P. Chase. Finally, after the Civil War, the original Executive Building designed by Hadfield and rebuilt by Latrobe facing Pennsylvania Avenue was replaced by the north wing of the Treasury in 1869. Alfred B. Mullet, the architect of the complementary Executive Office Building to the west and Rogers's successor, maintained the exterior design but created an interior Renaissance design most evident in the two-storied Cash Room.

The entire complex was completed in the early twentieth century by set of sculptures by James Earle Fraser, a student of Augustus Saint-Gaudens and a member of the Commission of Fine Arts. These are **Alexander Hamilton** on the south, Washington's great first secretary of the Treasury, and on the north, **Albert Gallatin**, secretary of the Treasury for both Jefferson and Madison. Gallatin was noted for an extensive career but perhaps best celebrated here for his unique role of reducing the national debt so that the Treasury had a surplus during his tenure.

Plate 2.2 The Old Patent Office

The Patent Office

Mills was also responsible for at least the interior plan and structure of original south wing of the **Patent Office** on F Street with its Doric-columned portico patterned after the Parthenon (See Plate 2.2). Made of the same Aquia sandstone as previous public buildings, subsequent portions were clad in marble while continuing the Doric porticos at the center of each side with compatible Doric pilasters on the sides. Mills later designed, but Thomas U. Walter carried out, the east wing for that same building including the Lincoln Gallery on its uppermost floor designed for display of patent models. The west and north wings were also carried out in the 1850s by Thomas U. Walter, the architect of the Capitol extension, thus completing the original quadrilateral design. The interior design of the wings differed with the wings by Walter using cast iron rather than Mill's heavier masonry for creating a fireproof building. After a fire in 1877, the top floors of both the west and south wings were rebuilt by Adolf Cluss and Paul Schulze with cast-iron round columns supporting iron balconies and tiled flooring. The thinking at that time precluded imitation of earlier wood or stone but reflect iron's own natural mechanistic properties with stylized plant forms at the capitals.

The Patent Office is particularly important for the role of patents and inventions confirmed the sense that American history was the fulfillment of the fruits of liberty. The inventions were an expression of American creative genius and technical superiority. The patent system promoted individual creativity and economic independence when those were some of the chief goals of the new country. The **Old Patent Office Building** was billed as "the Shrine to Genius," "the Temple of Invention," and "the Temple of the Useful Arts".[9] It expressed American aspirations and values more than any other federal building at the time. The number of patents issued each decade increased exponentially, far greater than in Britain or France, the major European industrial powers at the time.

It was the most prominent of the new buildings built during the 1830s. It is fitting that at that time, it was second only to the Capitol building in its volume. Mills claimed the gallery in the original south wing was the largest in the United States when built. The model room on the third floor of the east wing was large enough to house two thousand people for the gala ball for Lincoln's second inauguration on March 6, 1865, at the close of the Civil War.

"There shall be sung another Golden Age / The rise of Empire and the Arts." So sung as early as 1726 a poem by the famed philosopher George Berkeley, bishop of Cloyne, of the rise of America.[10] Published for the first time in his *Miscellany* in the 1750s, it resonated in the next decades with similar prophecies of imminent American greatness in the arts and sciences. There was great optimism after the success of the French and Indian War in the 1760s. Once the French were defeated in 1763, one could foresee another Augustan Age. In addition, after the Stamp Act, John Trumbull, the artist whose work is in the rotunda of the Capitol, spoke in a commencement address at Yale in 1770 of the connection between culture and freedom. "In mighty pomp, America shall rise / her glories spreading to the boundless skies . . . See bolder genius quit the narrow shore / and unknown realms of science dare t'explore." Philip Freneau, later the editor of a Jeffersonian newspaper and friend of his fellow Princetonian James Madison, wrote a poem in 1771 repeating the same idea in *The Rising Glory of America*. These ideas of the potential of an America freed by the revolutionary spirit were amplified by the actual growth in population and economic strength.[11]

These ideas seemed to gain some support by an outpouring of the arts that came after the American Revolution exemplified by Charles Willson Peale and his large family of artists. Indeed, Peale's Philadelphia Museum was an early version of a collection of objects having to do with both art and science as a source of knowledge.[12] However, any trappings of high culture that did appear did not receive governmental support and were denounced by some as anti-Republican. Benjamin Franklin clearly understood "the invention of a machine or the improvement of an implement is of more importance than a masterpiece of Raphael".[13] His own inventions of the Franklin stove, bifocal spectacles, as well as the lightening rod were examples along with his more theoretical work in electricity. Jefferson also was an inventor, most prominently of the moldboard, a curved iron plate attached to a plow more effective in turning the soil. It was this aspect of applied science that would find support.

Recognizing the importance of federal control as opposed to that of the states, the Constitution (Article 1, Section 8, Clause 8) explicitly empowers Congress "to promote the Progress of Science and useful Arts, by securing for a limited time to Authors and Inventors the exclusive Right to their respective Writings and Discoveries." The safeguard to authors was via copyright; the safeguard to inventors was via a patent, analogous to the system in Britain well-known to the framers. The Patent Act was one of the first laws passed by the First Congress in its second session in 1790. Noteworthy is an early patent issued to John Fitch in 1791 and others for a new way to propel boats. The cumbersome method for approval required at least two of three cabinet members. This was superseded by a new law in 1793 that issued patents as a matter of routine with payment of the fee of $30, far less than required in other European countries. Any invention had to be useful and new, but the system was widely abused and subjected the inventor to costly court cases to protect his rights. Noteworthy was the patent issued to Eli Whitney for his cotton gin in March 1794 that he could not easily protect against infringement.

In 1802, the Patent Office became a separate bureau in the Department of State. Until 1828, it was under Dr. William Thornton, the designer of the U.S. Capitol. He managed to protect the building containing the Patent Office from destruction by the British in August 1814, the only public building spared. Exemplary were patents for the Fulton steamboat in 1809, McCormick reaper in 1834, and the Colt six-shooter in 1836. By that year, a new law was passed to now require an examination to determine the novelty and usefulness of the invention, and the Patent Office was established as a distinct bureau, still in the Department of State. It is interesting that the first new patent under the new law was for a "locomotive steam engine for Rail and Other Roads".[14]

That same year of 1836, a fire destroyed the building that housed the Patent Office and its ten thousand models. The models of inventions and patent records were a treasury of American ingenuity and were popular as an educational exhibition and thus required suitable space for display. The display in the new building opened in 1840 was envisaged as a "national museum of the arts and . . . and the inventions and improvements in machinery . . . of which this nation can claim the honor . . . augmented by other government collections that would surpass any in the world".[15]

The importance of the theme of pride in the extraordinary American claim to creativity is further expressed in some of the Brumidi decorations in the Capitol. The Patent Corridor near the Committee Room of old Senate Committee on Patents contains several inventors. Lunettes commemorate Robert Fulton pointing to a steamboat, John Fitch working on his model of the steamboat, and Benjamin Franklin.

Plate 2.3 Minerva in the Apotheosis of Washington

This pride is made most explicit in his great canopy dome painting carried out in 1865 after the interior roof of the dome was completed. Brumidi's *The Apotheosis of Washington* achieved the long-held plan to make the rotunda a place commemorating the founder. It does so by evoking classical and religious motifs in the context of American nationalism. The picture is in the nature of Titian's famous *Assumption of the Virgin Mary* in the Franciscan Church of Venice. Allegorical figures from classical Roman mythology interact with the central figure of George Washington as he rises to the heavens to the level of a god flanked by Liberty and Fame surrounded by thirteen maidens representing the original states. Around the border are the six figures representing *war, science, marine, commerce, mechanics,* and *agriculture*. Moreover, associated with this paean to national spirit are some of the salient American inventors and inventions that may also lay claim to posterity. For example, the figure of Ceres, the Roman goddess of agriculture, is shown seated on a McCormick (otherwise called the American) reaper. In the section on marine, Neptune, the Roman god of the sea, is surrounded by image of the goddess Venus laying the Transatlantic cable and an ironclad ship with smokestacks. The latter is reminiscent of the Monitor designed by Ericsson that fought the Merrimac in the famous battle in March 1862. Science epitomized by the Roman goddess Minerva is surrounded by a generator creating power to be stored in batteries while Benjamin Franklin, Samuel F. B. Morse of telegraph fame, and Robert Fulton look on.[16]

It was on Mills's recommendation that the Patent Office building was placed between Seventh and Ninth streets NW just north of the site of the Post Office on the knoll between F and G streets. The site had been identified as suitable for a national pantheon by L'Enfant.[17] It contains since 1968 the **Smithsonian National Museum of American Art (since 2000 the Smithsonian American Art Museum) and the National Portrait Gallery,** the latter thus fulfilling the original L'Enfant notion of a place to honor great personages[18] **The Smithsonian American Art Museum** is the first apparently permanent home of what had started in the 1840s on the top floor of Robert Mills's original Patent Office Building as part of an eclectic collection known as the National Gallery. The collection included art, sculptures, natural wonders, and historical documents, as well as models of mechanical patents. Since art and science were both considered forms of knowledge of nature, there seemed to be no problem in combining them within a single setting.

The art was subsequently placed as part of the total eclectic collection in the West Gallery of the Smithsonian Castle Building. The art consisted mainly of portraits of American Indians painted on their visits to Washington seeking redress. Deposited in the Corcoran Gallery in the 1870s after a serious fire, the art collection remained there until given exhibition space in the early 1900s in the National Museum (now the **Smithsonian Art and Industries Building**) and then after 1910 in a specially dedicated hall in what is now the Smithsonian **National Museum of Natural History**. There it remained until 1968. As the fields of aesthetics and the fine arts diverged from science, there was less commonality of interest, and the art collection remained as a stepchild in institutions dominated by science.

In 1903, Harriet Lane Johnston, the niece of President James Buchanan, bequeathed works by both European and American artists to a "national gallery of art," not yet so designated. Subsequently, the title was given to the already existing collection in order to claim the bequest. Particularly important for the present collection was the 1907 gift of what was then mainly contemporaneous American art by William T. Evans, a New York textile magnate, including Winslow Homer's *High Cliff, Coast of Maine.* Another New York collector John Gellatly contributed in 1929 many of the American impressionists such as Childe Hassam and Albert Pinkham Ryder. The commitment to American art and to living artists became the collections exclusive focus with its move to the refurbished Patent Office Building. In the 1960s, a gift of twentieth-century art by S. C. Johnson and Son, the wax company owners, added to the quality of the collection, including Edward Hopper's *Facing the Sun*.

It became the National Collection of Fine Arts and entered bureaucratic limbo when in 1937, its previous title was transferred to the new Mellon *National Gallery of Art*. The Mellon collection was of old masters and limited at the time to artists dead at least twenty years. The commitment to American artists, including living artists, remained unfulfilled. Such commitment was limited since there was particular concern in the post-World War II era about the radical politics often found among artists and their art.[19] The collection is now finally committed to the collection of American artists, even those still living.

Another of the buildings designed by Robert Mills is the **Post Office** whose home was destroyed by fire in 1836 along with the Patent Office that shared its building. Adjacent to the newly built Patent Office, the Post Office lies to its south at E and F streets between Seventh and Eighth streets NW. Unlike the other buildings, it was clothed in marble from the start. With Corinthian pilasters and interspersed Corinthian pillars, it lacks the dominant façade of the Treasury and the Patent Office. It became the prototype for a large number of Beaux-Arts buildings in Washington in the early twentieth century. Now a hotel, it was the home of a series of government agencies including the Tariff Commission after the building in the 1890s of what came then to be called the **Old Post Office Pavilion** at Twelfth Street and Pennsylvania Avenue.

Manifest Destiny in the Capitol Rotunda

The expansion of the country involved both the subjugation of the indigenous Indians, the marginalization of the blacks, and the dispossession of the Mexicans. Manifest Destiny was the ideology that the European Americans, white and Protestant, would, by right, populate a country stretching from sea to sea. The term was coined in the context of the annexation of Texas in 1845, that such annexation represented the fulfillment of our *manifest destiny* to overspread the continent allotted by Providence for the free development of our yearly multiplying millions.[20] It was generally understood that civilization had throughout history spread from the Orient to the West in Europe and had now spread west to the New World and then to the Pacific. History was seen as the fulfillment of God's millennial plan. The foundation of the American republic was part of that plan. The country's progress was thus the unfolding of the millennial seed rather than merely historical change. The nation's aggressive growth and displacement of the Native Americans was thus felt necessary in order for America to fulfill its mission. Evidence of this doctrine appeared particularly in the additions that occurred in the **rotunda of the Capitol,** its ceremonial heart.

Coincident with the hanging of the four Trumbull paintings under Bulfinch between 1824 and 1829 (described in the previous chapter), reliefs over the doors to the rotunda documented prerevolutionary episodes that reflected the interaction between the indigenous Indians and the European Americans.[21] The relief over the west door, *The Preservation of Captain Smith by Pocahontas,* illustrates the act of intercession by the Indian princess that saved the Jamestown settlement and thus the beginnings of the United States. *The Landing of the Pilgrims* over the east door illustrates the equally important

Plate 2.4 The Preservation of Captain Smith by Pocahontas

landing by the founders of the New England settlement aided by the gift of corn by the subservient kneeling noble savage. *William Penn's Treaty with the Indians* over the north door shows a more egalitarian, peaceful relationship but one that ultimately succeeded in the loss of Indian land to the profit of Penn and his settlers. *The Conflict of Daniel Boone and the Indians* over the south door illustrates the fourth method of subjugation by war.

Plate 2.5 The Landing of the Pilgrims

The real person of Daniel Boone had become by legend a paradigm of the white hunter who led the chosen people westward as an agent of civilization opposed to the untamed wilderness and the savage and bloodthirsty Indian.

These images, actually created by émigré artists, nevertheless reflected the attitude widely held by Americans of the need for assimilation and subjugation of the uncivilized savage to ensure opportunities for settlers to create a superior and civilized culture. The solution to the "Indian problem" was very much in the minds of the legislators. The earlier policy of assimilation and conversion of Indians from hunters to farmers was thought by persons such as Jefferson likely to free up enough land to serve the needs of both Indians and whites. This policy was being questioned, both by the press of immigrants onto Indian lands and more specifically by the Cherokee settlement in northern Georgia. In accordance with the earlier policy, the Cherokees had become settled and created farms, become literate and

Plate 2.6
William Penn's
Treaty with
the Indians

Plate 2.7
The Conflict of
Daniel Boone
with the Indians

appeared to fulfill the goals of the Indian policy. Nevertheless, finding gold in their territory precipitated a gold rush that took precedence over any treaty commitment to their independence. Given the lands available from the Louisiana Purchase, the idea of removal became more acceptable. The Indian Removal Act of 1830 signed by President Jackson caused the migration of Indian tribes such as the Cherokees as well as other southeastern tribes to lands beyond the Mississippi with the resultant Trail of Tears in 1838.[22]

Trumbull's notion of the rotunda as the "hall of revolution" had thus begun to contain other images dealing with the entire range of experience from the time of the European discovery. Second only to George Washington, Columbus became the icon in the Capitol that connected the development of civilization in the New World from its initiator to his successors. Busts of Columbus as well as Raleigh, Cabot, and LaSalle had already been enshrined in the rotunda. Later, Randolph Rogers, an American-born sculptor trained in Florence and living in Rome, used motifs from the entire life of Columbus in 1858 to create a massive bronze door. What is now the **bronze entrance door to the rotunda** (known as the Rogers door) was originally placed in the House wing. The door echoes other artistic evidence of the role of Columbus as the person who brought Christianity and civilization to the New World and thus the United States as one of his heirs in its own civilizing role. There are ten instances, most importantly in the

**Plate 2.8
The Columbus (Rogers) Door**

rotunda, when Columbus is portrayed within the Capitol. His legend was that despite the opposition of Native Americans and others at the Spanish court, he persevered analogous to the pioneers of American folklore.[23]

**Plate 2.9 Upper Lunette of Columbus Door—
The Landing of Columbus**

Between 1840 and 1855, four additional paintings were created to fill the spaces available in the rotunda in the context of the rapid expansion of the country during this era. Trumbull's offer of four additional Revolutionary War images was turned down in favor of these others that came to be focused on the discovery and settlement of America, while also reflective of sectional rivalries.[24] The selection of topics by the artists arose out of the political setting that continued to emphasize the legitimization of national expansion following encounters between the Europeans and the Native Americans. Unlike Trumbull's use of classical references, the new set of paintings will use Christian events and Christian symbolism.[25] The provision of Christianity to the heathen Indian provides the moral basis for their conquest.

The paintings are in the romantic tradition of history paintings. The first is by John Gadsby Chapman, a close friend of a fellow Virginian Henry Alexander Wise, his congressional sponsor. Commissioned in 1837 and hung in 1840, it illustrates the *Baptism of Pocahontas at Jamestown, Virginia*. Rather than the better-known story of John Smith, it emphasizes the assimilation of the heathen princess into a Christian Virginian. Her eventual marriage to John Rolfe and the birth of a son made her the ancestor of several of Virginia's first families. With the choice of her baptismal name of Rebecca, there is a suggestion that she, like her biblical namesake, would be the forerunner of a Christianized Indian nation.[26]

Plate 2. 10 Baptism of Pocahontas at Jamestown

Appropriately, the next painting to be installed was by Robert W. Weir, a New York artist of the Hudson River school, that deals with the other founding myth. Commissioned in 1837 and hung in 1844, the New England founders are portrayed in prayer, in *The Embarkation of the Pilgrims at Delfthaven, Holland*. The image is that of the chosen people about to embark to found the nation of religious freedom. The evidence of arms and armor in the picture points to the use of force to accomplish their providential mission.

**Plate 2.11 The Embarkation of the Pilgrims at
Delfthaven, Holland**

The next was the *Landing of Columbus at the Island of Guanahani, West Indies*. The artist John Vanderlyn was trained under Gilbert Stuart but then went on as a protégé of Aaron Burr to be the first of the American painters to train in France. He painted portraits of many of the outstanding politicians of his day including John Calhoun and Zachary Taylor. Commissioned in 1842, his painting gave visual form to the actions depicted in Washington Irving's romanticized biography of Columbus and influenced from then on the image that Americans would have. In a recurrent theme in his portrayals in various media in the Capitol, the explorer stands triumphant in the center with a drawn sword while bearing the standard of the Spanish monarchs with a cross also present. The Europeans form the largest part of the picture with the natives on the side gazing in wonder or adoration. The European side is in light bringing civilization to the darkened area of the natives.[27]

Plate 2.12 The Landing of Columbus

The last, placed in 1855 but actually commissioned in 1847 during the Mexican War, was *Discovery of the Mississippi by DeSoto* by William Henry Powell (See Plate 2.13). A New York-trained painter under Henry Inman, Powell also painted *Perry's Victory on Lake Erie* on the north side of the Capitol building. Indian tepees and European flags frame the central regal figure of the explorer on a white horse juxtaposing the two cultures, one "savage," the other "civilized." Implements of war are also prominent while the Indians are shown as submissive.[28] The cross and the sword are both evident as the "civilizing" instruments being used.

Plate 2.13 The Discovery of the Mississippi by DeSoto

At one time, the ideology reflected by these paintings became even more explicit by sculptures placed in front of the very prominent east portico of the Capitol, but no longer there. Luigi Persico's *Discovery of America* showed the figure of Columbus standing upright with a seminude native female crouched beneath. James Buchanan, then a Pennsylvania senator, and later president, was effusive in his praise of his friend's statue: "the great discoverer when he first bounded with ecstasy upon the shore . . . presenting a hemisphere to the astonished world . . . a female savage, with awe and wonder in her countenance, is gazing upon him".[29] The companion Horace Greenough figure entitled *Rescue* had the white-clothed settler protecting his wife and children, overpowering the seminude male native warrior. These were removed in 1958 when the east front was being rebuilt. They were never returned most likely as a reflection of the changes in attitude toward the Native Americans during the second century of the republic.[30]

Part of **Brumidi's work in the rotunda** consisted of a frieze at the base of the new dome. Designed in 1859 in the model of the spiral of scenes on the columns of Trajan and Marcus Aurelius in Rome,[31] it was not started until much later and was incomplete at the time of his death in 1880. It was ultimately finished in the second century of the Capitol building.

The selection of scenes in Brumidi's work on the frieze was heavily influenced by his patron Meigs.[32] The history commemorates the New World's higher achievements of civilization. The scroll begins with several of the most frequently used symbols. The figure of *America* holding the shield in one hand and a spear in the other accompanied by the cap signifying liberty and an eagle. Once again, the *Landing of Columbus* is the first of the narrative describing the historical events of American history followed by *Cortez with Montezuma* and *Pizarro with the Incas* before coming to *The Burial of DeSoto in the Mississippi*. Inclusion of the Spanish conquests in the frieze in the rotunda suggest a connection between the Spanish conquerors and the fulfillment of their mission by the United States as their true heir. This notion was compatible with the stance of Jefferson Davis who sought expansion into Mexico and the conquest of the remaining Spanish possession of Cuba as consistent with the principle of Manifest Destiny.[33]

The next scenes replicate those already in the rotunda dealing with John Smith, the Pilgrims, Penn's Treaty, and the equivalent treaty with the Indians by Ogelthorpe, the founder of the settlement at Savannah in Georgia. The section of the American Revolution starts with the *Battle of Lexington* before it once again replicates Trumbull's topics of the *Declaration of Independence*, but of its public reading rather than signing, and the *Surrender of Cornwallis at Yorktown*. A new topic is the death of the Tecumseh, leader of the Indian Confederation supporting the British in the War of 1812. His defeat marked the opening up of Indian lands to settlers in the old northwest territory. The triumph of the Mexican War in the *American Army on Its Way to Mexico City* shows the surrender of the Mexicans to General Winfield Scott. The actual work by Brumidi on his frieze ends with the *Discovery of Gold in California*. Much later additions deal with the *Spanish-American War* and the *Wright Brothers Flight*.

Manifest Destiny in the Capitol Extension

As early as the 1820 census, the House had already expanded to 216 members necessitating a modification of the south wing to accommodate the larger number. States formed out of the old northwest territory and the Louisiana Purchase also required an enlarged Senate. By 1850, the nation had grown by the annexation of Texas and the formerly Mexican territories that form the southwest. California entered as a free state in exchange for a strengthened Fugitive Slave Law in the Compromise of 1850. Congress authorized in 1851 an extension of the Capitol to accommodate delegates from the expanded country and its enlarging population.

Thomas U. Walter, a Philadelphia-born and trained architect, was noted for his neoclassical Greek revival buildings, most particularly the Girard College complex in his native city.[34] Active from the last of the Greek revival era of the 1840s until 1870, he was the dean of American architects between the eclipse of Robert Mills and the work of H. H. Richardson. As architect to the Capitol in the 1850s until 1865, he completed the house chamber in 1857 and the Senate by 1859. During the Pierce administration ending in 1855, Jefferson Davis as secretary of war was in overall charge. West Point-trained Montgomery Meigs of the U.S. Army Corps of Engineers was directly in charge and primarily responsible until 1859 for overseeing the artists decorating the building. Broadly educated, Meigs had the vision of a Capitol that would be comparable to the temples and palaces of Europe. The pediments were to be reminiscent of the Parthenon; the bronze doors that of the Baptistry of the cathedral of Renaissance Florence.[35] The overall opulence of design and decoration drawing upon roots in the Italian Renaissance was meant to exemplify that the torch had passed from the age considered the epitome of European civilization to an America that had fulfilled its destiny uniting the west and east coasts of a continent.[36]

Walter added a marble wing to each of the original wings of the U.S. Capitol while maintaining an exterior similar to Thornton's earlier design, including Corinthian capitals on the columns and pilasters. His Victorian interpretation of the neoclassicism of the original introduced more windows and façades treated more three-dimensionally. Its breadth now extended 751 feet across the brow of Capitol Hill. The new rectangular chambers of the House and Senate were placed in the center of their respective wings, now each with a separate entrance reached by external stairs and pediment surmounting the Corinthian columns. The north wall of the House chamber contains medallions of the great lawgivers of the past such as Hammurabi of Babylon, Solon of Athens, and Tribonium alongside his patron, the Emperor Justinian, responsible for the codification of the Roman law in the sixth century CE.

The old House chamber eventually became the Statuary Hall; the old Senate chamber the home of the Supreme Court. Given the great lateral extensions, it was necessary to replace the old dome designed by Bullfinch. The new higher double cast-iron dome was patterned after that of Christopher Wren's St. Paul's in London and the Pantheon in Paris. It used technology developed for the newly completed St. Isaac's Cathedral in St. Petersburg. The use of cast iron would make it lighter and more easily constructed than the more common masonry construction of the time. Its "wedding cake" external appearance relates to the sculptural quality of the façades of the wings drawing the entire composition together, also becoming the model for the legislatures of many state capitols as well as capitols of foreign countries.

Although there was continuity in the exterior, the interior became quite different from the original building with a far greater variety of color and pattern. The opportunities that were now opened up for decoration of the new wings, the chambers, the corridors, and the rotunda under the newly completed dome were fulfilled mainly by Constantino Brumidi. An Italian artist well trained in Roman classical fresco painting, he brought prevailing themes into his work that reflect the ideology of national expansion. Although Meigs was satisfied that the subject matter was American and that no American could carry out fresco painting, his selection of a foreigner to execute the work was criticized. American artists sought the commission; a number of congressmen expressed concern about the extravagance of art. Indeed, it provided a pretext for forcing Meigs to leave his post supervising the Capitol. Brumidi, however, carried on. He replicated the Vatican work of Raphael in a Victorian version of Italian Renaissance style.

The triangular pediments on the east fronts of each new wing were also seen by Meigs as an opportunity to replicate classical models. Design of the sculptures for the pediment of the **north Senate wing** was assigned to Thomas Crawford. An American living in Rome, he had been trained by the Danish neoclassical sculptor Thorwaldsen and was considered, along with his fellow Italian ex-patriots Hiram Powers of *Greek Slave* fame and Horace Greenough, one of the leading American sculptors of his time. One measure of the esteem in which he was held was Crawford's statue, alone of Americans, placed among the great artists honored in the niches of the original Corcoran Art Gallery (now the **Renwick**

Gallery) completed in the late 1850s. Crawford was also a protégé of Charles Sumner, the Massachusetts senator and abolitionist, responsible for steering federal patronage his way.[37] Crawford was also apparently more willing than Powers to submit his designs to a mere engineer such as Meigs and to respond to Meigs's injunction to make his sculpture "intelligible to the entire population" and illustrative of American history and its themes.[38]

The Progress of Civilization (originally appropriately entitled *The Rise of American Civilization and the Decadence of the Indian Races* in the correspondence between Meigs and Crawford) is one of the fruits of this collaboration and is clearly in tune with the ideology of Manifest Destiny.

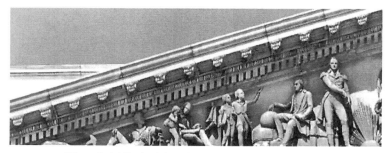

Plate 2.14 Left side of Progress of Civilization

On the pediment of the entry to the Senate wing, it recapitulated the story of American settlement across the continent "from sea to shining sea." Completed in 1863, similar to the initial figure in the Brumidi frieze in the rotunda, there is a central female figure of *America*. She looks heavenward in recognition of the role of Providence in the national expansion. There is a Phrygian cap signifying liberty that was in use on revolutionary times in France as well as America. However, unlike the earlier Persico sculpture on the east front, the sculpture is not limited to classical allegorical figures. On the right of the pediment (See Plate 2.15), the figure of the woodsman with his ax is emblematic of the progress of civilization as the adjacent Indian on the left as the hunter is emblematic of the wilderness. The role of the Indian is to give way and for his family to fade into oblivion ending in the grave. To the left of the central figure (See Plate 2.14) stands the soldier, then the merchant with his hand on the globe, and finally the mechanic symbolizing the industrial and agricultural accomplishment with standing clothed schoolboys in contrast to the crouching naked Indian boy on the right.[39]

Plate 2.15 Right side of Progress of Civilization

The **south House of Representatives pediment** *The Apotheosis of Democracy* was not completed until 1916 when the American culture had been well established. The sculptor, Paul Wayland Bartlett, born in New Haven, spent most of his life in Paris. The title derives from the character of the House as the direct representative of the people whereas the Senate represented the states. The central *Armed Peace* protects *Genius* nestled at her feet. The sides represent the great sources of wealth with motifs identifying *Agriculture* on the right and *Industry* on the left.

Plate 2.16 The Statue of Freedom (Armed Liberty)

The bronze doors to each of the new chambers inspired Meigs as an opportunity to replicate the impact of **Ghiberti's Baptistry of the cathedral in Florence**. Crawford embellished the entrances to each of the wings with scenes from the revolutionary and federal periods, incorporating themes from both war and peace. Crawford's other major contribution was the statue of *Freedom* that surmounts the dome. Next to the Washington Monument, it is the most prominent feature of the Washington skyline. Several metamorphoses were necessary before the present statue, more properly called *Armed Liberty* with a sword in hand and shield in the left, became acceptable to Jefferson Davis, himself of course a slaveholder. He particularly objected to the Phrygian cap, symbolic of manumission of Roman slaves with the statement that "its history renders it inappropriate to a people born free and would not be enslaved." A helmet with an eagle's head and feathers suggestive of an Indian headdress was substituted, obscuring any suggestion of the extremely sensitive issue of slavery. Although completed in 1857, the statue was finally placed after the completion of the dome in 1863, the year of the Emancipation Proclamation and Gettysburg. Its meaning then became seen as celebrating at the summit of the Capitol the reunification of the Union under Northern hegemony.[40] The image of *America* as a female with evidence of American Indian identity was a well-established motif from the earliest period of American settlement. Its lasting imagery is seen in Brumidi's 1870s mural in the U.S. Capitol of Columbus lifting the veil of the native Indian maiden exemplifying the discovery of the New World.

The theme of the "westward course of empire" implicit in much of the work in the Capitol was explicitly the title of painting by the German-trained history painter Emmanuel Leutze, depicting the immigration to the west for the **west stairway of the House wing** (the artist also responsible for the iconic *Washington Crossing the Delaware*), is in a prominent position used by persons on their way to the visitors gallery of the House. Completed during the Civil War, *Westward the Course of Empire Takes Its Way* (also called Westward, Ho) reflects a modification of the prevailing iconography. Less evident than in the rotunda and elsewhere is the subject of conflict between the Native Americans and the immigrants. The Indian figures are displaced to the periphery of the painting with the focus on the triumphant migration by the immigrants to the Pacific exemplified by the Golden Gate. There has indeed been a final realization of American Manifest Destiny in the New World Eden. The religious context is reinforced by side vignettes illustrating *Moses Leading the Israelites though the Desert* and the *Spies Bearing Fruits of Eschol from Canaan*. America had fulfilled its God-given role overcoming all obstacles.

Plate 2.17 Westward The Course of Empire Takes Its Way

This work carried out, in the context of the use of the Capitol building by soldiers during the Civil War, also marks for the first time the presence of an African American in the picture. A black young man stands in the center in the foreground of the completed painting, not present in the earlier sketches. Since Jefferson Davis no longer controlled the Capitol decoration, Meigs, in accordance with his own antislavery proclivity, allowed this innovation. The painting, along with the hoisting of Crawford's **Statue of Freedom** atop the completed dome, symbolized the continuity of the national mission despite the ongoing fratricidal war.[41]

Plate 2.18 Detail of the African-American in "Westward Ho"

For the Increase and Diffusion of Knowledge

One of the dreams of Washington for his capital on the Potomac was that it would be the site of a national university and a place for the amassing of knowledge to complement his hope for commercial and political success. Yet the ideology of republicanism evoked during the revolution was antithetical to such aims. Excessive devotion to the arts or pure science was considered by many as sinful, a mark of degeneracy. The democratic impulse found by Tocqueville in the burgeoning capitalist society was antithetical to the creation and appreciation of the arts or science other than those easily applied. They required special cultivation and leisure.

Theoretical science was regarded with the same distrust as the fine arts.[42] America, as a source of culture and the role of the federal government in encouraging this effort, required a major change from the context in which there was distrust of what is now called high culture and an essentially utilitarian attitude toward science. The difficulties to be faced became evident in the struggle over the use of the bequest by James Smithson from the time of its arrival in 1836. The illegitimate son of the Duke of Northumberland, Smithson had been a scientist and a member of the Royal Society. His estate of around $500,000 was to be used to "found at Washington, under the name of the Smithsonian Institution, an Establishment for the increase & diffusion of Knowledge among men".[43] Although a substantial amount of money at that time, it could soon be dissipated and very nearly was by investing the money in state bonds that lost value. The dogged persistence of John Quincy Adams, now in the House of Representatives, was essential to preserve the funds.

Not until 1846 was there some agreement as to how to proceed. In the bitter sectional rivalry of the time, there had been particular opposition by Southerners in Congress intent on reducing any expansion of activity by the federal government. A "national institute for the promotion of science" organized in 1840 by John Quincy Adams among others failed to achieve control of the bequest but did provide a model for its successor in combining patronage to the arts and sciences, technology and American history.[44] The act signed by President Polk in 1846 established an independent organization with a secretary and board of regents made up of luminaries and members of both houses of Congress headed by the vice president and chief justice ex officio.

Alexander Dallas Bache was a particularly important regent. He was a professor of chemistry at the University of Pennsylvania, the second superintendent of the U.S. Coast Survey. Very well connected personally (a great-grandson of Benjamin Franklin and a top-ranked graduate of West Point) as well as politically, he was instrumental in the selection of first Secretary.[45] Appointed the Smithsonian's first Secretary in 1846 was Joseph Henry, a close friend of Bache and a leading American scientist whose basic work on electromagnetism led to the Morse telegraph.

However, the building and its placement on a site on the Mall reflected the influence of Robert Dale Owen, a congressman from Indiana and the son of Robert Owen, the social reformer and founder of New Harmony,

Indiana. The young Owen had trained in Germany imbued with the theories of popular education espoused by Johann Pestalozzi and had tried to apply them in New Harmony. Owen had guided the bill though Congress and was also one of the Smithsonian Regents. The Act of Incorporation partly reflected Owen's wishes to create a wide range of functions for education of the common man. The building was to contain a museum based upon what had already been started at the Patent Office, a library, an art gallery, a chemical laboratory, and lecture rooms.

Owen also took a large role in selecting the architect and the design of the building based upon his love for German medieval architecture. **The Castle** came to be built on the south border of the Mall (the less marshy side) at the center of Tenth Street by James Renwick. Its medieval style was a forerunner of the Gothic revival of many churches including the architect's St. Patrick's Cathedral in New York City. It remains as a mediaeval-inspired Norman Romanesque building made of locally mined sandstone (from nearby Seneca, Maryland). Yet its style was deemed more functional than the pediments and columns of the Greek revival. For example, window ornamentation served as a drip mold above the windows; parapets were to serve for drainage; towers served as furnace flues.[46] It has both pointed and round arches with nine different turrets perhaps reflecting its ambiguous mission as well as the American nature of eclecticism in architecture. Owen went on to advocate the dissemination of this Romanesque round arch style as progressive and economical, compatible with the American republic. It was to be the forerunner of the acceptance of the work of H. H. Richardson later in the last quarter of the nineteenth century.

Unlike Owen, Joseph Henry wanted to use the income from the bequest to "increase knowledge." He sought to support original scientific research very much lacking in the United States at that time and to "diffuse knowledge" by the publication of such research. He was particularly active in the support of meteorological research and the foundation of what later became the Weather Bureau. Illustrative of its scientific publications was the first: *Ancient Monuments of the Mississippi Valley* that dealt with the Indian mound builders. The large size and expense of building the Castle, as well as its maintenance, detracted from the income to support the primary role as envisaged by Henry to fund science and a scientific clearinghouse.

Other efforts at the same time supported Henry in his efforts to advance science in the United States. Modeled after its British predecessor (BAAS), the American Association for the Advancement of Science (AAAS) was founded in Washington in 1848 as the first national organization to support the development of all the sciences in the United States. As a general organization, it spawned over the years many more specialized groups such as engineering societies, many of whom increasingly settled in Washington.

Throughout its early history, Henry also fought against the **National Museum** being part of the mission of the Smithsonian as well as several of its other assigned functions.[47] He was eventually successful in divesting its library to the **Library of Congress** to become the basis of the latter's science section. The art collection went to the **Corcoran Gallery of Art** (also then in a Renwick-designed Second Empire building now the **Smithsonian Decorative Arts and Crafts Museum** on Pennsylvania Avenue). That art collection eventually became the core of the **National Museum of American Art**, now in the Old Patent Office Building. The lecture hall was a victim of a fire in January 1865 and was not replaced. However, the fire had spared the museum collection in the west wing. Despite Henry's wishes, but now with federal appropriations, the **National Museum** component continued to grow. It spread to the **great hall** in the central building as well as the west wing containing material from archeological and ethnological explorations sponsored by the Smithsonian as well as a natural history section. For example, the large hall in the west wing on the second floor displayed the collection of American Indian artifacts. Each of its collections became forerunners of a series of museums over the years, several of whom placed on the Mall.[48]

Under the auspices of Henry's deputy and successor Spencer Baird, the **National Museum** component continued to proliferate particularly with material from the Centennial Exhibition in Philadelphia in 1876.[49] The Exposition coupled a patriotic theme with display of the flowering of American inventiveness, including Alexander Graham Bell's telephone. Finally in 1878, Congress appropriated money for the separate relatively utilitarian redbrick building for the **National Museum** (now the **Arts and Industries Building**). Placed adjacent to the Castle, it was built by Adolf Cluss, the leading Washington architect of the time, after a design by

Montgomery Meigs.[50] Adolf Cluss, born in Germany, was a refugee from the failed Revolutions of 1848. From 1862 onward, Cluss was the pioneer local Washington professional architect. He designed both private and public buildings throughout the city in a layered redbrick Victorian style derived from Northern German architecture that fell out of favor by the end of the century. His work on the Arts and Industries Building was replicated in other public buildings on the south side of the Mall, now replaced. Among those remaining are the public school buildings he designed that served to exemplify his consistent faith in the republican principles he had advocated in Germany.

The Arts and Industries Building was opened in time for the inaugural ball for President Garfield in 1881. Its continued presence, although shuttered at this time, reflects the initial success of the vision of Owens rather than **Joseph Henry** whose statue stands in front of the Castle he so disliked. It was the first of a proliferation of museums along the Mall associated with the Smithsonian with the clear mandate of public education rather than support for scholars. Other activities spread beyond the Mall. Baird's interest in fish led to the **Marine Oceanographic Institute** at Woods Hole, Massachusetts. The subsequent secretary Samuel Pierpont Langley established the **zoological park** in Rock Creek Park. Still others built astronomical observatories run by the Smithsonian in different sites in New Mexico and Peru.

Washington as a *City*

The Congress, with each delegate representing his own individual constituency, was reluctant to support the earlier vision of George Washington and other Virginians that the city would become a commercial center. The shallow harbor of Georgetown was inadequate as steam-powered ships began to appear. The Washington Canal designed to connect the costly C&O Canal to the Anacostia River had become a sewer as was the Tiber Creek. In addition to the technical advantages of its port, Baltimore had superior political access to its own state legislature. It was thus able to gain priority for the **Baltimore and Ohio Railroad** to tap the commerce of the west to the detriment of Washington's **Chesapeake and Ohio Canal** on the Potomac River.[51]

The stresses first demonstrated in the selection and design of the seat of government, the city, and its salient capitol became even more evident during the interval leading to the Civil War. The Chesapeake region had become the linchpin of a sectional division between the North and South.[52] The city was situated in the Tidewater section of the increasingly self-conscious and assertive South. It remained a Southern city despite its national ambitions.[53] The ongoing presence of slavery and the slave trade as well as Black Codes affecting free Negroes branded it Southern. Southern influence on the federal government was based upon equal number of states between the sections in the Senate and the three-fifth rule counting slaves in establishing congressional representation that magnified Southern influence in the House. Efforts of Northern abolitionists to call upon the power of Congress's "exclusive jurisdiction" to end slavery in the District were prevented. A "gag rule" forbade even the bringing of petitions to Congress to act toward abolition of the very active slave trade even in the shadow of the Capitol. Indeed, one of the reasons for the retrocession of the Virginian portion of the District of Columbia in 1846 was the desire to maintain the slave trade unhampered. The slave trade was finally abolished in the District of Columbia by the Compromise of 1850 but rendered relatively meaningless by the maintenance of the slave trade in neighboring Alexandria.[54]

Washington's development as a *city* was also constrained by the unchecked power of sectional and local interests in the Congress. An orphan of sectional interests without any federal representatives of its own, it was considered a Southern city by the North, a Northern city by the South. Particularly burdensome for this small city in the antebellum era was need for clearing and paving the far larger extent of the streets than towns of a similar size would normally have. The Congress contributed very little to the city and limited its contribution to improvements to the streets around the Capitol and Executive Mansion. The local government had a severely restricted tax base since most of the land was held by the federal government. Yet the municipality was expected to provide all the usual services in terms of roads, street lighting, markets, schools, etc.

One major development was the **City Hall** started in the 1820s rising on the knoll assigned by L'Enfant to the judiciary at Indiana Avenue and F Street between Fourth and Fifth streets NW. This building was a joint effort with the federal government since one wing was assigned to be a courthouse. The center portion served as the City Hall until 1873 when it was taken over by the federal government for use as courts. Its design was replicated in the subsequent adjoining court buildings built over the succeeding century. This Greek revival building with its Ionic portico is the only remaining building in the District that was the work of George Hadfield. A British-trained architect, he had been for a short time one of the series of architects involved in the U.S. Capitol in the late 1790s. He also was responsible for designing the earliest version of the executive buildings adjoining the President's House. His work can still be seen in the **Arlington House,** the Doric-pillared Custis-Lee Mansion overlooking Arlington National Cemetery.

On the eve of the Civil War, the city's population had reached 75,000 with 2,100 government employees. The franchise was limited to free white males meeting certain property requirements.[55] With the secession of Virginia and the Battle of Manassas in the summer of 1861, the city was on the frontline of battle. The Tidewater Southern city entered the war with its Capitol and the occupant of the White House besieged by Southern sympathizers in Maryland and within the District itself. Employees of the federal government were required to take an oath of allegiance or forfeit their property and leave the city. Many did, but in the aftermath of the Civil War, it became a much larger city and a truly national capital for the first time. Map 2.1 shows the City Canal replacing the original Tiber Creek and uniting the Potomac and Anacostia rivers, the Treasury just to the east of the President's House permanently obstructing the vista between the President's House and the Capitol, the nearly completed Patent Office and the Capitol extension, the Smithsonian Castle, and the still uncompleted Washington Monument.

Map 2.1 of 1860

CHAPTER 3
THE GILDED AGE /
THE NATIONAL CAPITAL (1860-1900)

Introduction

During the Civil War, Washington was both a "seat of government" and a "seat of war." With the secession of Virginia, Washington was on the front line of the Union and, for a time, isolated within the slave state of Maryland. Communication with the North via rail went through Baltimore. In the spring of 1861, military reinforcements on their way to Washington were attacked on the streets of Baltimore when they marched between rail terminals in that city. Secession was threatened. A circuitous route bypassing Baltimore was opened up that brought troops early on from the North to Washington by water to protect the city. Although there were many Southern sympathizers, Maryland stayed in the Union.

During the war, Washington was an important supply base for the Army of the Potomac. The Long Bridge connecting Washington to Virginia had been built initially in 1809 and recurrently replaced when destroyed by floods. A connecting rail line was laid on a parallel span for the first time during the war to expedite transport to the front lines.[1] The Chain Bridge was the other Potomac bridge during the Civil War, the sixth of a series. It received its name from the third bridge at that site in 1810, an unusual early chain suspension structure. The site three miles upriver from Georgetown at Little Falls, the narrowest part of the river, had been the site of a series of bridges since 1797. A bridge at this point was subject to recurrent flooding; hence, the short life of each bridge prior to the method that gave the bridge its long-lasting name.[2]

Cattle pens surrounded the uncompleted **Washington Monument**. Bread was baked in the basement of the **U.S. Capitol**. Washington's many churches and government buildings throughout the city served as barracks or hospitals. For a time in 1862-1863, the **Patent Office Building** provided space for one or the other. Clara Barton, a Patent Office clerk, was among those comforting the wounded. Soldiers could be brought by rail from the battlefields of Northern Virginia to Aquia Landing on the Potomac. From there, by boat, they came to Washington. Close by was one of the major hospitals named after the Armory on Seventh Street on the Mall (now the site of the **Smithsonian Air and Space Museum**). It was there that Walt Whitman mainly carried out his service to the more severely wounded soldiers.

Plate 3.1 The Exterior of the Armory Hospital

Plate 3.2 A Ward in the Armory Hospital

An earlier version of the present-day **Willard's Hotel** at Fourteenth Street and Pennsylvania Avenue was the center of many activities. The site has been used for a hotel since 1816. The Willard name became associated with the hotel in 1850. For the next one hundred years, it was the major hotel in Washington. The present Beaux-Arts building by Henry Janeway Hardenbergh, the architect of New York's Plaza Hotel, was built in 1901 and recently restored as the Hotel Intercontinental.

The home of the president, then called the Executive Mansion, changed its character. It became primarily an office building that also secondarily housed the president's family. Great events such as the signing of the Emancipation Proclamation took place there. Crowds appeared at its gates when major happenings occurred. Security for the president became an issue. The Executive Mansion, like the U.S. Capitol, became symbolic of the nation.[3]

The Union Army of the Potomac had a dual role, both to capture Richmond, the Confederate capital, and to protect the Union capital. Lee, commander of the Confederate Army of Northern Virginia, carried out offensive maneuvers ending at the Second Battle of Bull Run (Manassas) in the spring of 1862, to Antietam (Sharpsburg) in September 1862, and Gettysburg in July 1863 that appeared to threaten Washington. Lincoln, remembering the way Washington was beleaguered at the time of his inaugural in March 1861, insisted on the maintenance of the troops guarding the capital. The capture of Washington would be a devastating blow to the Union. A ring of more than sixty defensive forts arose completely surrounding the city. (See Map 3.1) Many of these sites still remain. Names such as **Military Road, Fort Totten** (named after the commander of the Army Corps of Engineers)**, Fort Reno** (with Reno Road)**, and Fort Stevens** still remain part of the Washington scene. Fort Stevens bore the brunt of the attack by the Confederates under Jubal Early in July 1864. A small **military cemetery on Georgia Avenue** near the District Line contains remains of those who died at **Fort Stevens**. The **Arlington National Cemetery** on the grounds of the former Arlington plantation surrounding the **Custis-Lee Mansion** attest to the very large number of those who died in and around Washington.

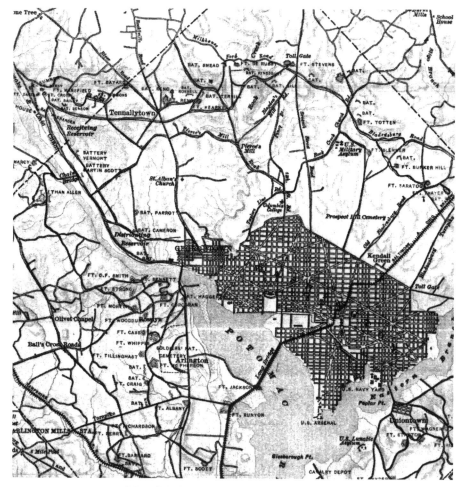

Map 3.1 The Defenses of Washington

The United States ceased to be a plural noun to become a singular one and its capital city the seat of a forceful central government. Architecture during the post-Civil War Gilded Age was eclectic in that any single building might contain a mixture of styles derived from the past. Influences from abroad could include the neo-Gothic, the French Second Empire, or the German Rundbogenstil (round arch style) that came to be equated with Victorian excess. Henry Hobson Richardson combined elements of all with the Romanesque into a monumental style that expressed "grandeur and repose" that transcended its sources to form a totality that was American in expression.[4]

Washington as *Capital*

At the time of Lincoln's first inauguration in March 1861, the new dome of the Capitol had not been completed. Its progress continued despite the Civil War. On a cold and windy December morning in 1863, a large crowd cheered and cannon boomed for each of the thirty-five states to announce the ascension of the statue *Freedom* atop the newly completed Capitol dome. It was cast at the Clark Mills foundry in nearby Bladensburg by men such as Philip Reid, one of the many slaves involved in the building of the Capitol. He was also one of those newly freed by the emancipation of slaves in the District. The statue symbolized more than it had been thought to represent when first designed by Crawford in 1856.[5]

The Capital of Northern Hegemony

The Grand Review started on May 23, 1865, as General Meade rode at the head of his Army of the Potomac from the Capitol going west along Pennsylvania Avenue to the reviewing stand at the White House. There stood President Andrew Johnson and General Grant among other dignitaries. The next day, General Sherman rode at the head of his troops from the armies that had fought in the West in the Army of the Tennessee. On the top of Pennsylvania Avenue and Fifteenth Street just south of the Treasury is the site of the very high equestrian **Sherman Monument**. Here, Sherman had reviewed his troops. Erected in 1903, it was the work of several different sculptors.

Born in Ohio, Sherman was near the top of his class at West Point and remained in the army until 1853. At the start of the war, he was teaching at a military school in Louisiana that became Louisiana State University. Although offered a commission by the Confederates, he joined the Union. After service at Vicksburg, he was appointed by Grant as his successor as commander of the Army of Tennessee. Sherman then carried out the famous March to the Sea through Georgia. Other generals who fought with Sherman are commemorated on his monument, including General James McPherson and John A. Logan, who were also otherwise commemorated on their own.[6]

The Grand Army of the Republic (GAR) was the organization of Union veterans representing the three million who fought in the Union military forces. Founded in 1866, it reached its largest enrollment in 1890 of nearly five hundred thousand. The first organized interest group in American politics, it was the most powerful single-issue political lobby in its era. It was active in the promotion of pension and veteran's benefits including the Soldiers' Homes, precursors of the Veterans Administration health care system. Its success led to the expansion of the **Pension Bureau**, to be housed in the monumental **Pension Building**. It helped elect Republican presidents from Grant to McKinley, all Union veterans. One of its lasting legacies is the celebration of Memorial Day (formerly Decoration Day). As its membership was dying, it set out in 1909 to memorialize its organization and its founder. **The Benjamin Franklin Stephenson and the Grand Army of the Republic Memorial** is a granite shaft at Seventh Street between Pennsylvania and Indiana avenues NW. It is dedicated to the organization's motto of "Fraternity, charity, and loyalty." Its sculptor in 1909 was John Massey Rhind. Born in Edinburgh and mainly English trained, he came to New York in 1889. He became famous early on by winning a commission to design a door in Trinity Church in a memorial to John Jacob Astor III. Rhind designed a large number of public monuments including several on the Gettysburg Battlefield.

Plate 3.3 Andrew Jackson

L'Enfant's plan provided for about 250 sites such as squares, circles, and triangular parklets where monuments could flourish. Indeed, Washington came to have more equestrian statues than any other city. There were just two such statues prior to the series placed following the Civil War: **General Andrew Jackson** in **Lafayette Park** in 1853 in front of the White House; and **General George Washington** in 1860 at **Washington Circle** at the confluence of Twenty-second Street, K Street, New Hampshire Avenue NW. Both were by Clark Mills who thus cast the first equestrian statues in the country.

Plate 3.4 General George Washington

Particularly noteworthy for their prominence were the monuments placed after the Civil War along the spine of Northwest Washington, mainly along Massachusetts Avenue NW. It was customary for each to be mainly sponsored by fellow veterans with varying amount of federal funds for the pedestal and for the grading of the site, dedicated by a military parade and usually the president among those speaking. Going from east to west: Formerly Iowa Circle (note the **Iowa Apartment house**) still with several 1870s Mansard buildings, **Logan Circle** is at the confluence of Thirteenth Street, Vermont Avenue, and P Street. It is now named after the equestrian statue of **General John A. Logan** sponsored by the Society of the Army of the Tennessee in 1903. He became colonel of his Illinois Regiment and fought as commander in the Army of Tennessee for a time after the death of James McPherson at the Battle of Atlanta. Moreover, he fought even longer and harder for the veterans after the war as a leading member both of the GAR and Society of the Army of Tennessee. He was first congressman in 1858 as a Democrat and then as a Republican in 1866 before becoming a senator from Illinois. The Republican candidate for vice president along with James G. Blaine, they lost to Grover Cleveland in 1884. He was noted for "waving the bloody shirt" and for keeping alive the memory of the North's victory and the South's treachery.[7]

The sculptor of the Logan statue was Franklin Simmons. Born in Maine and educated at Bates College, he was particularly active in sculpting members of Lincoln's cabinet and military officers during the Civil War. His statue of Roger Williams of Rhode Island is in Statuary Hall. The base of the statue reminiscent of a rectangular Renaissance tomb was designed by Richard Morris Hunt, the cofounder of the American Institute of Architects and the first of a series of Americans trained at L'Ecole des Beaux-Arts.

Thomas Circle at Fourteenth Street and Massachusetts Avenue NW is named after what is probably the best of the equestrian statues, that of **General George Thomas** by John Quincy Adams Ward in 1879. A Virginian and a West Point graduate, Thomas nevertheless opted for the Union. The statue was funded by the Society of the Army of the Cumberland. He became its commander after his stand as the "Rock of Chickamauga" at that battle. Ward was a preeminent sculptor of his era that spanned from 1860 until 1900. His most famous statue was of the oversize George Washington in front of Federal Hall in New York City. He also helped design with Paul Wayland Bartlett the figures on the pediment of the New York Stock Exchange.

McPherson Square is at Fifteenth Street between I and K streets NW. In the center is the statue memorializing **James McPherson,** the commander of the Army of the Tennessee. Born in Ohio, he was first in his class at West Point with John Bell Hood as his classmate. The latter was the Confederate commander at Atlanta where McPherson was killed by a Confederate picket. His was the first of the statues commissioned and unveiled in 1876 with addresses by Generals Sherman and John Logan, his colleagues in the Army of the Tennessee.

Scott Circle at Sixteenth Street and Massachusetts Avenue NW contains the statue of **General Winfield Scott** by Henry Kirke Brown completed in 1874. Born in Massachusetts, Brown trained in Boston and Italy. Noted for his equestrian statues, he designed his statue of George Washington for Union Square in New York City in 1856, the second one in America after Clark Mills's Andrew Jackson in Lafayette Park. The Scott statue was one of few memorials paid for by the Congress in its entirety. The commanding general in the U.S. Army at the start of the war, he soon retired after the First Battle of Bull Run in the summer of 1861. Serving from the time of Jefferson to Lincoln, he led in the capture of Mexico City. He earmarked the tribute exacted from the Mexican government to create the **Old Soldiers Home** off North Capitol Street. Formerly the home of W. W. Corcoran, its name **Harewood** became attached to the road lining the edge of the property. In recognition of his involvement, a statue of Scott also stands there. Because of the elevation of the site, **Anderson Cottage** (named after the commander of Fort Sumter) on the property was used as a Summer White House by Lincoln.

Dupont Circle, where Connecticut, Massachusetts, and New Hampshire avenues meet with P Street, is a major traffic center. Its monument to **Admiral Dupont** is uniquely a fountain among the Civil War commanders. Its base contains three allegorical figures representing the *arts of ocean navigation,* namely the male *wind,* the female *sea,* and goddess of the *stars.* Dedicated to a descendent of the famous Delaware munition makers, his family provided in 1921 the fountain by Daniel Chester French, the sculptor of Lincoln in his memorial, to replace an earlier bronze statue. Dupont's fleet captured Port Royal in North Carolina early in the war only to fail to capture Charleston Harbor. He retired with an undeserved stain on his reputation for that failure.

The westernmost of the equestrian statues is actually beyond the original boundary of the city of Washington at **Sheridan Circle** at Twenty-third Street and Massachusetts Avenue NW. Surrounded by embassies, **General Philip Sheridan,** the cavalry leader, is shown in his role of rallying his troops to win at the Battle of Winchester in the Shenandoah Valley of Virginia. Completed in 1908 by Gutzon Borglum, it was one of his early triumphs in beating out John Quincy Adams Ward in the competition. Born in Idaho, Borglum grew up in Nebraska and studied with Rodin in Paris. He dealt with figures of gigantic scale and themes of heroic nationalism as evidenced by his heroic presidential figures on Mount Rushmore.

Perhaps most noteworthy for its sculptress as well as is subject is that of **Admiral Farragut** at Farragut Square at Connecticut Avenue and K Street NW placed there in 1881. The admiral is standing as though on a ship deck with his telescope ready in his hand. The statue was cast from the propeller of his flagship the *USS Hartford.*

A career navy man since boyhood, Farragut was the first naval officer to achieve his rank of admiral in the U.S. Navy. He was responsible for aiding Grant in the crucial western campaign that eventually conquered the Mississippi, including the capture of New Orleans and Vicksburg, the latter in July 1863. He is particularly famous for his victory against great odds at Mobile Bay in August 1864 that closed that major port to the Confederacy.

The sculptress was Vinnie Ream (later Hoxie), the first woman sculptress to receive a federal commission. Born on the Wisconsin frontier in the 1840s, she first became famous for her sculpture of Lincoln from life just prior to his death in April 1865. Despite much opposition, she was later commissioned to do the life-size **Lincoln** statue in the **Capitol rotunda**. She had been attacked by the Radical Republicans in the Congress intent on impeaching President Andrew Johnson. The deciding vote preventing impeachment had been cast by a senator she was accused as having influenced. She was later asked to do the statue of Farragut by his wife.

These examples do not exhaust the list of Civil War monuments on the squares and streets of Washington. Nearly every military leader of note is commemorated in this militarization of the national capital to commemorate the Civil War, the great defining experience of the history of the United States and its capital.

The Executive Buildings

Under President Grant, the decision to have Washington remain the capital was decided anew despite efforts to move it to more central places such as St. Louis.[8] The term "Reconstruction" referred to the commitment of the Republican Party to reconstruct Washington, not only racially and socially, but also physically and symbolically. Even after the conclusion of the efforts to carry out the former, there remained the commitment to its physical reconstruction. The character of the buildings reflected the eclecticism of the Gothic and Renaissance revival that goes under the name of Victorian.

Plate 3.5 The State, War and Navy Building

One piece of evidence of this commitment starting in 1871 was the massive **State, War, and Navy Department Building (now the Old Executive Office Building)** on the site immediately west of the Executive Mansion. Designed by Alfred B. Mullett, the supervising architect of the Treasury, its Mansard roof (named after François Mansart) was reminiscent of the Second French Empire style that he used elsewhere in the 1870s. Monumental central porticoes project forward to provide separate entries for its three executive departments, one facing north on

Pennsylvania Avenue, another facing west on Seventeenth Street, and the last facing south. Insignia on the shield above each window identify the departments housed in each wing: the navy in the south, state on the east and war on the north and west. Unlike the recent additions to the Louvre considered the prototype of Second Empire design, Mullett turned to late-seventeenth-century models such as Jules Hardouin-Mansart's Church of the Invalides (the grandnephew of the earlier François Mansart). Mullett's two-story porticoes, like his prototype, are open and deeply recessed with pairs of columns but rather extend vertically through the three, four, or five stories. Multiple columnar elements further distort the prototype with longer Doric capitals below and shorter Ionic capitals above, contrary to standard practice and occasional Corinthian orders. Unlike the purer Second Empire style of the **Renwick Building** across the street, it is far more eclectic and was considered to be bombastic as well as excessively costly. Mullett was dismissed amid charges of graft. Out of favor since its completion in the 1880s and despite recurrent efforts in the Beaux-Arts period for its reconstruction in the style of the nearby neoclassical Treasury Building, the building still remains, its exterior unremodelled while adapted to its new use.

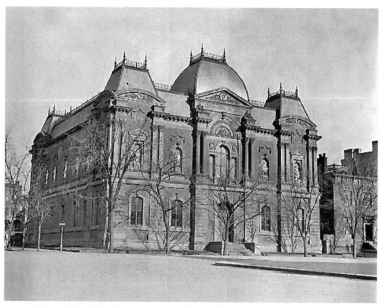

Plate 3.6 Old Corcoran Gallery (Now Renwick Gallery)

Plate 3.7 Frieze on the Pension Office

One measure of the growth of federal employment dealing with the effects of the Civil War was the very large brick **Pension Building (now the National Building Museum) in Judiciary Square.** It was built during 1882-1887 by Montgomery Meigs as a model office building in terms of light and ventilation.[9] The Pension Bureau had a staff of 1,500 in rented quarters to process the pensions of almost three million, mainly Civil War veterans and their dependents. Meigs devised the design from a synthesis of Renaissance models visited during his European travels following the Civil War. The famous sixteenth-century **Farnese Palace** in Rome by Antonio da Sangallo was the basic model but doubled in size from the original to four hundred feet east to west and two hundred feet north to south. The original model was followed, albeit in red brick, in the horizontal organization of the exterior into three equal stories also duplicating the fenestration of the original with alternating semicircular and triangular pediments. The cornices have military themes rather than the acanthus leaves and fleur-de-lis of the original. Particularly different is the terra-cotta frieze depicting the Union Army on the march that is more reminiscent of the religious **Panathenaic Procession on the frieze of the Parthenon** than the depiction of a military convoy in the campaigns of Napoleon's **Grand Armée on the Arc de Triomphe.**

The shallow risers of the interior staircases are designed to enable disabled persons to use them more easily. Still one of the great rooms of Washington is the interior-roofed **great hall** ringed with huge Corinthian columns. The columns were derived from the **Baths of Diocletian as modified by Michelangelo for the church of Santa Maria degli Angeli** in Rome. The great hall was used for the inaugural ball of President Grover Cleveland in 1885 and for President Benjamin Harrison in 1889. It is still used for large receptions. The interior consists of two levels of arches carried by slender columns modeled after Bramante's sixteenth-century Roman **Palazzo della Cancelleria**. The tenets of Renaissance architecture were freely violated when the roof was designed in accordance with the iron-trussed railway sheds of the Victorian era.[10]

Plate 3.8 Great Hall Pension Bldg on Occasion of the Inaugural Ball of President Harrison

A Temple of Learning

The Library of Congress was first opened in 1800 as a resource for Congress, but then for the government as a whole before becoming a resource for the general public throughout the country. Its size and scope changed as it mirrored the changes in the scope of its mission. After the destruction of the Capitol by the British in 1814, the acquisition of the private library of Thomas Jefferson in 1815 was an important milestone. A far greater variety of subject matter and languages than heretofore entered the collection consistent with Jefferson's wide-ranging interests. Thus was established the library's policy of comprehensive collections. Another clear watershed was the appointment of Ainsworth Rand Spofford as Librarian by President Lincoln in 1864. He increased the hours during which the library was open and permitted books to circulate to the general public. Early in his tenure, the Smithsonian transferred its collection to the library. In 1870, the library gained sole rights for the deposit of all copyright materials. After 1891, material of foreign origin was also deposited to ensure copyright. It had become *the* de facto national library. In 1897, it was truly designated as the national library with many of its present-day multiple divisions and activities.

The library was inundated by accessions from the 1870s onward. Its inadequate quarters in the west front of the Capitol building could not expand. Spofford gained the support of influential members of Congress including the fellow Ohioan and later president Rutherford B. Hayes. He also traded on the nationalist spirit of the Gilded Age to move the library to the status of the world-class national libraries of Britain and France. In 1873, Spofford achieved authorization for a new separate building to be placed across from the east plaza of the U.S. Capitol.

Its design became a victim of congressional politics. The plan by John Smithmeyer and Paul Pelz, both German immigrants after the Revolutions of 1848, had first been selected in 1873 for an Italian Renaissance building. It was not finally approved until 1886 after multiple revisions. Its construction was also controversial. Smithmeyer was removed with General Thomas Lincoln Casey of the Army Corps of Engineers assigned responsibility in 1888. As the engineer in charge of the completion of the Washington Monument and the State, War, and Navy Department Building, Casey was noted for keeping costs down while carrying out difficult monumental buildings and ensured not only the library's completion but its decoration.[11] Pelz was then replaced in 1892 by Edward Pearce Casey, a young architect and son of the general in charge. Trained with Charles McKim, young Casey had newly returned from having spent several years at L'Ecole des Beaux-Arts in Paris. He took responsibility for overseeing the internal decoration already mainly designed by Pelz. After the dismissal of Pelz, controversy arose as to the proper credit and payment for the work with attacks on the number of persons with German background employed to the detriment of "Americans." As immigrants, they were disdained by the native-born architectural elite, and credit was inappropriately given to Edward P. Casey. This could be consistent with the aim of establishing the Library of Congress as proof that American culture could be taken seriously and the contribution of foreigners be denied.[12]

The present-day **Thomas Jefferson Building** was opened in 1897. The aim was not only to provide a functional building but an inspirational one. A relatively large amount of almost $400,000 was made available from the funds unexpended for construction. The dome with its gilded *Torch of Learning* epitomizes its grandeur. The multiplicity of subjects to be included in its decoration reflected the tenor of the nineteenth century with its bias toward ornament. The content and quality of its art was taken to reflect the maturity of American art of its time. All twenty sculptors and nineteen painters were required to be American citizens although sometimes foreign born. Many had also been involved with the Columbian Exposition of 1893 in Chicago when painter, sculptor, and architect had all worked together to achieve a greater whole. The library was indeed an expression of the American Renaissance, drawing upon its European antecedents in the earlier Italian Renaissance but also the expression of the sense of American optimism and possibilities for the future.

Plate 3.9 The Great Hall of the Library of Congress

Its **great hall** replicates the entry into impressive entry courtyards of baroque or Renaissance palaces. Prominent are allusions to the goddess Minerva (the Roman counterpart of the Greek goddess Athena) representing wisdom. Its arched openings are suggestive of Roman triumphal arches. The elaborately decorated interior is reminiscent of Brumudi's earlier work in the U.S. Capitol building. It is also important in its association of grandeur with democratic citizenship in a library open to all.

In accordance with the sense of American arrival on the world scene, American figures were interspersed with the great figures of the past. Spofford, for example, selected the figures to be sculpted on the outside of the building. He included his personal favorites: Benjamin Franklin, Emerson, Hawthorne, and Irving along with Sir Walter Scott, Macaulay, Goethe, Dante, and Demosthenes.

The design of a **main reading room** (See Plate 3.10) was patterned after that of the British Museum but also of Jefferson's concept of a circular library at the University of Virginia.[13] The highlight of the entire building is the **central dome of the main reading room** with its decoration by Edwin Howland Blashfield of *The Progress of Civilization*.[14] Born in New York City, Blashfield studied in Paris. He painted large murals in many state capitols and at the Chicago World's Fair of 1893. He was appointed to the Commission of Fine Arts in 1912, carrying on the connection of its members with the Chicago Fair. The collar of the dome is a ring of twelve-seated figures representing the twelve countries or epochs which have contributed most to the development of nineteenth-century civilization in America. Starting in the East are the contributions of Egypt (*Written Records*), Judea (*Religion*), Greece (*Philosophy*), Rome (*Administration*), Islam (*Physics*), the Middle Ages (*Modern Languages*), Italy (*Fine Arts*), Germany (*Art of Printing*), Spain (*Discovery*), England (*Literature*), France (*emancipation*), and, finally, its culmination in America (*Science*). The oculus in the center illustrates *The Evolution of Civilization*. The female figure of *Human Understanding* floats upward looking toward the figures on the collar of the dome representing *Finite Intellectual Achievement*.

Plate 3.10
The Main Reading Room of the Library of Congress

The statues placed on the balustrade of the **main reading room** once again placed the Americans Joseph Henry (representing *Science*) alongside Newton; Robert Fulton (representing *Commerce*) alongside Columbus.

The other figures were Moses and Saint Paul (representing *Religion*); Herodotus and Gibbon (representing *History*); Michelangelo and Beethoven (representing *Art*); Plato and Bacon (representing *Philosophy*); Homer and Shakespeare (representing *Poetry*); and finally, Solon and Chancellor James Kent (representing *Law*).

The dramatic colorful mosaic by Elihu Vedder is on the steps leading to the visitors' gallery overlooking the **main reading room**. **Minerva**, the goddess of *civilization*, holds the scroll listing the various arts and sciences that flourish in a civilized society. Born in New York City, Vedder was a symbolist painter

Plate 3.11 Minerva

living mainly in Italy in Rome and Capri. When in the United States, he was a friend of Walt Whitman, Herman Melville, and Richard Morris Hunt, the last the early Beaux-Arts architect. He was a friend in England of the pre-Raphaelites and interested in mystics like William Blake. He was best known for his extraordinarily successful illustrations for Edward FitzGerald's translation of the *Rubaiyat of Omar Khayyam*.

Since the move to the Jefferson Building in 1897, the library has continued to expand into the adjoining Adams Building in the 1930s art deco style reminiscent of the adjoining Folger Library and the 1970s Madison Building with a range of flat columns reminiscent of earlier Beaux-Arts architecture. The library's books and other materials derived from copyright deposits have been augmented by several additional divisions. Lessing Rosenwald, the son of Julius Rosenwald, the founder of Sears, Roebuck and Co. provided his collection to the rare book division. The music division has been particularly affected by the legacy of Elizabeth Sprague Coolidge. A. A. Sprague, her father, was a successful wholesale grocer in Chicago. A musician, thwarted by her class and time in the late nineteenth century from a musical career, she used her fortune to endow musical performances by string quartets and an eponymous performance space at the library. She particularly sponsored new music and American music such as Aaron Copeland's *Appalachian Spring*. Contemporaneously, Mrs. Gertrude Clarke Whittall provided a collection of violins by Stradivarius for use by those string quartets playing at the Coolidge Auditorium as well as support for poetry readings and literary lectures.

Washington as *City*

By the end of the decade of the war, the city had become truly a national capital grown to a population of seventy-four thousand whites and thirty-five thousand blacks.[15] The total number of government employees had tripled to seven thousand. With the departure of many Southern sympathizers and arrival of persons from the North, the city's white population both increased and changed its character.

To an even greater degree, its black population increased. Although oppressed by Black Codes in effect, the overwhelming majority of blacks in the District were free on the eve of the war. Emancipation (with compensation) of the relatively small number of slaves took place in the

District of Columbia on April 16, 1862, on the basis of congressional "exclusive jurisdiction" to pass laws in the District. The more general Emancipation Proclamation that took effect on January 1, 1863, applied only to slaves being held within states in rebellion. Thus although it would apply to Virginia, it would not apply to Maryland. Nevertheless, many former slaves escaped from Maryland to come to the District. The Fugitive Slave Law still applied to them, and for a time, a number of such persons were returned to their owners. The Union military authorities then acted to maintain these escapees as "contraband" and offered them work and protection. By the end of the war, there were twenty-five thousand additional Negro inhabitants in the District, almost entirely uneducated and destitute. Many of the newly freed were housed under poor conditions in the "alley dwellings" that sprung up in the southwest area and elsewhere to deal with the influx.

The Washington Aqueduct

The first of the many great achievements that Montgomery Meigs contributed to the embellishment of Washington is that which underlies its very development as a city. Until 1852, the water supply was dependent on wells and cisterns, and thus both insufficient and liable to cause illness. In the course of the years ending finally in 1863, an aqueduct brought water from **Great Falls** on the Potomac through a series of tunnels mainly to the western portion of the city of Washington, bridging Rock Creek at present-day Pennsylvania Avenue. The level of the river upriver from Great Falls seventy feet above that of the city enabled the water to flow by gravity without the need for a pump.[16]

Plate 3.12 Union Arch of Washington Aqueduct

Meigs in his planning invoked not only modern waterworks such as those of New York and Boston but also the great aqueducts of Imperial Rome worthy of emulation if not to be surpassed by our own republic.[17] Under the direction of fellow West Pointer Jefferson Davis as secretary of war in the administration of Franklin Pierce, the job was assigned to Meigs. The conduit from Great Falls carried water over the masonry **Cabin John Bridge** (the longest in the world at the time) to be discharged into a reservoir near the District line, now the **Dalecarlia Reservoir**. From there, it is carried under what is now **MacArthur Boulevard** to the **reservoir** near the Palisades. Carried further west along **Reservoir Road,** it was pumped up to a high-level reservoir atop **Wisconsin Avenue at R Street NW** (now site of the D.C. Public Library George Town Branch). Other mains carry water to Capitol Hill and the Navy Yard to the east over **Rock Creek** along Pennsylvania Avenue. However, the water supply to the eastern portion of the city remained inadequate and subject to many complaints by its citizen's associations until the building of the McMillan Reservoir near Howard University in the first decade of the twentieth century.[18]

Montgomery C. Meigs, an 1836 West Point graduate, carried out his work as a member of the U.S. Army Corps of Engineers on the **Washington Aqueduct** during the 1850s while also working on the **Capitol building extension** and the further extension of Robert Mills's **Post Office** near the Patent Office. Quartermaster General of the Union Army during the Civil War, he was able to provide logistical support for what was then the largest army operations in American history. He recommended the transformation of Robert E. Lee's former plantation into **Arlington National Cemetery**. His only son, killed in the Civil War, was interred in a monument showing him as he had fallen next to the one of the father. After the war, as a general in the Army Corps of Engineers, he advised on the **State, War, and Navy Building (now the Old Executive Office Building)** and on the **National Museum (now the Arts and Industries Building)** both designed by others. Adolf Cluss was responsible for the design of the latter with the exterior similar to the appearance of the buildings at the 1876 Centennial Exposition but with polychromatic brick and large arched windows. The interior is in the form of a Greek cross with a central octagonal rotunda. Meigs continued his extraordinary career with the **Pension Building,** his last great effort.

The Governance of Washington

Reconstruction in the city immediately after the war was led by the Radical Republicans Charles Sumner of Massachusetts in the Senate and Thaddeus Stevens of Pennsylvania in the House. They saw an opportunity for Washington to be in the forefront of renewal in the aftermath of the war. In the first instance, they sought the renewal of the destroyed physical fabric of the city.

Moreover, they also sought the renewal of the population to include the newly freed. Immediately after the end of the war, laws were passed that gave Negroes the vote and access to public accommodation within the District. These laws were additional to the passage of the Fourteenth and Fifteenth amendments that had general applicability. The Freedman's Bureau headed by General Oliver Otis Howard was active until its abolition in 1871 in establishing schools and a hospital including what became **Howard University. Freedman's Hospital (the forerunner of present-day Howard University Hospital) was** at Sixth Street and Boundary Road (Florida Avenue) in the area of the former Campbell Hospital used during the Civil War. First mainly a secondary school and then also a teacher training school, Howard University soon became a full-fledged college and then university. A line item on the federal budget, it has continued to be the centerpiece of the nationwide system of traditionally black colleges.

Plate 3.13 The Home of General Howard,
the original building of Howard University

There was some initial success. The Congress passed a Negro suffrage bill in early 1867 and overrode Johnson's veto despite the overwhelming opposition of the white inhabitants of the city. A Republican mayor was elected in 1868 along with several Negroes to the city council. A civil rights bill initially offered by Lewis Douglass, the son of Frederick Douglass, was passed in 1870 ensuring entry of blacks to public accommodations. Negroes received government jobs.

Schools, however, remained segregated. An 1862 law had mandated for the first time the setting aside of specific funds for Negro schools and a board of trustees for "colored schools". In 1864, the money to be devoted to Negro schooling was to be determined by their percentage in the decennial census. Later, laws in 1871 and 1878 continued to emphasize the duality of the system but maintain the appropriate equality of resources. Negro educators had a nearly autonomous role in running "their schools" with parity of salaries. The unique opportunities for employment for such educators attracted the best-educated Negro men and women in the country to D.C. with equivalent quality of student achievement.[19] Institutions since 1822 such as the **Metropolitan AME Church** (now at 1518 M Street NW) attest to the size and prosperity of the community. The present redbrick neo-Gothic building was built in 1886 and is considered the national cathedral of the African Methodist Episcopal Church. Frederick Douglass preached at its dedication.

It was also during this time that several new schools were built: the **Franklin School** by Adolf Cluss still remains on **Franklin Square** that won prizes in Vienna in 1873 for its quality of school architecture. Its redbrick design he called Renaissance combines elements of Second Empire style with a polychromatic Mansard roof coupled with the round arches of his native Germany. The **Charles Sumner School** at Seventeenth and M streets NW, named after the abolitionist senator from Massachusetts, is also by Cluss and, also still remaining, was the first permanent school building constructed for Negro students.[20] In his schools as well as numerous other buildings (now mainly gone), Cluss built with cast iron covered with pressed brick heavily ornamented in the Victorian style.[21] Cluss worked as part of a larger group of German-born and trained architects active in Washington in the 1870s, many of whom immigrated to the United States after the failed Revolutions of 1848. His outstanding public school buildings were a reflection of his ongoing belief in republican principles.

Incorporating the newly freed was not accepted by all parts of the population; most of the white voters were firmly opposed. However, the threat of moving the seat of government to a more central place such as St. Louis did unite all segments of the population on the need for physical improvement, Maryland Avenue leading to the Long Bridge and Pennsylvania Avenue leading to the Capitol were the only paved roads.[22] They, along with the other streets, had been destroyed by the army convoys. The sluggish canal filled with sewage running by the Mall brought recurrent epidemics of typhoid fever and malaria.

From 1802 there had been a municipal government with an elected mayor and city council with the franchise limited to white males meeting a property standard. Claiming corruption and inefficiency of the social program, the Board of Trade representing conservative business interests managed to have Congress abolish the long-standing municipal government. The hope was that the new governance would lead the Congress to contribute more to the public works program but would also deal with the concern of the same interests to prevent Negro control of the government.

A territorial government took effect in early 1871 with a governor appointed by the president, a board of public works, an appointed upper house, and an elected lower house. The effect of the local Negro vote was diluted. One goal that was achieved was that only two Negroes were elected to the twenty-two seats in the lower house (House of Delegates). Grant did appoint Republicans to office so that some of the gains achieved were maintained. For example, Frederick Douglass was defeated for nonvoting delegate to the Congress but was appointed to the upper house or governor's council.

A side effect was to combine for the first time into the one government of the District of Columbia the former city of Washington, the previously independent municipality of Georgetown, and the remainder of the District previously known as the county of Washington. Georgetown had been incorporated in 1751 as a tobacco port settled mainly by refugees from the unsuccessful Scottish revolts of 1715 and 1745. Its economy began to founder with the decline of the C&O Canal in the nineteenth century and the end of the gristmills along Rock Creek. Its main east-west street, now called M Street, was initially called Bridge Street as a continuation of Pennsylvania Avenue crossing Rock Creek close to its mouth. The one-

and-a-half-story **Old Stone House** remains on M Street as the prototype house of eighteenth-century artisan. Its main north-south street, now called Wisconsin Avenue, was originally part of the first military road laid out by General Braddock in the French and Indian War reaching eventually the site of present-day Pittsburgh.

The southeast area across the Eastern Branch of the Potomac was not laid out by L'Enfant as part of the city of Washington. As part of the county of Washington, it remained rural with tobacco and then wheat grown on plantations worked by slaves. James Barry was a leading landowner, one of several speculating that the area would be the basis for the expected industrial and commercial development of the city. The silting of the Eastern Branch ended the commercial use of the river. Development lagged dependent as it was on connection to the remainder of the city. The first major land development was Uniontown laid out in the flat land adjacent to the river in 1854 to house workmen at the Navy Yard accessible via the recently constructed bridge. It was unsuccessful due to the reduced employment at the Navy Yard during the 1850s.

Due to the efforts of Dorothea Dix, the tract known as St. Elizabeth on the high ground was purchased by the federal government in 1853 for use as the U.S. Government Insane Asylum. Its name was changed to the original title of the land during the Civil War when it was used as a general hospital for wounded soldiers. **Uniontown's** name was changed to **Anacostia** in this same period after the Civil War. The southern tip became Congress Heights.[23]

Barry Farms, laid out by the Freedman's Bureau as self-help housing for freed slaves east of the Anacostia River, became a long-lasting Negro community known as Hillsdale, after its public school. The sons of Frederick Douglass were heavily involved in developing the educational opportunities for the families of the freed in expanding the public schools in this area. Eventually destroyed by the building of Suitland Parkway in 1940 that bisected the property, the area was then converted to a public housing with the same name.

Alexander Shepherd, already the driving force on the Board of Public Works, became territorial governor in 1873. He was an active builder, with Adolf Cluss acting as the architect on many of the projects. A large-scale plan for public works was carried out to lay sewers and grade streets, mainly in the northwest quadrant, to which Congress ended up contributing only a small amount. The pestiferous Washington Canal was finally covered over to become B Street and then **Constitution Avenue**. Streets were "parked" with trees on either side and in the central median, all designed to diminish the amount to be paved but ensuring the future of the city as being tree-lined for both the health and beauty of the city.

Cluss was the engineer member of the Board of Public Works but testified against Shepherd in the congressional investigations that led to Shepherd's downfall. Although much had been done, debt had mounted far beyond expectations. Millions of dollars had been spent, mainly in the western portion of the city that enhanced even further the area whose water supply was best served by the aqueduct and where Shepherd himself built for speculation. The Northwest clearly from then on became the fashionable area. "Boss Shepherd's" actions had been reckless and inefficient. His own real estate speculative holdings were lost as was his mansion near Dupont Circle. Bankrupt, he went to Mexico. His reputation eventually rehabilitated, a statue of **Alexander Shepherd** now stands in front of the **District Building** on Pennsylvania Avenue.

The Congress abolished the territorial government in 1874, and by 1878, had set up total control of the District by a set of commissioners, one of which from the Army Corps of Engineers responsible for public works. In exchange, the Congress would make an annual payment for the District of Columbia from the federal budget. The long-standing 50 percent contribution was based on the estimate that the value of federally owned property was approximately equal to nonfederal property. This arrangement ensured relatively low taxes for Washington residents and encouraged the establishment of palatial residences by wealthy persons from outside the city.

The experiment in democracy had ended. The issue of suffrage and integration was submerged beneath the commitment in favor of public improvements to be funded by the Congress. The citizens of the District of Columbia were to remain totally disenfranchised until the 1960s.

Frederick Douglass and Reconstruction

The life and career of Frederick Douglass in Washington reflected the opportunities that Reconstruction offered and its limitations. He was the famous orator and abolitionist whose life story as a former slave on Maryland's Eastern Shore had great value in achieving support for emancipation. He had enormous faith in the effects of the Thirteenth Amendment abolishing slavery but only as the first step. Civil rights appeared to be guaranteed by the Fourteenth Amendment in 1868. He looked further. Voting rights were still not guaranteed until the Fifteenth Amendment was ratified by 1870. He still thought a major deficiency was that no effort at land distribution ever succeeded at providing economic opportunities to the former slaves.

Living in Washington since 1872, he was editor of *The New National Era* newspaper that until 1874 sought to lead Negroes to participate in the political life of the country. Douglass was initially supportive of the territorial government for the District of Columbia and was appointed to the upper house (governor's council). Although concerned about the dilution in voting power, he approved it since it applied to both whites and Negroes. However, the election of Rutherford Hayes in 1876 was part of a bargain that ended Reconstruction in the South. Ironically, Douglass received from Hayes in 1877 his first federal appointment as Marshall of the District of Columbia.

As his political power waned, Douglass in his personal life carried on as a representative of Negro emancipation, but now in terms of being a respectable property owner. He owned two houses at **310-318 A Street NE on Capitol Hill** (later the temporary site of the Museum of African Art) that he had

Plate 3.14 Cedar Hill Estate House

joined together to provide a home for his children. They were in the Second Empire Mansard style prevalent in the still fashionable 1870s Capitol Hill. In 1877, Douglass bought a property he called **Cedar Hill** from **Uniontown's** bankrupt segregationist developer, thus ending the exclusion of Negroes.[24] His message of the last decades of his life when segregation was intensified was to fight back by accumulating property and leading an integrated life. The image he presented was as a man of letters and property owner.

The Cedar Hill estate (See Plate 3.14) containing approximately fifteen acres (now a National Historical Site) was thus an important part of his life and career as a pioneer in Negro rights. The white pillared house with a verandah on a hill is part of the message. Like the plantation on which he had been born in a slave cabin, he created on his property a garden and woodland. The "big house" in which he lived counters the previously despised maternal black side of his ancestry. He built as his study as a man of letters what could have been a small slave cabin on the property. He invoked the cedars on the property as similar to the one near the slave cabin of his grandmother with whom he had lived and brought soil from there to Cedar Hill to nourish the trees.

The furnishings of the interior also project an image consistent with his message. The **west parlor of Cedar Hill** has a picture depicting Othello confidently and comfortably telling his life story, the scene that Shakespeare alludes to in his play as leading Desdemona to fall in love with him. The room also includes a copy of *The Greek Slave* by Hiram Powers, so often used as an icon by abolitionists. Pictures and heirlooms are displayed as though of his abolitionist "family." These include among others both Wendell Phillips, the white abolitionist, and Blanche K. Bruce, the black senator from Mississippi elected in 1878. **The east parlor** has a table formerly owned by the abolitionist senator Charles Sumner and a rocker given him when Douglass was Minister to Haiti. Finally, a picture at Cedar Hill shows him from behind at work at his desk surrounded by books. Only his shock of white hair identifies him.

Cultural Life

The dream of George Washington for a national university sited in Washington was not achieved. One possible exception was **Howard University,** the most prominent Negro university from its start. In addition to the original Mansard-roofed **Howard Hall**, the **Rankin Chapel** was completed in 1895 patterned after the Romanesque style of H. H. Richardson. **Gallaudet University** was first founded in 1856 as the Columbia Institution for the Deaf, Dumb, and Blind under federal auspices. It is sited on Kendall Green, the former farm of Amos Kendall, postmaster general in the Jackson and Van Buren cabinets. During the

1860s, additional buildings arose under the direction of Emil Frederich, the former draftsman for Robert Mills, in brick in the Italianate style. During the next decades, buildings including the noteworthy **Chapel Hall** arose in the high Victorian neo-Gothic style by Frederick Clarke Withers, an associate of Frederick Law Olmsted and Calvert Vaux in their landscape work.

Private universities such as **the Catholic University of America,** opened in 1889, did not achieve national prominence among Catholic schools. The bishops throughout the country who were its trustees were more interested in developing schools within their own sees. Other schools such as **Columbian College** (now George Washington University) and **Georgetown University** were mainly local in terms of students and financial support. After 1900, George Washington University began to secure a foothold in the Foggy Bottom area where it has proliferated since. Georgetown University had been founded by Father John Carroll, a member of the leading Catholic Maryland family, in 1789 on the heights overlooking the Potomac River. The Jesuit-run academy was chartered by Congress in 1815. A medical school was started by 1850. Its student body returned to

Plate 3.15 Healy Hall of Georgetown University

its Southern homes during the Civil War, and the buildings were used for Union soldiers. Father Patrick Healy, the biracial son of a plantation owner and a slave, transformed the small college into a university after becoming president in 1874. Unable to earn a postgraduate degree in the United States due to his race, he was forced to receive his PhD at the Catholic University at Louvain, Belgium. Smithmeyer and Pelz, the architects of the Jefferson Building of the Library of Congress, during its namesake's presidency of the university, designed **Healy Hall**, still the centerpiece of the main quad.

The situation in higher education illustrates once more the antebellum problem of inadequate private commercial capital as well as lack of governmental support. Most telling was the foundation of the exemplary Johns Hopkins University in nearby Baltimore by a very large legacy derived from the Baltimore and Ohio Railroad stock or universities that arose as legacies of wealth in other centers such as Boston, New York, Chicago, and even Palo Alto. Washington was beginning to be "the intellectual switchboard [but] for information originating elsewhere".[25]

Building the City

As the City of Magnificent Distances, the development of the city was heavily dependent on internal transportation. In 1862, during the Civil War, a charter was granted for the first of several horse-drawn omnibus lines, one between Georgetown and the Navy Yard that is still the basis for today's Metrobus east-west number "thirty" line. With the improvements in the water supply and asphalt-covered streets came the development of areas beyond the boundaries of the city of Washington. The trolley made it possible to extend areas for residence beyond the flat area served by horse-drawn transport. By 1890, there were various electrical trolleys with lines throughout the city and extending into the suburbs. Starting with **Mount Pleasant** at the top of Sixteenth Street came other areas served by streets and streetcars or railroads. **Eckington** and **Brookland** were on the east via the B&O Line. On the west were **Kalorama, Cleveland Park** (named after the use by Grover Cleveland for his summer residence during his presidency), and eventually **Chevy Chase** across the district line in Maryland.

LeDroit Park, one of the earliest subdivisions immediately beyond the boundary of **Florida Avenue**, to ensure its isolation and privacy, had a street system deliberately designed to prevent continuity with the L'Enfant street system. The decision made in 1888 to prevent further efforts of this kind was not fully implemented even as late as 1893.[26] However, major streets such as Massachusetts Avenue and Sixteenth Street were extended to the District Line. The naming of the second tier of alphabetized east west streets was carried out initially with two syllable names of famous Americans starting with Adams, Bryant, and Canning; then three syllables starting with Allison, Buchanan, and Crittenden; all the way to the district line east of Rock Creek and Albemarle, Brandywine, and Chesapeake, etc., to its west.

The row house became characteristic of Washington. This is attributed in part to the provision suggested by Jefferson to permit a party wall enabling the builder to put half the wall on the neighbor's land. The easy availability of clay encouraged the use of brick. The unusually wide streets permitted front gardens and permission to build projecting bays beyond the property line—thus, the variety of styles of architectural details.[27]

By the 1880s, Capitol Hill, less fashionable than Northwest, became an area of modest houses for government clerks or persons in the building trades such as carpenters, bricklayers, etc.[28] The area was representative of Washington's relatively stable industries of real estate and government. Consistent with the conservative character of the community was the use of red brick as exemplifying the practical, aesthetic, and even moral virtues associated with that building material. The newly developed "pressed bricks" were particularly used. Machine made, they were uniform, cheap to make and use, fireproof, and less subject to weathering. Their aesthetics represented modesty, simplicity, and stability as opposed to the excesses of Victorian ornamentation in the more fashionable buildings. In the 1890s, the earlier "vertical" Queen Anne style became the broader more horizontal of the Romanesque revival of H. H. Richardson.

Although there is but one house by H. H. Richardson that remains at least semi-intact at 2633 Sixteenth Street (the **Benjamin Warder House** transferred from 1515 K Street), the architect had a major influence on the architecture of the 1870s and 1880s in Washington. He designed the famous twin houses of John Hay and Henry Adams (now the site of the **Hay-Adams Hotel** at Sixteenth and H streets) that played an important role in the social life of the city. Born in New Orleans to a mercantile family, Richardson enrolled at Harvard in 1856 where he was known as a bon vivant. He made influential friends as a member of Porcellian Club while in college. Living in Paris during the Civil War, he was only the second American architect to be trained at L'Ecole des Beaux-Arts. Haussmann, the prefect of Paris during the Second Empire, was rebuilding Paris during this time. Richardson eventually returned to Boston to build his masterpiece of Trinity Church and to live in suburban Brookline, a close friend and neighbor of Frederick Law Olmsted. He died young in 1886 of kidney disease.

His romanticist Romanesque style with round arches was much copied in the 1870s and 1880s and even into the 1890s. It was also compatible in Washington with the work done by German builders-architects derived from their own Rundbogenstil (round arch style). His premature death and the resurgence of academic classicism exemplified by the Columbian Exposition of 1893 brought his influence to an end by the start of the new century. **The Old Post Office,** completed at the very end of the nineteenth century, represented the last of the Victorian structures in the Richardsonian mode. The

Plate 3.16 The Old Post Office

first of the buildings in the Federal Triangle at Pennsylvania Avenue and Twelfth Street NW, it remained at variance from the neoclassical structures that came to surround it. Out of fashion almost immediately after its completion, it was soon superseded by the neoclassical Post Office to its west across Twelfth Street. It became the focus for preservation efforts in the 1970s, leading to the beginning of the movement's "Don't Tear It Down." The statue of Benjamin Franklin in front recognizes Franklin's role as the founder of the Postal Service even before the American Revolution.

Thomas Franklin Schneider was Washington's preeminent developer-architect of the much more prevalent row house during this last quarter of the nineteenth century. Originally an apprentice in the office of Adolf Cluss, Schneider developed the area to the east of Dupont Circle, particularly Q Street NW. His townhouses in the 1700 block remain in his idiosyncratic adaptation of a Romanesque-Richardson style with low arches in stone rather than the brick of Capitol Hill. On the 1600 block of the same street, he completed in 1894 **the Cairo Hotel**, now a condominium, with a low-arched entrance reminiscent of Louis Sullivan's Transportation Building at the Columbian Exposition of the previous year. It is a ménage of architectural motifs and much too high for its street. It has however remained. At first, a luxury apartment house, it became unfashionable in the 1920s when it was converted to a tourist hotel and then a rooming house after WWII. Its renovation in the 1970s and conversion to condominium status removed a blight and was instrumental in the gentrification of the entire area.[29]

Plate 3.17 The Cairo Hotel

The Cairo's height of 146 feet has never been exceeded in Washington since all subsequent construction has been limited to 90 feet on residential streets and 110 feet on commercial streets. The general rule is that the height of a building cannot exceed the width of its street. This height limitation has produced a uniformity of height of office buildings throughout much of the downtown area. It emphasizes the subordination of the commercial core of the city to the monumental core of the capital in which the Capitol dome and the Washington Monument remain preeminent.

The 1875 Mansard-roofed British legation at the corner of Connecticut Avenue and N Street (now the **Parish House of St. John's Church**) was the impetus for the development of the West End. **Dupont Circle,** formerly known as Pacific Circle, was the westernmost circle within the boundaries of the original city. There is the still somewhat extant Second Empire—Queen Anne Victorian highly decorated 1882 **Blaine House** at 2000 Massachusetts Avenue just west of the circle (now an office building). Later, the home of George Westinghouse, the inventor of the air brake and the developer of alternating current electrical system, it was originally the home of James G. Blaine. He was a longtime congressman and Speaker of the House as well as senator from Maine. The Republican candidate for president in 1884, he lost to Cleveland in the latter's first term.

Plate 3.18 Heurich Mansion

Another still extant late Victorian house is the 1892-1894 redbrick-brownstone **Heurich Mansion** at 1307 New Hampshire Avenue, long used as the headquarters of the Historical Society of Washington. Plate 3.18

illustrates the "conspicuous consumption" of the Gilded Age mansions in the Richardsonian-Romanesque-Queen Anne eclectic style. In addition, each of the major rooms are in a decorated style: the salon is in a rococo style of Louis XV and the dining room in an oak-paneled German Renaissance style. It was built for the leading German-born Washington brewmaster by one of the lesser known of the large number of German-speaking architect-builders active in that era. John Granville Meyers was born of German-speaking parents in the Moravian area of eastern Pennsylvania. Moving to Washington in the 1860s, he prided himself on his fireproof construction of which the Heurich Mansion was the largest and most important. It was also one of the last of its genre with classicism of the Chicago World's Fair and the McMillan Commission becoming dominant after the turn of the century.

No longer seeking to be a commercial or industrial city, the role of Washington was clearly to be a government town. Its major business became the buying and selling of real estate to house its growing population. Washington had more apartment houses than any other city after New York and Chicago. In addition, there was a large transient population during the winter season when Congress was in session. The season was amplified by the arrival of those with self-made fortunes not yet accepted by the upper level society of settled places such as New York or Philadelphia. Their mansions remain to become the embassies of the future[30]

Map 3.2 of 1894 shows Public Reservation land under the control of the U.S. Corps of Engineers. It demonstrates the obliteration of the City Tiber Canal, delineation of the site of the Library of Congress but not yet its building, the Pension Office at the top of Judiciary Square that held the district courts and the State, War, and Navy Department Building just west of the Executive Mansion.

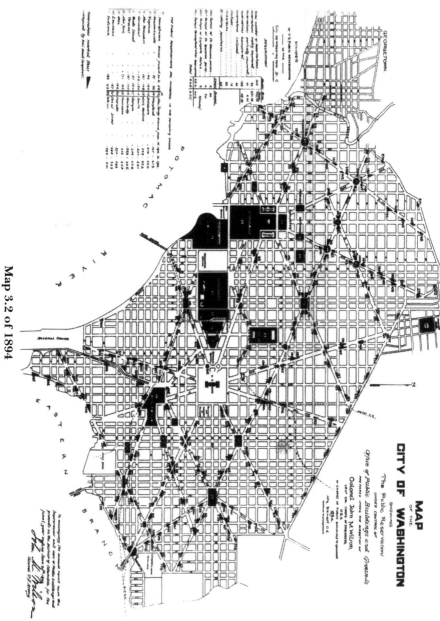

Map 3.2 of 1894

CHAPTER 4
THE PROGRESSIVE ERA /
THE CITY BEAUTIFUL (1900-1930)

Introduction

By the end of the nineteenth century and the centennial of Washington as the national capital, the population had reached 275,000, buoyed by the continual increase in civil service jobs. There were nearly thirty thousand federal employees living in Washington in 1901, around 20 pecent of all those working in the city.[1] The Civil Service Act of 1889 ensured job security for the first time. The stable above-average income ensured the building of housing for government workers and those servicing them in rows of attached houses into the rest of the District of Columbia. Moreover, the industrial growth of the United States since the end of the Civil War and its international role as an imperial power in the Spanish-American War contributed to the importance of its national capital. The reconciliation of the North and South exemplified by representatives of both in the recent Spanish-American War seemed to confirm their reunion since the end of Reconstruction. Despite its role as a symbol of a reunited nation, the city was once again clearly Southern in its culture and character of local government by its white elite.

One of the attractions of the city was its lack of significant commercial and industrial development. It was touted as made up of "Americans" from every state and largely free of the "low foreign element," that is, non-Anglo-Saxon immigrants. Characteristic of the Progressive Era extending from the 1890s through the 1920s was the use of professionals such as city planners in the reorganization of cities to deal with the sense of disruption by the increase in diversity caused by immigration. The centennial of Washington was an opportunity to create the image of the City Beautiful that could serve as a model for other cities while also creating a national shrine where all Americans could come together.

L'Ecole des Beaux-Arts in Paris trained architects in what was considered an eclectic Roman-Renaissance-baroque historicist style that also emphasized a massive aggregation of buildings. Symmetry was important as well as axes intersecting at right angles. Clad in white stone, the interior framework was iron. The American Renaissance found its roots in the earlier Italian Renaissance by combining ideas such as the use of architecture to enhance public order and refined taste with the sense of the newly achieved national wealth and power of the United States.[2] Charles F. McKim of the important New York firm of McKim, Mead, and White was particularly instrumental in establishing this neoclassical style as the American national style for public buildings. It is appropriate that he also founded the American Academy in Rome. Washington became rebuilt in this style during this period.

Washington as *Capital*

The number of states had grown to forty-five by the turn of the century. The inclusion only of Oklahoma, Arizona, and New Mexico by 1912 were necessary to achieve the long-term complement of forty-eight states. Concomitantly came the increase in accommodation required for the number of senators and representatives. The first of a series of office buildings were built along the flanks of the U.S. Capitol. John Merven Carrere and Thomas Hastings of Carrere and Hastings both trained at L'Ecole des Beaux-Arts and worked at McKim, Mead, and White before forming their partnership. They were one of the leading firms building mansions in New York, as well as the New York Public Library. They designed in 1905-1908 the **Joseph Cannon House Office Building** (named for the longtime, 1903-1911, and very powerful Republican Speaker) on Independence and New Jersey avenues NE and its companion **Richard Russell Senate Office Building** (named for the longtime Democratic senator from Georgia, 1933-1971, and leader of the conservative coalition that ruled the Senate from 1937 to 1963) on Constitution and Delaware avenues NW. In the Beaux-Arts style, ranges of colonnades on the façades along the respective main avenues of Independence and Constitution are coupled with pilastrades along the secondary avenues. Each have two-story circular entry vestibules leading to the equivalent ornate Caucus Room. Both buildings were designed with their scale to be in relation to one another and to the Capitol. They were reminiscent of Parisian models by Gabriel on the Place de la Concorde and Perrault on the east front of the Louvre.

Plate 4.1 The Columbian Exposition

The McMillan Commission

President William McKinley, celebrating the centennial of Washington as the capital on December 12, 1900, emphasized the contribution of L'Enfant to the creation of the distinct beauty of the capital. The American Institute of Architects (AIA), under its secretary Glenn Brown, was instrumental in responding to these comments. AIA's interest included reducing the influence of political appointees and military engineers in the public works of the capital and promotion of use of the "best artistic talent" such as its own professionally trained architect members. Glenn Brown himself had become interested in L'Enfant and in reviving his almost forgotten plan in the course of his study of the U.S. Capitol. Brown was well connected politically and instrumental in moving the AIA to Washington and making its headquarters at the **Octagon House** (at Eighteenth and New York avenues NW) designed by William Thornton (the first architect if the U.S. Capitol).[3] The AIA convention in Washington at the time of the centennial further proposed to reorder public building in Washington according to the formula of those trained at L'Ecole des Beaux-Arts in Paris.

Starting in 1890, James McMillan, the wealthy Republican senator from Michigan, was chairman of the Senate District Committee. Born in Canada, he had a variety of business interests in the Detroit area, starting with the building of railroad cars. During his tenure on the District Committee, he encouraged the development of the city in association with the local business interests. His aide on the Senate committee, Charles Moore, participated in the publication of the 1900 AIA convention proposal as a Senate document. Not withstanding the opposition of the House under Uncle Joe Cannon, a *Senate* Park Commission (the McMillan Commission) was authorized in an unusual executive session. A group of outside consultants were to study the development of parks and public spaces in the District of Columbia.

The group reassembled that had been associated with the recent wildly successful neoclassical "White City" of the Columbian Exposition in 1893 in Chicago. (See Plate 4.1) The modernized classicism of the Fair was to dominate the architecture of Washington for the next generation. Daniel Burnham was in overall charge. As partner in Burnham & Root, he was Chicago's leading architect in building office buildings in the Loop and mansions for their owners. Burnham brought in Charles McKim, partner of McKim, Mead, and White, the leading New York architects of the time. Born in an abolitionist family, McKim had trained at L'Ecole des Beaux-Arts and then worked with H. H. Richardson before setting up his own firm with his two partners. His works by then had included the American Renaissance Boston Public Library that had been original in merging sculpture, painting, and architecture. McKim considered Beaux-Arts design to represent the timeless, universal architecture. Burnham also recruited Augustus Saint-Gaudens, the greatest American sculptor of his time, who had also trained in Paris as well as New York.

Frederick Law Olmsted Jr. was selected for the Commission on the request of Senator McMillan himself on the basis of his experience with the senior Olmsted in designing Belle Isle Park in Detroit.[4] The son, his father's successor, was to be the "parks" consultant. Olmsted Senior, now incapacitated, had been the architect of parks throughout the country including the U.S. Capitol grounds and the terracing of the West Front in the 1870s. He had also designed the "White City" grounds. Olmsted Senior, starting with Central Park and many other sites in otherwise urban areas, had emphasized proper urban design as part of transforming the "behavior and moral outlook" of the teeming working and immigrant class in the cities.[5] The McMillan Commission now applied these same principles to the national capital.

The well-received 1902 Report of the Commission went far beyond its original focus on the parks to deal with the entire ceremonial core of the district. A very successful presentation took place at the Corcoran Art Gallery. It recommended a unified ceremonial core based on the Mall no longer to be a "romantic landscape" but now a more formal "tapis vert" analogous to the work of Lenotre in Paris. In tune with the policies of the reigning Republican Party, its Federalist forbearers of Washington and the almost forgotten L'Enfant were frequently invoked as the basis of what was being recommended.[6] However, the Commission's recommendations rather derive from the ideology and aesthetics of the City Beautiful Movement of the time.[7] Although not an official member of the Commission, Charles Moore, Senator McMillan's secretary, was intimately involved, writing its report and moreover was to have a crucial role in its ongoing implementation over the next generation.

The Development of the Mall

The first important decision to be dealt with by the Commission was the accommodation of the railroads on the Mall. L'Enfant's original idea was of a partially sunken road lined by museums and theaters. An equestrian statue of George Washington was to be at the juncture of the major western axis of the Mall and an arm southward from the President's House. Robert Mill's **Washington Monument** came about at that point but somewhat off center. This placement has been attributed to the marshy ground unable to support a heavy masonry structure. Actually, the site was at a central point derived from Renwick's **Smithsonian Castle** on the southern side and the then existing canal along the northern side of the Mall. **The Botanical Garden** at the foot of the Capitol building was complemented by a series of individual public parks centered on each of the redbrick buildings in place. The model for the others was the original picturesque park with many trees native to the Washington area centered on the **Smithsonian Castle.** It was designed by Andrew Jackson Downing in the 1850s before his untimely death in 1852 in a steamboat accident. Downing was the premiere landscape architect at the time. He was the partner of British-born Calvert Vaux and responsible for the latter meeting Frederick Law Olmsted, the team that planned New York's Central Park.

Moreover, there was since 1878 the Victorian Gothic terminal of the Baltimore and Potomac Railroad (B&P) on the north side of the Mall at Sixth and B streets (now Constitution Avenue NW, the present site of the **National Gallery of Art**). There was the terminal since 1852 of the then competing Baltimore and Ohio Railroad (B&O) at New Jersey Avenue and C Street NW at the foot of the U.S. Capitol. Each of the stations was connected by its own dangerous ungraded street crossings of tracks. Tracks (for the B&P) went south through city streets and then via a railroad bridge parallel to the Long Bridge (now the **Fourteenth Street Bridge)** crossing the Potomac.[8]

The solution generally credited to Burnham in cooperation with A. J. Cassatt, the then president of the Pennsylvania Railroad, was the removal of the station on the Mall to be incorporated in a "union" station at the then site of the B&O Station near the U.S. Capitol.[9] In any event, both lines were being merged into the Pennsylvania Railroad. Ultimately, the tracks would run from the north into the new station now to be placed in a relatively undeveloped area called Swampdoodle, slightly further north of the existing B&O train station. There would be no further use of city streets. A tunnel would bring the tracks to the south across the river along a newly built railroad bridge that replaced the old twin Fourteenth Street bridges dating from the Civil War. The idea of tunneling the now recently electrified railroads had been pioneered in the Gare d'Orsay in Paris and by Cassat in the North River tunnels in New York City leading to Penn Station.

One of the first fruits of the McMillan Commission Plan was the neoclassical **Union Station** designed by Burnham with statuary by Louis Saint-Gaudens, the younger brother of the more famous Augustus Saint-Gaudens. The exterior contains the threefold arch characteristic of the **Arch of Constantine** with the central porch surmounting the Ionic columns supporting allegorical figures representing *fire, electricity, freedom, imagination, agriculture, and mechanics.* Central panels quote the then Harvard president Charles Eliot extolling the railroad as the culmination of the American destiny for westward expansion. The interior with its coffered ceilings replicates the **Baths of Diocletian**, visited during their European tour by the McMillan Commission members.

The Union Station Building was not merely a railroad depot, but in the great era of railroad travel, the main portal of entry to the national capital and a vestibule to the Capitol itself[10] Under Daniel Burnham, the "design of the station is intended to be monumental . . . and in keeping with the dignity of the chief city of America." The architects used modern materials such as steel but maintained the traditional masonry and granite and an axial neoclassical design. On the north-south axis, the central portion of the entrance leads through the central element of the **main hall waiting room** to the **concourse** and the trains. On the intersecting axis, the **west hall lobby** is counterbalanced by the **east hall.** The situation of Union Station with a clear vista to the Capitol, the axial arrangement of its interior and the building's identity as a "temple of transport" were all consistent with the Beaux-Arts style of an ensemble of buildings to create a whole. (See Plate 4.2)

Plate 4.2 Union station and Plaza

The complementary **United States Post Office** completed in 1915 by Burnham's firm continues the Beaux-Arts tradition. A giant Ionic colonnade along Massachusetts Avenue NW obscures the several floors of offices contained within. The building also continues the Vermont granite used in the Union Station and the earlier station's end pavilions at a time when the railroad and the delivery of mail were so interdependent.

Completing this monumental gateway to an increasingly imperial capital in 1912 is the **plaza** with its statue and **Columbus Fountain** by Lorado Taft. Born and trained in Illinois but also at L'Ecole des Beaux-Arts, his career was mainly connected with the Art Institute of Chicago. His first sculptures were those for the horticultural hall at the Columbian Exposition of 1893. The fountain in front of Union Station has Columbus standing at the prow of his ship flanked by crouching figures representing both the Old and New Worlds. All is surmounted by a globe supported by the American eagle. Once again as in the Capitol, the United States draws its roots from its European origins with the discovery of the New World the beginning of its quest for mastery of the continent.

According to the Parks Commission, **the National Mall** was projected to be no longer merely a means to connect the two great branches of government but to serve as a sacred space—the nation's civic center. It was a much expanded public space performing national functions extending from the Capitol and the Washington Monument and now extended to the reclaimed land on the west. The earlier image of the Mall as a series of gardens had represented America as a novel seminatural environment distinct from and superior to other nations. Rather, the Mall was now to become a formal site in the mode of European parks.[11]

The first test came quickly. Crucial to the integrity of the newly designed Mall was the replacement in 1905 by a neoclassical building of the former redbrick **Department of Agriculture** with its attached gardens extending across the Mall. Placed on the southern rim at Twelfth and Independence Avenue SW, the direct intervention of President Theodore Roosevelt was required for the new building to be aligned with the recommendations of the Commission. The outcome was to maintain the unimpeded central vista offered by the Mall between the Capitol and eventually the Lincoln Memorial.

Established in 1862 during the time the Congress was depleted of the secessionists, the Agricultural Bureau grew out of the agricultural division of the Patent Office. Its formation was part of the large-scale effort to develop land-grant colleges. Moreover, for the first time, there was a clear mandate to provide jobs for scientists in Washington doing research in fields such as animal breeding and seeds for planting. By 1913, there were over a thousand scientists employed by the Department of Agriculture. Its gardens on the Mall had played an important role in its mission. After several intermediate sites, the gardens were eventually replaced by the present-day **Beltsville Agricultural Research Center** in nearby Maryland.

The Commission of Fine Arts

The next decades saw implementation of the McMillan Commission's vision of the Mall lined with neoclassical monumental buildings. With the death of Senator McMillan and impeded by its lack of official status, the establishment of the U.S. Commission of Fine Arts in 1910 by Congress made it ultimately possible to shepherd the Senate Park Commission Plan through the political shoals. Particularly noteworthy in the early years was the ongoing opposition of the House Speaker Joe Cannon. With Charles Moore as its secretary and then longtime chairman, the Commission of Fine Arts served "to guide the architectural development of Washington so that the capital city would reflect, in stateliness and grandeur, the emergence of the United States as a world power".[12]

Its early members drew heavily from the composition of the McMillan Commission with Daniel Burnham as chairman and Frederick Law Olmsted Jr. The other five members included outstanding neoclassically trained architects such as Cass Gilbert and Thomas Hastings (of Carrere and Hastings) as well as sculptor Daniel Chester French, all connected to the Chicago Fair in some way. Daniel Chester French was born deaf in Exeter, New Hampshire, a neighbor and friend of Ralph Waldo Emerson and Louisa May Alcott's family. His first major commission was *The Minuteman* in Concord dedicated on April 19, 1875, in conjunction with the centennial of that battle. He also sculpted in 1884 the *John Harvard Monument* in the Harvard Yard as well as *Republic*, the centerpiece of Columbian Exposition of 1893. Wealthy and wellborn, he epitomized the other "clubbable" members of the Commission of Fine Arts during the years of leadership by Charles Moore ending in the 1930s.

The Natural History Museum, with classical portico and central dome in 1911, was first of the museums on the northern rim of the Mall. Its collection grew out of that of the **National Museum** on the south side east of the **Castle** (now the **Art and Industries Building of the Smithsonian Institution).** Its original French design was scrapped in favor of suggestions by McKim for a classical design compatible with the McMillan Plan[13] The centerpiece of its collection is now the Hope Diamond noted for its history as a treasure. Its last private owner was Evelyn Walsh McLean, one of the doyennes of Washington society during the 1920s and 1930s.

The Freer Gallery of Art was built alongside the western side of the Smithsonian Castle in 1923-1928 as the first modern Smithsonian museum of fine art. Freer's contribution of his collection to the Smithsonian is attributed to the influence of Charles Moore, a fellow Detroiter.[14] The Freer Gallery's subdued sixteenth-century Renaissance design by Charles A. Platt, a member of the Fine Arts Commission at the time, derived from the Palazzo del Te in Mantua. Platt was noted for his work on Italian gardens and was influential on the design of formal gardens for the Rockefellers and others. His own house and gardens were at Cornish, New Hampshire, near to the studio of Augustus Saint-Gaudens. **Charles Freer** was a Detroit manufacturer of railroad cars and an avid collector of art. He was particularly involved with his friend James McNeil Whistler whose Peacock Room is in the Gallery.

Freer's main interest was in Asian art. The Freer collection has been augmented subsequently by the Asian art collection of Eugene and Agnes Meyer. Eugene Meyer was a Wall Street investor and the publisher of the *Washington Post.* Born in Los Angeles, Meyer grew up in San Francisco. After Yale, he went into banking and became successful on the stock market. He married a much younger **Agnes Ernst** in 1910, a friend of Georgia O'Keefe and Edward Stieglitz. After amassing a fortune, he turned to government service and worked for President Wilson during World War I. He then went on to found Allied Chemical in 1920 that later became Honeywell Corporation. President Hoover made him head of the Federal Reserve and then also head of the Reconstruction Finance Corporation designed to aid business during the Depression. In 1933, he bought the bankrupt *Washington Post,* sustaining it until it finally became profitable after the purchase of its competing *Washington Times-Herald.* In 1946, Truman made him for a time head of the newly formed **World Bank.**

He first made his son-in-law Philip Graham publisher of the *Washington Post*. His daughter Katherine Graham took over in the 1960s when her husband committed suicide and went on to build one of the country's great newspapers.

The Mall

In further fulfillment of the McMillan Commission's plan, the last of the pre-World War II buildings on the northern rim of the Mall at Fifth Street was Andrew Mellon's **National Gallery of Art** opened in 1941. Although much later, it may be considered the capstone of the effort initiated by the McMillan Commission. It was at the site of the removed B&P Railroad Station. The architect, John Russell Pope, represented the last of the neoclassical tradition. He was the recipient of first fellowship from the American Academy in Rome founded by Charles McKim followed by training at L'Ecole des Beaux-Arts in Paris. Pope was noted for his use of classical motifs, particularly the domed center with two lateral wings.

The National Gallery of Art was carried out in an elegant manner to be a sanctuary to house valuable and important works of art. Since much of the art was of the Renaissance, the interior incorporated Renaissance elements in its design. In the Beaux-Arts tradition, there is a long horizontal axis with three great trans-axial spaces intersecting in the center and both ends. The solid blocks of pink Tennessee marble vary in shade with the lightest used in the dome and with the inner Ionic columns of the portico lighter than those on the outside. Ionic order is repeated in the massive green marble in the interior of the central rotunda; the more austere Doric is used for the columns of the twin garden courts. This neoclassical building, closest to the Capitol, served to buttress the relationship of the Capitol to the Mall.

The Federal Triangle

The recommended removal of the marshy low-lying slum and red-light district called Murder Bay area south of Pennsylvania Avenue led to the building of the neoclassical **Federal Triangle**. It started in the

1920s under the Secretary of the Treasury Andrew Mellon but was not completed until the 1930s during Roosevelt's New Deal. Made up of several separately designed buildings with a variety of classical columns, the massive blocks clearly represent the triumphant bureaucracy with sculptural elements intrinsic to the design. It is the embodiment of the City Beautiful Movement in which the whole ensemble comes together greater even than the sum of its parts with uniformity of setbacks, cornice heights, and limestone façades. These government buildings were clearly not merely functional but symbolic. They also epitomize the horizontal character of the entire city where height is constrained so as to maintain the priority of the salience of the U.S. Capitol. Their evolution marked the apogee and also the ending of the impetus created by the Chicago World's Fair as embodied in the 1901 McMillan Plan nurtured by Charles Moore and his Fine Arts Commission.[15] The completion of the Federal Triangle during the Depression clashed with the complaints that it was too ornate and too expensive.

Ranging along **Constitution Avenue** NW (formerly B Street, the roofed over sewer of the City Canal that had united the Potomac and Anacostia rivers) from west to east are the following: **the Department of Commerce** with a monumental one thousand feet long Fifteenth Street façade reminiscent of Robert Mill's Treasury to its north but with Doric colonnade. The Department of Commerce was split off in 1913 from its previous status as Department of Commerce and Labor. It was designed by Louis Ayres, one of the members of the Board of Consulting Architects, each of whom created one of the buildings in the Federal Triangle. Herbert Hoover had unsuccessfully sought to place the department on the Mall along with the Department of Agriculture. Filling the entire base of the triangle, it was the largest office building in the nation when built. Its great size was in accordance with the wishes to unite all its activities under one roof by Herbert Hoover, then commerce secretary (after whom it is now named). The great hall, previously used by the Patent Office, is now the White House Visitor Center. The four pediments along Fifteenth Street by James Fraser illustrate the activities of the department such as *foreign and domestic commerce, fisheries, aeronautics, and mining.*

Ranging along Constitution Avenue from Fourteenth Street to Twelfth Street are **the Customs Service of the Department of the Treasury** at Fourteenth Street, **Interstate Commerce Commission** at Twelfth Street with the **Departmental Auditorium named after Andrew Mellon** in the center portion. The founding ceremony of North Atlantic Treaty Organization (NATO) took place there. It was designed by Arthur Brown who had trained at L'Ecole des Beaux-Arts along with John Russell Pope and who had also designed the neoclassic buildings of the San Francisco Civic Center. The dramatic **Post Office Building** is a hemicycle along Twelfth Street reminiscent of the London County Council Building along the Thames. It was designed by William Adams Delano of the blue blood firm of Delano and Aldrich. Both former employees of Carrere and Hastings, they built mainly neo-Georgian residences and clubs in New York City for the Rockefellers and Astors among others. Delano, a relative and friend of President Franklin Delano Roosevelt, was also a member of the Commission of Fine Arts.

The Internal Revenue Service at Eleventh Street was unique in having been designed by Louis Simon, not a private architect but part of the office of the supervising architect of the Treasury. The entire scheme had been designed to further the use of private architects, and they unfairly attacked the work of Simon as being inferior. The **Department of Justice** is between Ninth and Tenth streets. The latter, completed in 1931-1934, shows the transition from the traditional neoclassic to modernism by combining elements of both. There is extensive use of aluminum art deco as well as colonnades.

Completing this range of buildings between Seventh and Ninth streets is the freestanding massive **National Archives Building** conceived by John Russell Pope in the style of the classical Mausoleum at Halicarnassus with impressive use of Corinthian columns. It replaced the redbrick Central Market built by Adolf Cluss. Its main attractions are in the dimly lit central room containing the U.S. Constitution, the Declaration of Independence, and the Bill of Rights. The murals on either side are in the classical motif but of inferior quality echoing the Trumbull paintings in the rotunda of the U.S. Capitol.[16]

Completed last in 1937 is the **Federal Trade Commission** at the apex of the triangle at Sixth Street. A product of the New Deal era, it is the least ornate building in the Federal Triangle with only several Ionic columns facing the U.S. Capitol. The municipal **District Building** with ornate Corinthian-capped columns on Pennsylvania Avenue NW between Thirteenth and Fourteenth streets, completed in 1904, preceded the

Federal Triangle but was also in accordance with McMillan Commission criteria. Since 1994, it is named after John A. Wilson, former chair of the D.C. City Council in the 1970s after the council again became an elected body.

A monumental classical central core had been established. It was not merely an end itself. The idealized aim of the City Beautiful Movement was to generate in the national city, as a prototype for cities elsewhere, an expansive sense of public activity consistent with the reform politics of the era.[17] Civic center replicas by Burnham and his pupils did appear in Cleveland, San Francisco, and Chicago. However, in Washington itself, government by the commissioners appointed by Congress divorced the political life of the city from its inhabitants, particularly from all of its black inhabitants. A civic core developed that reflected the capital but remained isolated from the surrounding city.[18]

The other aim of the City Beautiful Movement in the national city was to enhance the sense of commitment to the idea of America as a nation. The large scale immigration starting in the 1880s made America a country more variegated in its politics, its religion, and its origins. One of the more benign forms of nativism was to inculcate a sense of unity by the use of shrines celebrating the principles of national power and solidity. Washington became increasingly a place for pilgrimage with the further development of presidential memorials.

The Grant Memorial

General Grant was still at the head of the pantheon of American heroes in 1900. Recently completed had been his tomb on New York's Riverside Drive. Although his presidency had been marred by scandal, he still remained the commander of the victorious army. Instigated by the Society of the Army of the Tennessee, of which he had been commander, **the Grant Memorial** Commission was set up in 1901, funded by Congress with the largest amount thus far. Proposals were elicited for a site just south of the **State, War, and Navy Building,** parallel to the recently erected statue of **General Sherman** south of the **Treasury.** Rather, under the auspices of then Secretary of War Elihu Root, the decision was to coordinate with the plans of the Park (McMillan) Commission. Part of the twenty-year delay before its completion in 1922 was due to the conflict of the concurrence of the competition with the recent McMillan Report. Charles McKim from the now-defunct McMillan Commission was placed on the advisory board of the **Grant Memorial,** along with the other past members Burnham, Augustus Saint-Gaudens, and Daniel Chester French. The original suggestion of the Park Commission had been an arch at the head of the planned **Memorial Bridge** (now the site of the **Lincoln Memorial**), thus facing his counterpart of the **Lee Mansion** crowning the **Arlington National Cemetery**. The memorial to Grant had been thought to be central to the monumental character of the expanded Mall along with a projected Lincoln Memorial and the existing Washington Monument. Indeed, the overall theme of the expanded Mall to the west was to celebrate the victory of the Union in the Civil War. **The Lincoln Memorial** was to be at the present site of the **Jefferson Memorial** on the **Tidal Basin**.

Contrary to the original proposal near the State, War, and Navy Building, McKim now proposed three large equestrian statues to form a plaza arrangement at a site at the foot of the U.S. Capitol. This was envisaged to become a focal point at the western head of the Mall, to be called **Union Square** and analogous to **La Place de la Concorde** in Paris in its significance. The accepted design of Henry Merwin Shrady and Edward Pearce Casey (the latter earlier involved with the Library of Congress) was of Grant as a military figure flanked by Generals Sheridan and Sherman who had helped win the war. The entire ensemble was to function as a military reviewing stand. The height of the memorial is just short of the height of the contemporaneous monument to Victor Emmanuel in Rome. As built, Grant is the quiet even taciturn central figure on horseback flanked by artillery and cavalry groups. The figures portray war as demanding courage and sacrifice suggestive of the militaristic and nationalist stance of the times exemplified by the new president Theodore Roosevelt.

Opposition to the implementation of the Grant Memorial site over the years was tied to overall opposition to the implementation of the McMillan Plan by various local and national interests, particularly related to the removal of trees from the U.S. Botanic Garden. The intervention of then Secretary of War William Howard Taft was necessary on several occasions to maintain the decision to proceed.[19] Finally completed in 1922, ultimately the memorial as now placed with its reflecting pool at the confluence of Maryland and Pennsylvania avenues (covering the freeway) fails to realize the aims fought over so bitterly.

At this very time, Elihu Root as Secretary of War was carrying out major reforms by expanding the regular U.S. Army, incorporating the state militias into the Federal National Guard and establishing the **Army War College** (at **Fort McNair at Fourth and Points SW**). The fort, named after the commanding general of Army Ground Forces killed on active duty in France in July 1944, is at the confluence of the Potomac and Anacostia rivers—a place that has been a military installation since 1790. Designed by Charles McKim of McKim, Mead, and White, the main domed building is surrounded by U-shaped cluster of residences analogous to Jefferson's University of Virginia (where McKim also designed the rotunda when it was replaced after a fire). The present-day postgraduate **National Defense University** was founded in 1902 by Theodore Roosevelt to modernize the military just after the Spanish-American War when United States was starting to play an increased role in world affairs. This was also a time when schools in the model of Johns Hopkins providing professional-level education had begun to proliferate.

The Lincoln Memorial

The development of Washington as a city of grandeur was part of an effort to unite the country on the basis of a national public interest as opposed to ethnic, class, section, or vested interest. The policy of reconciliation of the North and South became even more evident in the role that the **Lincoln Memorial** was to play. After his death in 1865, Lincoln had become the Christlike martyr evoked by the Republican Party to justify their policies. Yet no major memorial to Lincoln had yet appeared commensurate to his importance to the history of the country. In the 1890s, the theme was to stress that which Americans had in common. Lincoln had become by now a less partisan figure idealized as a philosopher-statesman.[20] With the Republican Party firmly in control following McKinley's 1896 election and with a strong presidency under Roosevelt, honoring Lincoln would be as the strong Civil War president, a heroic figure. The time of the centennial of Lincoln's birth in 1909 saw an even greater deification, but now as a titanic but humane "man of the people." His appeal transcended Republicanism to be seen as a progressive figure compatible with the ideology of the Progressive Party and even Democrats.

The McMillan Commission offered the opportunity to create a memorial at the west end of the expanded Mall, commensurate with and directly in line with that of the Washington Monument and the U.S. Capitol. At the beginning, Charles McKim had visualized a standing figure of Lincoln silhouetted in front of a temple with a Doric-columned portico in the center of a *rond-point*. This memorial connecting the North and South via the Memorial Bridge could be compared with the **Arc de Triomphe** crowning the **Place d'Etoile** in Paris.

The original Lincoln Memorial Commission was set up in 1902. It was met headlong with delays and the adamant opposition of Joseph Cannon, now the Republican Speaker of the House. One important reason was that he could not forgive McMillan for having bypassed him and the House of Representatives when setting up his Park Commission. To counter Cannon, John Hay was called upon to testify. Hay had been Lincoln's Secretary and then Secretary of State under McKinley and Roosevelt, and supported placement of the Lincoln Memorial on the West Potomac site. Caught in a battle between the aggressive stance of Roosevelt versus Joseph Cannon's Congress, no decision as to the kind and place of the memorial could take place until William Howard Taft took office. The deposition of Cannon from his Speakership permitted the establishment in 1910 of the U.S. Commission of Fine Arts "to advise upon statues, fountains, and monuments."

A new Lincoln Memorial Commission was quickly organized with President Taft as chair that deferred to the Fine Arts Commission and its not unforeseen choice of the site in West Potomac Park. One persistent alternative was for a highway from Washington to Gettysburg to be called the Lincoln Highway, a name eventually used to designate the main national north-south road. Part of the urgency in 1910 was recognition that the Republican control of Congress was in jeopardy and the Democrats were far less likely to establish a memorial to the Republican president.

Charles Moore, the former clerk attached to Senator McMillan's district committee and secretary of the Senate Park Commission, returned to Washington to serve as secretary and then, from 1915, long-term chairman of the **Commission of Fine Arts**. Moore had been born in Ypsilanti, Michigan, of transplanted New Englanders. After the early death of his father, his guardian arranged for him to attend Phillips Andover Academy and then Harvard where he came under the influence of Charles Eliot Norton, the professor of art history. Starting his journalistic career on the *Harvard Crimson,* he continued to be a reporter in Detroit before coming to Washington to be an assistant for Senator McMillan. His success in his position on the Fine Arts Commission was due to his social and political connections with the local business leaders on the Board of Trade as well as his experience in Congress.[21]

Moore spoke in 1933 of his credo formed under the tutelage of Charles Eliot Norton. In Washington, it was necessary to renew devotion to the "classical" tradition as carried out by Thornton, Latrobe, Bulfinch, Mills, and Walter. He singled out the **State, War, and Navy Building** by Mullett and the **Pension Building** by Meigs as epitomizing the "debasing" of architecture that occurred in the "disorder" after the Civil War. He also was critical of the **Jefferson Building** of the Library of Congress as cutting off the vista from the Capitol as envisaged by L'Enfant as well as its dome in competition with that of the U.S. Capitol. With the Chicago World's Fair came the "most momentous event in the history of Fine Arts in America" by a return to the classical tradition, but now with a far greater grandeur and sumptuousness expressing "the dignity of the Republic and the exuberance of a happy and prosperous people." The men of the McMillan Commission found no need for innovation but the restoration and enlargement of the L'Enfant Plan and the style of architecture favored by Washington and Jefferson. The Lincoln Memorial, the removal of the railroads from the Mall, and the Federal Triangle were some of the fruits, as was the Parkway to Mount Vernon.[22]

The Fine Arts Commission selected Henry Bacon as architect for the Lincoln Memorial. Burnham viewed Bacon as one on whom "the mantle of Charles McKim had fallen." McKim, until his death in 1909, had taken the greatest role in maintaining the principles of the Park Commission Plan throughout the fight over the Grant and Lincoln memorials. Bacon had worked for McKim and served as his representative on the 1893 Columbian Exposition before founding his own firm.

The Lincoln Memorial, Bacon's last project, is a Greek temple reminiscent of the Parthenon but without its pediments. The statue within is visible from one of the sides of the building rather than from the front as in the Parthenon. The names of the thirty-six states in the Union at the time of Lincoln's death are inscribed in the frieze above.

Plate 4.3
The Lincoln Emancipation Monument

At the time of the dedication of the memorial in 1922, Lincoln had clearly become the symbol of reunion rather than the Republican Northern hero of emancipation. He had become the godlike larger than life as the "preserver of the nation." The speakers made few if any references to the Civil War and the few grizzled veterans were from both sides. It may then not be surprising that there had been segregated seating of the audience and only a single Negro speaker. Robert Moton was Booker T. Washington's successor at Tuskegee Institute, a Republican and an "accomodationist" in the tradition of his predecessor. His speech mentioned the tension in American society between its principle of liberty and that of bondage. As the only reference to slavery, it was ignored by the press. The dedication was a microcosm of its times when the Ku Klux Klan paraded openly down Pennsylvania Avenue and frequent lynchings occurred throughout the South.[23]

The huge seated statue by Daniel Chester French is enshrined like a god on a thronelike seat based, like Greenough's Washington, on Zeus but, in this instance, realistically dressed. The statue is flanked in adjacent rooms by his Gettysburg Address and Second Inaugural Address, the latter a plea for "binding wounds" and reconciliation. Prominently displayed on the arms of the chair and elsewhere are the Roman "fasces," a bundle of rods bound around a battle-axe, traditionally a symbol of authority and justice but also of unity. The entire Lincoln Memorial site, including **the reflecting pool,** was created out of the previously filled tidal flats. The pool completes the ensemble in accordance with the long basin canal projected by the McMillan Commission in the style of Versailles.

Completing the symbolism of reconciliation was the **Memorial Bridge** by the firm of McKim, Mead, and White replicating a Roman aqueduct connecting the Lincoln Memorial to the **Custis-Lee Mansion**, home of Robert E. Lee, and the **Arlington National Cemetery**. Indeed, a very tall **Confederate Soldier's Monument** had been placed in Arlington National Cemetery in 1914. The sculptor, Moses Jacob Ezekiel, was born in Richmond to a Jewish family of Sephardic origin. He fought as a young cadet in the Confederate Army before graduating from Virginia Military Institute (VMI) and remained an unreconstructed Confederate. Funded by the United Daughters of the Confederacy, the dedication was witnessed by President Wilson, a son of the South. The theme of the speakers was mainly the spirit of common sacrifice and a common glorious future.

The few earlier statues of Lincoln as the emancipator had included the fundamentally flawed **Freedman's Monument** erected in 1876 at **Lincoln Park** at East Capitol and Eleventh Street NE designated by L'Enfant to be a square one mile east of the Capitol. Initiated by contributions in gratitude by those freed, its design came about under the rather unusual auspices of the Western Sanitary Commission founded to provide quality health and social services to Union soldiers in the Western theater of operations. Frederick Douglass was the lead orator at its dedication attended by President Grant, the Congress, the Supreme Court, and a crowd of fifty thousand, mainly Negro. It was widely considered an expression of Negro attitude of gratitude. (See Plate 4.3)

Lincoln, with the Emancipation Proclamation in his hand, stands above the kneeling man with clearly African features breaking free, said to be the likeness of a man called Archer Alexander. Alexander was actually a man who escaped from slavery in Missouri and was saved from the effects of the still-existing Fugitive Slave Law only by the protection of the antislavery Federal army area commander. In actuality, his freedom was not achieved under the Emancipation Proclamation, which freed only those slaves in states that were "in rebellion," thus excluding Missouri.

Although the right hand of the kneeling figure ends with a fist, the relationship between the two figures and the relative passivity of the Negro was part of the reigning iconography. Douglass noted the absence of a standing figure that might have signified equality and "manliness." Yet this monument became known as **the Emancipation Monument** and was replicated elsewhere, even on a postage stamp. The Lincoln Square monument became less well-known in the context of the suppression of Negro rights that ensued after 1877. It remained as the *Negro monument*. The subsequently far more popular monument of Lincoln in the next decade by Augustus Saint-Gaudens in Chicago's Lincoln Park chose to portray him standing alone.[24]

Lincoln Park became the focal point for celebrations of April 16 Emancipation Day and, in the 1960s, of civil rights demonstrations. Opposite Lincoln is the statue of the Negro educator **Mary McLeod Bethune** by Robert Berks, a black sculptor. Born in South Carolina, the daughter of former slaves, she founded what became Bethune-Cookman College in Daytona Beach, Florida. One of the founders of the National Council of Negro Women and a close associate of Eleanor Roosevelt, she was frequently the only prominent Negro woman in public settings in the 1930s and 1940s. In the tradition of Booker T. Washington, she sought to build economic self-sufficiency of her students while courting white support.

The White House

Commensurate with the strengthened more muscular presence of America on the international stage was the character of President Theodore Roosevelt who was very conscious of the enhanced role of the president. **The Executive Mansion** officially became the **White House** during his administration and was refashioned by Charles McKim to reflect the new imperial presidency. Space, always a premium in light of its usage as an official residence, home, and office, was more problematic with Roosevelt's large family and increased presidential role. Suggestions for the building of a new mansion for the president elsewhere, including upper Sixteenth Street, were shelved by the decision by the Roosevelts to remain in the existing building.

Charles McKim was called in by Mrs. Roosevelt to offer his suggestions that were in turn immediately supported by Senator McMillan with appropriation of money. The president's office on the second floor was removed and the area later converted to the use of the family. The State Dining Room was enlarged into the west end of the hall and the stairway moved to where the office stairway had been.

Jefferson had modified the central portion of the building early in the nineteenth century by adding service pavilions extending both east and west as he had done in Monticello. McKim rebuilt the east and west wings connected by colonnades to the central portion. The **east portico** became the ceremonial entrance to the White House leading via a corridor to a visitor's center. The West Wing was now a building exclusively for staff offices, called for a time the **Executive Office Building.** Originally planned to be temporary, the West Wing became permanent.[25] Under President Taft, the **West Wing Executive Office** was reconfigured with the addition of the **Oval Office** for the president designed to replicate the oval Blue Room in the central portion of the White House.

Washington as *City*

The Park Commission

Perhaps as significant as the Mall for the evolution of the entire Washington area in the twentieth century were the proposals for the park system embodied in the very name of the commission. Indeed, a larger portion of the report was given over to the park components than to the monumental core. Frederick Law Olmsted Jr. was the member of the commission most responsible for that component. The younger Olmsted's work carried on his father's tradition of creating within the urban setting places reminiscent of nature. The elder's work was based on the premise that such landscapes were designed to shape and uphold American national values growing out of its start as a wilderness. The work of the Olmsted firm in its Boston home for a comprehensive park system for that city was the model for Washington.[26]

At the time of the commission, **Rock Creek Park** had already been set aside after a long struggle led by Charles Glover, a partner of the Riggs National Bank, who gave his name to a segment of the park. It also contained since 1890 the **zoological park** of the Smithsonian. Its road system skirting the creek was laid out by the eponymous army engineer Captain Beach.

Moreover, the Army Corps of Engineers had carved out of the Potomac as yet undeveloped **East and West Potomac Parks**. A parkway along the lower portion of Rock Creek (the present-day **Rock Creek Parkway**) became the connecting link between the extended Mall in West Potomac Park and Rock Creek Park. The parkway connecting Arlington National Cemetery and the home of George Washington at Mount Vernon was also realized, as was its northern extension as the **George Washington Memorial Parkway** along the river. A National Park at **Great Falls** preserves that natural beauty. The enlarged park system ranging from Great Falls to Mount Vernon recognizes the regional setting of the city.

There has been continual tension between those who wish to retain the sylvan character of Rock Creek Park versus those seeking a direct commuter route downtown. The best known of the old bridges built to reflect a rustic character is still extant, **the Boulder Bridge,** built with boulders removed from the Rock Creek. It is on **Beach Drive** north of **Broad Branch Drive** at the site of a dam for the former **Argyle (Blagden) Mill**.[27] The restored **Pierce Mill** at Tilden Street and Beach Drive NW is a reminder of the time when Rock Creek was the site of a large number of working mills in the nineteenth century. Other reminders are street names such as **Adams Mill Road** (reflecting ownership by the Adams family) on the lower portion of the creek and **Jones Mill and Viers Mill** in Maryland.

Analostan Island in the Potomac opposite Georgetown was acquired as **Theodore Roosevelt Island** to serve as a nature preserve (in recognition of that president's role in building the National Parks System) and also contain his memorial. Earlier, a plantation owned by George Mason, it was now uncultivated. Completed in 1967, sculptor Paul Manship portrays Roosevelt standing in a characteristic pose with his arm outstretched. Trained in Rome and highly influenced by Egyptian antiquities, Manship's work was highly compatible with the art deco of the 1930s. He is most noted for the Prometheus Fountain in Rockefeller Center.

Given the Washington climate, there was much attention in the report of the commission on the development of fountains like those in Rome. This recommendation has not been realized. Several fountains were built including the **Andrew Mellon Fountain** (opposite the National Gallery of Art) sculpted by Sidney Waugh in 1952. He was also responsible for designing many of Steuben art glass products. **Andrew Mellon** was a wealthy Pittsburgh banker and industrialist. His business interests included but were not limited to the Aluminum Corporation of America (ALCOA) and the Koppers Company (coke ovens). One of the wealthiest men in America, he was secretary of the treasury from 1921 to 1932. During his retirement, he became an even more avid art collector. He gave the National Gallery of Art and his collection to the nation.

The **Oscar Straus Fountain** sculpted by Adolph Weinman in 1947 is now placed in front of the recently completed **Ronald Reagan Building and International Trade Building in** the Federal Triangle. He also sculpted portions of the Supreme Court pediment. Trained with Augustus Saint-Gaudens and Daniel Chester French, Weinman was noted for his work on the Pennsylvania Station in New York City in association with McKim, Mead, and White. His membership on the Commission of Fine Arts was still another example of the intimate connections between the various members. **Oscar Solomon Straus**, a member of the family owning the Macy's department stores, was the first Jew to be a member of the cabinet as the secretary of commerce and labor under President Theodore Roosevelt. He was on several occasions minister to the Ottoman Empire and finally ambassador there, last under President Taft.

Only the **Dupont Fountain** given by the wealthy munitions making family in honor of their naval ancestor is a central focus of a circle such as those in Rome. Similarly, recommendations for bathing facilities and water recreation are exemplified today only in the flotilla of pedal boats on the Tidal Basin and several boathouses along the Potomac. The recommended reclaiming for park purposes of the Anacostia Flats is still not accomplished.

Like the Commission of Fine Arts in respect to the monumental core, the broad outlines of the recommendations of the Park Commission became the basis for the ongoing work of the National Capital Park and Planning Commission from the 1920s. Frederick Law Olmsted Jr. continued the premise of the McMillan Commission in maintaining the rustic nature of Rock Creek Park as well as serving on the NCPPC. In 1917, Olmsted developed an overall plan for the park, which has been followed in large part since then. He was also responsible for the founding of the National Park Service in 1916. His concern extended to the development of recreation spaces within the natural areas and landscaping city areas such as Sixteenth Street.

Cultural life

The process of centralization of local and regional professional organizations had already started with the formation of national organizations that increasingly found their home in the national capital. The **AIA** was one of the first when it established its headquarters in the **Octagon House** in 1902 in conjunction with its role in the implementation of the McMillan Commission report. The **National Geographic Society** was founded in the Cosmos Club in 1888. Its popular *National Geographic* magazine supported the building of its original **Hubbard Memorial Hall** in 1902 with an expansion in 1932 at Sixteenth and M Street NW. Hubbard was the father-in-law of Alexander Graham Bell and instrumental in the organization of the Bell Telephone system. **The Volta Bureau for the Increase and Diffusion of Knowledge Relating to the Deaf** at 1537 Thirty-fifth Street in Georgetown was built by Alexander Graham Bell, originally a teacher of the deaf, in 1894 with his Volta Prize money and the royalties arising from the use of the telephone. Its design is attributed to the Volta Temple at Lake Como in Italy dedicated to Alessandro Volta, the pioneer in the use of electricity.

The **District of Columbia Public Library** was built in the Beaux-Arts style in 1902 even prior to the McMillan Commission. Funded by Andrew Carnegie to a greater extent than any of his other libraries, it was to be his monument in the national capital. Placed in the center of Mount Vernon Square facing south at Eight Street at the confluence of New York and Massachusetts Avenue, its vista extends south to the Doric-columned **Old Patent Office.** Replaced in 1970 by the Mies van der Rohe contemporary **Martin Luther King Jr. Library** on Ninth and G streets, it is has been renovated as the new home of the **Historical Society of Washington.**

The **Folger Shakespeare Library** on East Capitol Street NE was built in 1928-1932 by Paul Philippe Cret. French born, he settled in Philadelphia where he taught at the University of Pennsylvania. He designed many memorials to those who, like him, had fought in WWI. He is particularly noted for his design of the campus of the University of Texas and its signature central tower. In his later career, he was noted for his adaptation of classicism to art deco modernism. This is evident in this building that recalls classicism by its repetitive pilasters along the East Capitol Street front but also uses aluminum art deco motifs and the **Puck Fountain** on its west side.

The founder Henry Clay Folger was born in New York City, descended from an old New England family that included the mother of Benjamin Franklin. His roommate at Amherst College was the son of Charles Pratt, one of the owners of Standard Oil. His entire career was with that company. After the break-up of the Standard Oil Trust, Folger became head of Standard Oil of New York (Socony, later Mobil Oil). He and his wife became avid collectors of Shakespeareana—not only the books and manuscripts but also pictures and art objects dealing with Shakespeare and his times. The collection provided them with the "larger purpose in life" that his mentor Emerson had recommended. The site of their library in Washington, adjacent to the Library of Congress, came about because of the interest of Herbert Putnam, the Librarian of Congress.

The mansions of the Gilded Age along Massachusetts Avenue west of Dupont Circle became even more grand in the era during the first decade of the twentieth century prior to the institution of the income tax. Along with a large number of such mansions still in use converted to embassies are several houses that can be visited more easily by the public. They represent the development of Washington as a cultural and artistic center, as well as the sources of the fortunes that found expression in the social life of the capital. Those built after 1900 discarded the Victorian style in favor of classical buildings.

The first of these is the neo-Georgian **Phillips House** built at 1600 Twenty-first and Massachusetts avenues. The main house was built in 1897. Additions to the building in 1915 by McKim, Mead, and White included a wing containing the music room and art gallery above it. Other buildings have been added, but the original mansion remains intact. The heir to the Jones and Laughlin steel fortune in Pittsburgh, Duncan Phillips opened here in 1921 the first gallery of "modern art" in the United States. Starting in 1918, Phillips collected what was then considered contemporary art. The highpoint of an extensive collection of mainly French and American art is Renoir's *The Boating Party*. **The Phillips Collection** bears the mark of one person's highly developed and idiosyncratic taste displayed still in part within the rooms of a private house.

Across the street at 2118 Massachusetts Avenue is the palatial late baroque style 1902-1903 **Larz Anderson House**, the **headquarters of the Society of Cincinnati.** The Andersons both had wealthy antecedents. She was born in Boston, the granddaughter and heiress to the Weld fortune made in shipping under the *Black Horse Flag*. He was born in Cincinnati, Ohio, to Nicholas Longworth Anderson. His ancestor Nicholas Longworth had been a vintner and the first millionaire in the Northwest. One of his other relatives had been Major Robert Anderson, the Union commander of Fort Sumter at the start of the Civil War.

A Republican, Larz Anderson III served in the diplomatic corps in London and Rome and finally, in 1912-1913, as ambassador to Japan. As the eldest male descendent of a Revolutionary War officer, he was a member of the hereditary Society of Cincinnati. The house, willed to the society after the death of the widow in 1937, contains a heterogeneous collection of the couple's possessions gathered throughout the world as well as material related to the society.

Founded by Washington's officers in 1783, the society commemorates Washington in his role of Cincinnatus, the Roman general during the era of the Roman Republic who renounced his power and returned as a farmer to his plow after his victory. Henry Knox, the Boston bookseller turned general and Secretary of War in Washington's first cabinet, was a founder along with Lieutenant Colonel Alexander Hamilton. One may recall that Pierre L'Enfant, one of its earliest members, designed the seal of the society featuring the eagle, like that on the Great Seal of the United States.

George Washington was the first president general of the order that seemed to represent to its critics such as Jefferson and Franklin the establishment of a hereditary elite redolent of the British aristocracy. As a Federalist and Washington's political heir, it was appropriate that Alexander Hamilton served as its second president general. Members of the Society of Cincinnati were instrumental in establishing Pittsburgh as well as the settlement on the Ohio that bears its name. The society was successful in achieving pensions for Revolutionary War veterans that became the precedent for veterans of subsequent wars and is thus credited with the principle that underlies today's Veterans Administration.

The largest fortunes of this era derived from railroads. **The Townsend House** at Massachusetts and Florida avenues is a copy of the Petit Trianon at Versailles. Carrere and Hastings in 1902 built a French château connected to a previous Second Empire central portion. The house was based on combining the husband's fortune from the Erie Line and the wife's from the Pennsylvania Railroad. Their only daughter was the wife of Sumner Welles, Franklin Roosevelt's undersecretary of state during much of his administration. Welles was particularly involved in the "good neighbor" policy in relation to Latin America and preparations for the postwar United Nations. A museum of Gilded Age splendor, since the 1950s, it has housed the **Cosmos Club**.

Founded in 1878, the **Cosmos Club** is a private social club whose members include many outstanding persons in the fields of science, literature, and art. Its title infers an interest in the widest possible intellectual range. Its founding members included leaders of the relatively small scientific community in Washington at that time. One was **John Wesley Powell** a geologist and explorer of the American West. He is most famous for his three-month river trip down the Colorado River in 1869 that included a passage through the Grand Canyon. In 1881, he became the second **director of the U.S. Geological Survey** and **director of the Bureau of Ethnology of the Smithsonian Institution. John Shaw Billings** was head of the **Library of the Surgeon General's Office** (the forerunner of the National Library of Medicine now on Rockville Pike in Bethesda). He created the catalogue called the *Index Medicus*. There were also several astronomers working at the **Naval Observatory** (now at the Observatory Circle at the top of the Massachusetts Avenue) hill. The club met in a townhouse in Lafayette Square formerly owned by Dolley Madison from 1882 until its move to the present home in 1952.

The still extant Philosophical Society of Washington was founded in 1875, the first of the scientifically oriented organizations founded by members of such governmental agencies as the Army Medical Museum, the United States Coast Survey, and the United States Naval Observatory and was a forerunner to the more widely ranging Cosmos Club. The

Anthropological Society of Washington and the Biological Society of Washington were but two of the many founded in this era concerned with the advancement of science along with its diffusion.[28] A number of professionally based national scientific organizations arose out of the umbrella American Association for the *Advancement* of Science (AAAS) such as the **American Chemical Society** on Sixteenth and M streets NW. National associations representing every professional group increasingly found their headquarters in Washington.

Along with the AAAS, Joseph Henry and Alexander Dallas Bache had nurtured governmental support of "pure science" rather than merely its diffusion. They encouraged Congress to form the **National Academy of Science** (NAS) in 1862 and in the 1870s clarified its role in providing evaluation of quality science.[29] Its development marked the eclipse of the Smithsonian in the pursuit of science in favor of the latter's museum role. The large building of the NAS at Twenty-fourth Street and Constitution Avenue NW was completed in 1924 by Bertram Grosvenor Goodhue. It shared the neoclassic style of its neighbors but without the classical colonnades and pilasters. Goodhue was noted for his neo-Gothic churches early in his career in association with Ralph Adams Cram. More recently, the statue of a benign **Einstein** by Robert Berks (also the sculptor of the Kennedy bust at the Kennedy Center for the Performing Arts and the Mary Bethune statue in Lincoln Square) has been placed on its Constitution Avenue side.

Corcoran Gallery of Art

The major artistic life of the city arose out of the private collection of W. W. Corcoran, a principal in the banking firm of Corcoran and Riggs. He amassed a fortune selling, mainly to British investors, U.S. government bonds to finance the Mexican War. The first of the series of wealthy American art collectors, he was particularly interested in American landscapes such as the Hudson River school and, after the 1840s, scenes of the American West. He began to open his art-filled home to the public in the 1850s. Built by John Renwick, it stood at the corner of at Connecticut Avenue and H Street NW overlooking Lafayette Park (since 1922, the **U.S. Chamber of Commerce** site).

Also built by Renwick, the first art gallery at Seventeenth Street and Pennsylvania Avenue was completed in 1861. It was for a long time the U.S. Court of Claims. Now called the **Renwick Gallery**, it is the American decorative arts and crafts museum of the Smithsonian. The façade is a relatively pure adaptation of the design of the 1624 Pavilion d'Horloge of the Louvre, but with the American touch of Indian-corn capitals. Also significant in its design was the remodeling of the Louvre that had just gone on under Napoleon III in French Renaissance style. Derived from it, the Second Empire court style of straight-sided Mansard roofs had become fashionable. With its Mansard roof, Renwick's design was the first major French-inspired structure in the country and is mirrored somewhat across the way by the even more eclectic Second Empire style of the **Old Executive Office Building**.[30] The Renwick Gallery's brick walls with Aquia sandstone trim is also reminiscent of the **Place des Vosges** in Paris.

Although the building was completed in 1861, the opening of the **Corcoran Gallery of Art** was delayed until 1869 while Corcoran, a Southern sympathizer, was in exile in Europe. A highlight of the collection was Frederic Church's 1857 *Niagara*, an icon of Manifest Destiny, as an expression of American energy and promise.[31] Church, the son of wealthy parents, was a student of Thomas Cole, the great American landscape painter. Church, like Cole, came under the patronage of Daniel Wadsworth, the founder of Hartford's Wadsworth Atheneum. Wadsworth was related by marriage to John Trumbull, the painter of historical pictures in the U.S. Capitol Rotunda.

Still another highlight of the early collection was the notorious *The Greek Slave* by Hiram Powers for which a special circular room was designed. It had been exhibited at the center of the Crystal Palace exhibition in London (to be discreetly covered when Queen Victoria visited), and Elizabeth Barrett Browning wrote a sonnet about it. It became an icon of the abolitionist cause, and copies of it appeared in many Union-supporting settings including Frederick Douglass's home of **Cedar Hill**. Powers grew up in Ohio near Cincinnati. He was given his first solo show in that city at the home of Nicholas Longworth in 1842. Moving to Florence in 1837, he lived there until his death in 1873 as one of the American expatriate colony in Italy.

The growth of the Corcoran collection brought about its move in 1897 down several blocks to a Beaux-Arts building at Seventeenth Street and

New York Avenue by Ernest Flagg, noted also for the Singer Building in New York City. The **Corcoran Gallery of Art** remains as a unique privately supported major museum and art school in Washington. For a long time, it was *the* art museum and in 1865 received the art collection of the Smithsonian. The original collection, mainly American art, particularly of the Hudson River school, was augmented by the eclectic Clark Collection of mainly European art. William A. Clark was a wealthy Montana copper baron whose only connection with the national capital was as a one-term senator in 1901-1907.

The relatively short duration of the successful American involvement in the Great War led to a large number of "temporary" buildings that actually lasted for the next fifty years. The most lasting were those placed along Constitution Avenue, finally removed in the 1960s to form what is now called **Constitution Gardens**. There is also the lasting memory of the **Tomb of the Unknown Soldier** with relief figures reminiscent of ancient Greek tombs within a neoclassic amphitheatre in **Arlington National Cemetery**. Several relatively inconspicuous monuments honoring the dead are the column for the men of the **First Division** (south of the Executive Office Building) and the **Second Division** (on the Ellipse near Seventeenth Street NW). These have since added lists of the dead of subsequent wars.

Building the City

"Negroes" made up 30 percent of the population, the majority poorly housed and limited to menial jobs. The tiny sliver of Negro professionals supported by government jobs such as the segregated D.C. schools and **Howard University** remained, albeit diminished by the end of Reconstruction. Segregation in government employment and public accommodation became even more rigid in the era of *Plessy vs. Ferguson* that enshrined "separate but equal" in 1896.

The housing pattern of Washington was similar to other Southern cities in that there were relatively few immigrants. Unlike Northern cities with relatively compact but large immigrant ethnic enclaves, Washington's Negroes and whites lived interspersed but with rigid social segregation. In contradistinction to the City Beautiful, arising on the Mall were the "alley dwellings" without running water or toilets. Shacks arose in the rear of row houses inhabited by whites to be rented to the poor, particularly following the influx after the Civil War.[32] Inhabited mainly by working-class Negroes, they were in sight of the Capitol; and in the Southwest quadrant, the "alley dwellings" were the object of recurrent reform efforts, one led by the first wife of President Wilson and later by Eleanor Roosevelt.

Plate 4.4 The Scottish Rite Temple

The "island" was the name given to the small Southwest quadrant. It had been isolated from the Mall on its north by an odoriferous canal and surrounded by the water of the Washington Channel and the Anacostia River. A run-down area, it was almost totally destroyed and "redeveloped" starting in the 1950s.

In segregated Washington, the leading Negro commercial and entertainment area was centered around U Street between Fifth and Fifteenth streets NW near the Negro academic polestar of Howard University.[33] The development of Negro-owned businesses in Washington reflected a national response to the increased rigidity of the "color line." Starting in the 1880s, segregation became even more prominent after the turn of the century. In response, in the spirit of Booker T. Washington, a new group of middle-class Negro businessmen advocated separate economic and institutional development. Despite enormous difficulties, a variety of businesses arose.

Evidence of the success of the community is the still extant 1903 building **True Reformers Hall** at Twelfth and U streets NW. The True Reformers were a fraternal order that served as a bank and insurance company and whose building contained various community services such as a pharmacy. As the Pythian Temple, it was the site for the professional debut of the locally born Duke Ellington. His fame is recognized in the **Duke Ellington Bridge** crossing Rock Creek Park at Calvert Street NW by Paul Cret. Successor to the earlier Industrial Savings Bank is the present-day **Industrial Bank** still at Eleventh and U streets, founded originally by a hod carrier to provide loans to Negroes unable to get them from white banks.

The **Whitelaw Hotel** (now restored as an apartment house) at 1839 Thirteenth and T streets NW was built in 1919 by Negroes as a first-class hotel that hosted many of the famous entertainers who played in the nearby U Street theaters. The **Lincoln Theater** at 1215 U Street NW is the only one remaining of the segregated theaters that formed the Negro Broadway prior to the 1960s. The earlier commitment of the Negro community to civil rights during Reconstruction once again became a focus with the organization of the NAACP in 1909-1910 and its eventual success in the 1960s.[34]

One of the leading builders in the white areas of the city of this era was Harry Wardman. Born in England to textile workers, he immigrated to New York, then Philadelphia, before moving to Washington in 1893 when he was twenty years old. He worked as a carpenter and soon began to build homes and apartments. Starting on Longfellow Street and Ninth Street NW at the turn of the century, he built a large proportion of the townhouses in the city. He was particularly active in neighborhoods such as Columbia Heights where buildings still exist now once again being gentrified like **Clifton Terrace** and **Highview** along Thirteenth Street.

Along Sixteenth Street, Wardman built the recently gentrified **Chastleton** at R Street next to the **Scottish Rite Temple** built by John Russell Pope in 1911-1915. (See Plate 4.4) The latter is a replica of the Hellenist tomb of King Mausolus at Halicarnassus, one of the seven wonders of the ancient world. The building, following Masonic custom, is symbolic of some of the fundamental rules of the universe. For example, the steps leading to the entrance are arranged in clusters of three, five, seven, and nine and flanked by two sphinxes. The latter are sculpted by

Adolph Weinman, a sculptor frequently associated with work by Charles McKim and his successors such as Pope.

On even more fashionable **Connecticut Avenue** is the 1909 **Dresden** following the curve of the street. At that point, public transportation by trolley car crossed the ravine formed by Rock Creek Park via the precast concrete bridge embellished by sitting lions. Built between 1897 and 1906, it is named after William Howard Taft. Nineteen sixteen saw the building north of the bridge of the long fashionable **Wardman Park Hotel with the adjoining apartments.** The latter neocolonial **Wardman Towers** built in 1928-1929 is still at Connecticut Avenue in Woodley Park. That same year in 1928, Wardman built the **Hay-Adams Hotel** on Sixteenth Street overlooking Lafayette Park that replaced the H. H. Richardson designed twin homes of Henry Adams and John Hay. The Hay-Adams was originally built as an apartment hotel but was converted into a transient hotel when it went into receivership in the early 1930s as did many others of Wardman's properties. Overextended at the time of the Crash in 1929, Wardman still continued to build good quality middle-class homes until his death in 1938. His name on a house still commands a premium.

The 1920s were a period of great change in the customs and morals of the country but not of the political life. However, the stage has been set for the development of Washington not merely as a place for national decision, but as an "open air cathedral for American patriotism" with tourism its other great industry. Map 4.1 shows the completion of the Department of Commerce Building as the first part of the "executive group" of the Federal Triangle, the Treasury annex opposite the Treasury, the completion of the Memorial Bridge, "Union Square" incorporating the Grant Memorial at the foot of the Capitol, Union Station, and Union Station Plaza.[35]

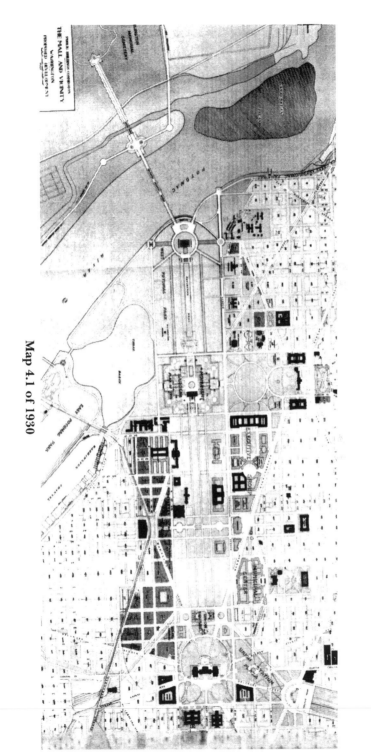

Map 4.1 of 1930

CHAPTER 5
THE NEW DEAL /
THE NATIONAL NERVE CENTER (1930-1960)

Introduction

In 1930, on the eve of the Great Depression, Washington had lost federal jobs during the preceding decade even as its population had grown somewhat overall. Led by the Secretary of the Treasury Andrew Mellon, the policy of the Republicans in the 1920s had been national debt reduction and retrenchment of federal services. The white population, particularly the elite members of the Board of Trade, had become increasingly Southern in origin.[1] The Negro population also tilted southward with migrants from Georgia and the Carolinas along with the usual migration from the Chesapeake area. The decade just ending under Republican administrations had been concerned with reducing the impact of federal action on the businesses of America.

While President Herbert Hoover was still in office, the Bonus March in 1932 of unemployed veterans of the Great War was the first evidence of the changes that would come to Washington during the activist Roosevelt administration. These changes extended even beyond the United States into American mobilization and leadership of the Grand Alliance during World War II that would end with America as the great power and leader of the Free World.

The number of federal jobs doubled during the 1930s and increased another 50 percent by 1950. The population grew along with the growth in federal employment to expand to the limits of the District of Columbia and beyond into Maryland and Arlington counties in Virginia. Moreover, as during the Civil War, there was once again an infusion of Northerners into a Southern city.

154

The style of architecture under federal auspices remained conservative in the neoclassical style under the continuing influence of the Fine Arts Commission. The Jefferson Memorial was the last of the classical monuments by one of the students of Charles McKim. The exigencies of the Depression and war modified the grandeur of the past generation while retaining much of its spirit.

Washington as *Capital*

The Bonus March

Over the summer of 1932, an army of veterans descended on Washington to lobby for payment of money promised those who had served in the military during the war ending in 1918. The money promised to be paid at the time of death or by 1945 seemed too far off in light of the widespread unemployment and poverty. It was commonplace to lobby Congress. What was not commonplace was for the lobbying to be done by thousands in the halls and galleries of Congress and ultimately seeking political redress for economic problems traditionally attributed to the workings of the marketplace.[2]

The then chief of D.C. Police Pelham Glassford tried to accommodate the marchers, even giving them the quasimilitary title of Bonus Expeditionary Force (BEF) reminiscent of their wartime title of American Expeditionary Force (AEF). Glassford had been a World War I hero recently brought in to reform the corrupt D.C. Police and was anxious to accommodate the veterans.

Men (and some families) were camped throughout the city on federal property including buildings being torn down for the Federal Triangle. Money was collected to provide food and shelter. Although the military had been racially segregated during the war, there was relative camaraderie with men of different races and ethnic backgrounds mixed in the parade down Pennsylvania Avenue. The marchers were orderly and remained under military discipline. On June 15, the House voted for the Bonus Bill. Soon after, the Senate turned it down. The marchers stayed on, and their number increased while their demands came to include more general relief in recognition of the economic conditions and to move public opinion rather than specific political objectives. Newspapers followed their activities, but the newsreels and radio, the principal news outlets, were more likely to ignore them.

To exert control, marchers had been diverted as much as possible to "Camp Anacostia" on the poorly drained mudflats where the **Eleventh Street drawbridge** could be raised to prevent entry into the main center of the city. The fifty-acre camp, officially called Camp Marks in honor of the police commander of the neighboring District, had grown to include as many as fifteen thousand persons, living in relatively squalid conditions. After the Congress had gone into recess, there could no longer be clear justification for their ongoing presence.

Herbert Hoover was president. Born in Iowa of Quaker parents and orphaned at age ten, Hoover had become wealthy as a mining engineer, mainly in Australia. Famous during World War I for his relief work, he had been a hardworking longtime Secretary of Commerce during the Republican administrations of Harding and Coolidge. He had been elected by a large margin over Al Smith in the 1928 election but was overwhelmed when confronted by the unprecedented problems of the Depression. Unhappy about the Bonus Marchers, he refused to meet with their leaders but was disinclined to oust them by force.

Patrick J. Hurley was Secretary of War. He had been born in Texas and raised in poverty in Oklahoma. He became wealthy as a lawyer in Tulsa working on oil and gas leases for the Indian tribes. Active in Republican Party politics and married to a wealthy socialite, he became Secretary of War in 1929 and was being considered as a vice presidential candidate for Hoover's second term. Hot-tempered, he was firmly opposed to the Bonus March.

In 1930, Hurley appointed the legendary World War I hero **Douglas MacArthur** as army chief of staff. MacArthur had prepared long in advance for military participation in the ouster of the Bonus Marchers. **Dwight Eisenhower** was in turn MacArthur's aide and appointed liaison to the District Commissioners in relation to the Bonus Marchers. **George**

Patton, the cavalry leader in the eviction of the Bonus Marchers, was a close friend of MacArthur.[3] The future career of these figures in World War II overcame their tarnished reputations arising out of their roles in the ouster of the Bonus Marchers.

There was relatively peaceful eviction from the abandoned buildings on Pennsylvania Avenue during the day of July 28. Then one Bonus marcher was killed and another wounded by police. That same night, flouting Hoover's policy of restraint, Douglas MacArthur as army chief of staff took personal control and ordered the army using tear gas to drive the marchers from Anacostia and destroy their shelters. Dwight Eisenhower was at his side.

Rather than address the demands directly, there was attempt to delegitimize their protest. The specter of Communist revolutionary activity had been raised but was discredited despite the efforts of J. Edgar Hoover of the FBI, MacArthur, and others. Public sympathy flowed toward their cause expressed in the defeat of Hoover and victory for Roosevelt in November 1932. The legacy of the Bonus March was that large-scale demonstrations in the capital appeared to be a legitimate part of the American political culture. Subsequent demonstrations of veterans were met with more generous support, and repression was avoided. The bonus was finally paid in 1936 after having first been vetoed by Roosevelt.

An Activist Federal Government

The proliferation of laws and regulations to deal with the Depression was associated with the proliferation of federal bureaucracy in Washington but also throughout the country. Washington became more clearly connected as a nerve center collecting information monitoring the expenditure of much larger sums in a much larger number of areas of activity such as agriculture and natural resources. Change is most evident in the executive offices and the enlargement of several of the federal departments such as agriculture and interior and agencies such as the Federal Trade Commission.

Plate 5.1 The Apex Building of the FTC

The White House executive office staff proliferated. The **Executive West Wing** was to be rebuilt, and President Roosevelt, priding himself as an amateur architect, participated in its design. One aim was make his working areas more accessible to Roosevelt in his wheelchair. A devotee of Charles McKim, the architect Eric Cugler was also personally associated with the Roosevelts. He built Eleanor Roosevelt's house at Val Kill and some of FDR's buildings at Warm Springs. Charles Moore, the longtime chairman of the Commission of Fine Arts and the guardian of the flame of the McMillan Plan, had expressed his concern about the projected changes that would have distorted the appearance of the White House. However, he no longer had the close relationships he had counted upon during the Republican Party rule in Washington. Cugler was successful in offering a design acceptable to Roosevelt that maintained the spirit of the work done by McKim in 1902 so as to receive the approbation of Charles Moore. The site of the Oval Office used by the president now looked out to the Rose Garden via French doors and a porch through which Roosevelt could enter directly Given Roosevelt's disability, he confined his activities to relatively few rooms. The most used was the second-story oval room over the Blue Room in the White House itself.[4]

The power concentrated in the White House during World War II exceeded any previous president. **The East Wing** was also rebuilt and expanded to two stories as a result of the increased staff. Its neoclassical entrance is reminiscent of the West Wing and its previous appearance as designed by McKim.[5] By the end of the war, there were 225 employees of the executive office, and their accommodation was highly inadequate. Portions of the old State, War, and Navy Building became the Executive Office Building, and West Executive Avenue was permanently closed to traffic under Truman. The entire White House building was gutted and rebuilt during the Truman administration.[6]

The Department of Agriculture was much enlarged in 1930 with a central block with Corinthian columns facing the Mall, incorporating the previous (1904-1908) neoclassical wings with Ionic columns. Botanical motifs adorn the pediments of the four-wing porticoes executed by Adolph Weinman in 1908. An American order involving cornstalks line the vestibule leading to the office of the secretary. As were many of neoclassical Beaux-Arts buildings, the façade was inspired by Gabriel's work on the Place de la Concorde in Paris.

The further extension of the very large south building by supervising architect Louis Simon between Twelfth and Fourteenth streets faces the south side of Independence Avenue and is connected by bridges to the earlier buildings. As a mark of the significance of federal involvement in agriculture under Roosevelt, at the time of completion in 1937, it was the largest single office building in the country.

The much enlarged **Department of Interior Building** was the first structure completed under the New Deal in 1935-1936 between Eighteenth and Nineteenth streets NW. The department had been founded originally in 1849 as the "home department" when Western expansion accelerated. Until 1917, its offices were in the Old Patent Office Building. **The Department of the Interior** under Harold Ickes had much greater responsibilities than before in the management of natural resources. There were accordingly more than two thousand rooms with three miles of corridors. Its utilitarian external appearance with flat pilasters represents the much less ornate façades characteristic of the New Deal architecture approaching modernism rather than Greek-inspired columns characteristic of the various buildings in the Federal Triangle.

Perhaps most emblematic of the activist government was the **Federal Trade Commission** (FTC) designed to regulate business and protect consumers. Established by President Wilson in 1914, it had additional responsibilities as a result of the New Deal. Completed in 1938, the **Federal Trade Commission Building** is at the apex of the Federal Triangle between Sixth and Seventh streets NW. It is stripped of much of the ornamental details of the earlier buildings but does have a monumental Ionic colonnade facing the Capitol. (See Plate 5.1) The sculptures adorning the building are a good expression of the art deco style of the 1930s and are symbolic of the purpose of the FTC.

The two large statues at the apex of the building by a young WPA sculptor, Michael Lantz, show a muscular man straining to control a balking horse emblematic of the control of monopolies. The huge horses are reminiscent of Bucephalus, the giant horse tamed by Alexander the Great. Other limestone reliefs called *Americans at Work* are placed over the four entrances. One shows two steelworkers with the simple lines and geometric figures characteristic of New Deal Depression art. *Shipping* depicts seamen hoisting a cargo; *Agriculture* depicts trade in wheat; and *Foreign Trade* depicts the ivory trade with Africa, each containing two human figures. The four identical doors, each with six panels illustrating *American Transportation* are made of aluminum, the new metal favored in art deco.

The activism was not limited to the executive branch. The congressional staffs also expanded as evidenced by the proliferation of office buildings serving the Senate and House. Built during 1929-1933, the **Longworth House Office Building** named after Nicholas Longworth (the Republican Speaker from Ohio 1925-1931) followed a simplified Beaux-Arts pattern. The Ionic-columned portico facing Independence Avenue is reminiscent of Robert Mills's work but overall the main part of the building is more austere than the adjoining earlier **Cannon Building**. Even less pristine in its execution, in the early post-World War II period is the mainly stripped-down **Everett Dirksen Building** with a nonfunctional pedimented southern portico as if to echo in a limited degree the Russell Building opposite. Built for the Senate, it is named for the longtime Republican senator from Illinois during the 1950s. The overdone neoclassic style of the Samuel Rayburn House Office Building in the 1960s is named for the longtime Democratic Speaker from Texas 1940-1961 (with some short interruptions). The building tries to overwhelm by sheer size and shows the decadence of the earlier Beaux-Arts pattern whose time had past. Even later, in the modern style in the 1970s is the Philip Hart Building (named after the Democratic senator from Michigan serving in 1959-1976).

Plate 5.2 Monument to Suffrage Pioneers

The Hart Building surrounds the eighteenth-century **Sewell-Belmont House**, since 1929 the headquarters of the National Women's Party (NWP). The longtime property of the Sewell family, it was acquired by Alva Smith Belmont, the wife of Oliver Hazard Perry Belmont, builder of the New York IRT Subway, son of the financier August Belmont and the grandson of the famous naval commander Oliver Hazard Perry. Alva had also been the wife of William Vanderbilt, most famous for the building of the Marble House in Newport.

The NWP, the more militant branch of the women's suffrage movement was led by Alice Paul. Paul, Quaker born, even as a child accompanied her mother to suffrage meetings. While living in London in 1907, Paul became part of the more militant "action-oriented" approach led by the Pankhursts that involved civil disobedience, imprisonment, and hunger strikes. Upon her return to the United States, in order to gain greater visibility for the movement, Paul organized a demonstration for women's suffrage that took place in Washington on the day before the Wilson inauguration in 1913. Called the "Suffrage Procession and Pageant," despite jeering, the women marched "with beauty and dignity" down Pennsylvania Avenue. They used that street, the central and most potent national space, despite its reputation as an area tainted with drinking, gambling, and prostitution. A pageant was also performed on the southern steps of the Treasury that emphasized the role women's suffrage could play toward the achievement of an "ideal" nation. The procession established the principle that there was a right to use public spaces for orderly parades, and it was the responsibility of the authorities to protect the marchers.[7]

In 1916, the NWP finally broke away from the larger National American Woman Suffrage Association (NAWSA) that had pursued a genteel policy with only limited results in achieving women's suffrage at a state level. To the contrary, the NWP sought a constitutional amendment and, after entry into World War I, began a campaign of civil disobedience analogous to what had been successfully carried out in Britain. There was success in gaining Wilson's support as a "war measure," and the Nineteenth Amendment was ratified by the required number of states in 1920. The NAWSA morphed into the nonpartisan League of Women Voters while the NWP, in pursuit of broader women's rights, continued to push unsuccessfully for an Equal Rights Amendment.

The most prominent representation of the women's suffrage movement is the *Portrait Monument to Suffrage Pioneers*, a gift of the NWP, placed eventually in the sacred space of the rotunda of the U.S. Capitol. (See Plate 5.2) The monument by the female sculptress Adelaide Johnson consists of busts of Lucretia Mott, Elizabeth Cady Stanton, and Susan B. Anthony. Lucretia Mott, born in 1793 of Quaker parents, was the organizer of the first women's rights convention in Seneca Falls, New York, in 1848. She remained faithful to the connection between women's rights and the abolition of slavery unlike Elizabeth Cady Stanton and Susan B. Anthony. The latter two broke with Frederick Douglass after the passage of the Fourteenth and Fifteenth amendments gave African American men the vote and protection but not women of any race.

Along with Stanton, Anthony founded in 1869 the National Woman Suffrage Association (NWSA) uniquely dedicated to women's suffrage that pursued a relatively conservative program throughout the nineteenth century. In 1890, the NWSA merged with the American Woman Suffrage Association to form the NASWA that continued to pursue a policy of achieving suffrage without the broad interest in the larger issue of women's rights or civil disobedience.

The Jefferson Memorial

The Tidal Basin had been established in 1882 to regulate the flow of the Potomac River in the area near the White House when the former tidal mudflats had been dredged. In 1912, on the instigation of Helen Taft while first lady in 1909, a gift of three thousand Yoshino cherry trees formed what became the iconic landscape of Washington. With the successful completion of the neoclassical Lincoln Memorial, there remained the one memorial site on the Tidal Basin at the southern tip of the Mall to fulfill the original McMillan Plan. First proposed as the site for the Lincoln Memorial, there had been no final decision as to the memorial to be placed there. There had been interest in placing on this site a memorial to Theodore Roosevelt. Roosevelt had already been immortalized along with Jefferson, Washington, and Lincoln on Mount Rushmore in South Dakota and he was eventually honored on the eponymous island in the Potomac devoted to nature.

In the 1930s, President Franklin Roosevelt, who took a personal interest in his Democratic Party predecessor, spoke of Jefferson as an American hero compatible with his own activist government experimenting to solve the problems of the Depression. Jefferson had after all been the founder of the Democratic Party, the author of the Declaration of Independence, and showed concern with social welfare and the welfare of the many over the privileged few.[8] The Jeffersonian principles of minimal government and an agrarian economy was no longer the principles for which he was to be remembered. Rather, he had become the "apostle of freedom." The quotation eventually chosen to circle the memorial was "I have sworn upon the altar of God eternal hostility against every form of tyranny over the mind of man".[9] Like the *Republican* Lincoln, the *Democratic* Jefferson could be accorded entry into the select trio who represented American history along with Washington.

The approaching bicentennial of Jefferson's birth in 1943 was occasion for the formation of a new Jefferson Memorial Commission in 1934. By 1936, the commission had decided on the Tidal Basin site after several other sites were considered around the city, including Lincoln Park.

A major issue was the design of the memorial. The Mall had become the symbolic heart of American history. The Democratic Party had come to power by acknowledging the interests of ethnic groups, city dwellers, and organized labor. The concept of American culture defined as outgrowth of classicism would have to respond to diversity and conflict. However, the Jefferson Memorial Commission was under the influence of Fiske Kimball, an expert on Jefferson the architect and the recent restorer of Monticello (opened in 1926). The commission, without the formality of an open competition, contracted with John Russell Pope. The architect of the National Archives and the National Gallery of Art, Pope was the last of his generation of Beaux-Arts architects to build a great neoclassical building in Washington. Pope ultimately created the memorial patterned somewhat after Monticello in that there was a domelike building, reminiscent of the Roman Pantheon for which Jefferson was an advocate. One of its advantages was its difference from the Greek temple of the Lincoln Memorial and the Egyptian obelisk of the Washington Monument.

Arguments as to style were couched in terms of being undemocratic, pompous, "dead," and lacking "virility." In response, partisans for Pope accused their opponents as being "overemotional and unstable," too concerned with subjective and individual interpretation evident in modern art, and denying the eternal universal values. Despite the opposition of architects arguing for a different style, adherents of classicism continued to have the support of public officials. The criticism about the closed process of selecting the architect led to an open competition for the figure of Jefferson. Nevertheless, the selection by the jury for a somewhat elongated cubist version was rejected by the commission for the traditional Jefferson that is in place. At its dedication in 1943 during World War II, President Roosevelt invoked Jefferson not as the father of architecture that had inspired Fiske Kimball, but as "leader in the philosophy of government, in education and the arts, in efforts to lighten the toil of mankind . . . and his love of liberty".[10]

The debate over style was actually a debate about cultural values. Young urban planners and architects criticized the McMillan Plan as divorced from "American living values" with particular criticism of the just completed Federal Triangle.[11] Moreover, the argument over the memorial was the argument as to what is now to be the common American culture that could bridge the diverse American social groups.

Charles Moore had finally retired in 1937. The Jefferson Memorial was the last purely Beaux-Arts memorial. The chairman of the Commission of Fine Art in 1944 noted a departure "from the slavish adherence to classical forms" and alluded to the recent Folger Library and the National Academy of Sciences buildings that maintained "beauty of form, the excellence of proportions and permanence of materials," as exemplary of the spirit of the architecture of the past.[12]

The Supreme Court

Unlike the president and the Congress, each with their distinct accommodation, the Supreme Court made do with borrowed space for the first 145 years of its existence. With the move to Washington, rather than the Courthouse in Judiciary Square anticipated by L'Enfant, the Supreme Court was placed in the north wing of the U.S. Capitol. It initially met in Washington for only a month each year with the justices each riding a circuit. In 1800, its staff included but one clerk. First, in a ground floor room, the Court was given the Senate's old chamber in 1860 where it remained until 1935. It has been suggested that, as an expression of republican ideals, the design of the successive court chambers with their half domes and the placement of the justices opposite enabled them to hear better the people before them. This is to be contrasted to the original Roman placement of the authority figure within the domed portion or apse to enable that figure to be heard better by the people.[13]

The Court's borrowed quarters represented its early ambiguity. The Judiciary Acts of 1789 left vague how the decisions of the court were to be enforced. The first chief justice John Jay determined that writs would be issued in the name of the U.S. president. This placed the Court dependent on the Executive and required the Court to tread carefully in its early opinions to establish the dignity and respect that it eventually gained.

The decision in 1803 under Chief Justice John Marshall in *Marbury vs. Madison* explicitly established for the first time the principle of judicial review that had been only implicit. While doing so, the Court managed to avoid a direct confrontation with the executive upon which it is ultimately dependent for enforcement.[14] Judicial review became enshrined only over the years.

Some of what seem like hallowed traditions actually were far more pragmatic. For example, the number of justices, at first six, became nine in 1837 when their role as circuit riders had increased in response to the increased number of circuits. The Court only gradually developed the principle of coequal power of the judiciary with the executive and legislature that was quite unlike its British parent.[15]

The Supreme Court was placed opposite the Capitol to its east in accordance with the recommendation of the McMillan Commission. The McMillan Commission assigned it the place opposite the east front of the U.S. Capitol at First and East Capitol streets NE. With support from president (and later chief justice) William Howard Taft, it finally had its own building in 1935. The architect Cass Gilbert, a member of the Fine Arts Commission, was the architect of the Woolworth Building in New York City as well as the Treasury Annex and the Chamber of Commerce buildings in Washington. He was a namesake and distant relative of Lewis Cass, enshrined in the Statuary Hall representing his state of Michigan. Lewis Cass was cabinet member in the Jackson and Buchanan administrations and also unsuccessful Democratic candidate for president in 1848.

Gilbert designed a monumental building that has the dignity commensurate with its coequal stature. In doing so, the Court was still in the shadow of the Congress and without an independent site commensurate with its independent role in the workings of the present-day Constitution. The motto "Equal Justice Under Law" leads to a marble Roman temple. The main west portico has on its pediment *Liberty Enthroned* holding the scales of justice guarded by Roman soldiers representing *order and authority* surmounting sixteen huge Corinthian columns. Other figures to either side giving *counsel* are the architect Cass Gilbert and Elihu Root (a leading corporate lawyer and Secretary of War in 1899-1904 under McKinley and T. Roosevelt) to the left and Chief Justice Charles Evan Hughes and the sculptor Robert Aitken to the right. Beyond these pairs representing *research* are in the same order, respectively, Chief Justices William Howard Taft and John Marshall. The great lawgivers of Moses, Confucius, and Solon are on the pediment of the east portico above the motto of "Justice, the Guardian of Liberty."

The Court's move into its own magnificent building was at a time when it was under attack by President Roosevelt. Charles Evans Hughes replaced Taft as Chief Justice in 1930. In 1935 and 1936, his conservative court majority struck down several of the basic New Deal measures for regulating the economic life of the country, thus questioning the ability of Congress to enact laws to deal with the economic effects of the Depression. After his overwhelming electoral victory in 1936, Roosevelt attempted to "pack the court." He failed in his attempt to replace justices over age seventy. However, following 1937, a more liberal new majority of the Court was able to change its previous support for laissez-faire just as the country had. For example, the Court upheld use of a minimum wage and the right of workers to organize in labor unions and the Social Security Act. The constitutional crisis was averted.[16]

The Lincoln Memorial Revisited

It may be noted that during the 1909 Lincoln Centennial its "Lincoln birthday call" marked the founding of the National Association for the Advancement of Colored People (NAACP). A membership organization with branches throughout the country, it provided leadership in advocating Negro civil rights henceforth.[17]

The Lincoln Memorial would remain, but its context would be revised. Conceived to mark Lincoln as the savior of the Union and conciliator of the North and South, it came to take on quite a different meaning. Marian Anderson, the famous contralto singer, had refused to sing before a segregated audience at DAR Constitution Hall and had thus been denied permission to use what was at that time the major concert hall facility in the city. Under the auspices of the Negro civil rights organizations and with the cooperation of the Department of the Interior, on Easter Sunday 1939, the steps of the Lincoln Memorial were the site of an open-air concert by Marian Anderson to an integrated audience of seventy-five thousand.

It was the first black mass action that evoked a positive response in the country at large and became part of the collective American past. Blacks over the next years were effective in appropriating Lincoln's memory and graft on the meaning of what had become an American icon to include his role in emancipation.

It was in the context of this concert and the experience that had occurred during the 1930s since the Bonus March that A. Philip Randolph conceived the idea of a Negro March on Washington in 1941. The route would go down Pennsylvania Avenue past the White House to end at the Lincoln Memorial. The symbolism of "Lincoln the Emancipator" had grown recently as a result of the Marian Anderson concert. As head of the entirely Negro Brotherhood of Sleeping Car Porters, part of the American Federation of Labor (AFL), he had successfully contracted with the Pullman Company, then the operator of railroad sleeping cars. Randolph was connected with all the existing Negro political network including NAACP.

Plate 5.3 National Airport

With mobilization for war 1940-1941, employment had increased, but not for Negroes. Every branch of the military discriminated against or, in the case of the Marines, excluded Negroes entirely. The organizing group met with President Roosevelt without concrete results. Indeed, the Democratic Party in the Congress and the ruling Democratic coalition was heavily dependent on Southerners. In frustration, Randolph began to organize what he initially hoped would be ten thousand marchers for jobs.

"The Negro March on Washington" was couched in terms of the government's concern for "economic security," a feature of the New Deal markedly different from the previous ethos of "pioneer and rugged individualist" prevalent even in the program of the Bonus Marchers. Power politics by interest groups had received popular sanction during the activist 1930s. The newly activist Supreme Court had established the rights of citizens to use public spaces, albeit under regulation. What was new was the demonstration that Negroes could organize themselves and in large number without the need for whites and thus possible Communist taint.

The march enlisted widespread support from a coalition of Negro organizations ranging from the NAACP and Urban League to the Elks and Negro churches. Some, however, were concerned that the approach had become confrontational and too unlike the quiet lobbying efforts of the past by individual Negro leaders. Exposure of the thin nature of American democracy would embarrass the United States internationally and at a crucial time in mobilization for war in the spring of 1941. In return for cancellation, Roosevelt issued an executive order forbidding discrimination in federal defense jobs and establishing a Committee on Fair Employment Practices to which one could appeal. Segregation in the military was not addressed.

With the outbreak of war in December 1941, the paper victories failed to translate into what the organizers had hoped. Although never carried out, the principle of a march on Washington had become more firmly established. It became used by a variety of organizations that would become even more widespread in the postwar period.[18]

War Mobilization

The role of the federal government based in Washington as the center of power expanded exponentially in response to the approaching war. In addition to the large number of "temporary" buildings on places such as the National Mall, several other buildings built during this era are still in use.

National Airport was built on made land across the Potomac. It replaces on its new site an earlier airport called Hoover Field that required planes to compete with traffic on the adjoining roads. The completion of the National Airport finally provided Washington with a portal of entry compatible with the air age.[19] Like the Union Station of the previous generation of rail travel, the selection of the site and the design of the airport for this new era of travel were determined by its relationship to the grand design of the nation's capital. Roosevelt compared the disagreement over the site for the airport to George Washington's struggle to place the capital on the Potomac River at the center of what was then the major channel of transportation.

Roosevelt made the decision in 1938 to support the new airport at Gravelly Point on landfill from the Potomac River rather than expansion at the old site further north or at places more distant from the city center. To overcome legal difficulties, under his direction, the financing was from the federal budget. The airport remained under direct federal control until recent times. More controversial was the president's participation in the design of the terminal building. He wished to make the appearance compatible with the classic architecture of the nation's capital with the design somehow reflective of Washington's home of Mount Vernon just downriver. Its central façade and spreading wings drew on Mount Vernon's form. To Roosevelt also was credited the inclusion of the columned portico in accordance with that of the original eighteenth-century model. (See Plate 5.3)

Moreover, the impetus for the replacement of the old inadequate airfield adjacent to the Fourteenth Street Bridge was in the name of "national defense." In his speech at the laying of the cornerstone in 1940, Roosevelt invoked the development of American airpower to counteract the threat posed by the growth of the use of military air power by Germany, Italy, and Japan. An air armada of American warplanes filled the air immediately after his speech.

The projection of American power in the world was even more clearly reflected in expansion of the departments previously housed in the State, War, and Navy Building. Even before the start of the war in 1941, a new building was being constructed at Twenty-first Street in Foggy Bottom for the War Department. Found inadequate before completion, it was later assigned to the **Department of State**. In the 1950s, an extension was added in recognition of the increased scope of American foreign affairs. Seemingly permanently fixed in this area, the department has acquired its name from the area.

The very much enlarged War Department site needed to be compatible with the grand design of the capital. The original plan was to build near the entrance to Arlington National Cemetery across the Potomac from the Lincoln Memorial. Roosevelt agreed with the Commission of Fine Arts in finding that site objectionable. Having such a large building so close to the Memorial Bridge would spoil the plan of the national capital. Recalling his error as assistant secretary of the navy in allowing the erection of the temporary buildings for the navy during World War I, he approved the final site to be south of Arlington Cemetery. The site for the **Pentagon** replaced that of the old airport and the agricultural experimental farm now transferred to Beltsville. This new office building, the largest in the world, has become the epitome of that military power that now characterized Washington. It was the nerve center no longer merely of the country, but of the world. It also marked the start of the great proliferation of development that occurred in Northern Virginia during the post-World War II period.

Most emblematic of the price of war was the building in Bethesda in nearby Maryland of the first portion of the **Bethesda Naval Hospital**. President Roosevelt had maintained his interest in the navy since his World War I office as assistant secretary of the navy. To him is attributed the selection of the site on then way off Rockville Pike and the design of the tall central tower with the two low wings. The design was in line with the state capitol of Nebraska by Bertram Goodhue that Roosevelt had noted on one of his campaign trips.

The War Memorials

Exemplary of the role of the United States as the leader of the grand coalition that liberated Europe is monument north of Arlington National Cemetery commemorating the liberation of Netherlands. **The Netherlands Carillon and Tower** recalls the ringing of bells throughout the country announcing the liberation from the Nazis in May 1945. This theme of international contribution to the landscape of Washington was continued even by former enemies. The monumental sculptures of horses exemplifying the **Arts of War** by Leo Friedlander are at the edge of the Lincoln Memorial Circle at the entrance to the Arlington Memorial Bridge. *Valor* is on the left and *Sacrifice* on the right; each a rider representing Mars as the nation's manpower astride the steed. **The Arts of Peace** by James Earle Fraser are at the entrance to Rock Creek Parkway; on the left is *Music and Harvest* and on the right is *Aspiration and Literature*. They were all completed in 1951, cast in bronze and gilded by the Italian government as a measure of goodwill.

The **Marine Corps War Memorial** was completed in 1954 north of **Arlington National Cemetery** in Northern Virginia as the first of the war memorials commemorating World War II. It replicates the famous photo of the raising of the American flag at the summit of the extinct volcano Mount Suribachi on Iwo Jima in February 1943. Iwo Jima was one of the series of Pacific islands hard-won from the Japanese in the march to the conquest of Japan's home islands. The Felix W. de Weldon statue incorporated the real faces of the men who had participated, one of whom was a Pima Indian, along with the steel pole and a real American flag that still flies. The base is inscribed with the names of the Marine Corps engagements since 1775 and with the tribute by Fleet Admiral Nimitz to those who fought to conquer Iwo Jima: "Uncommon Valor Was a Common Virtue."

The definitive **World War II Memorial** on the National Mall was long delayed until 2004. On the former site of the Rainbow Pool, it lies at the eastern end of the reflecting pool between the Lincoln Memorial and the Washington Monument. Its position in the monumental center of American patriotism recognizes its central position in the history of the United States in the twentieth century. Considered by some as "vainglorious," it is clearly grand in the tradition of earlier monuments albeit differing from the themes of more modern monuments to the Korean and Vietnam wars elsewhere on the Mall.

The **Franklin Roosevelt Memorial**, honoring the wartime president, was also long delayed. Following his death in April 1945, acting on his stated wishes, his only memorial was a marble slab "the size of my desk" in front of the National Archives Building on Pennsylvania Avenue. Although designed in 1977 before the Vietnam Veterans Memorial, the Roosevelt Memorial was completed only in 1997 during the Democratic

Clinton administration. The **Roosevelt Memorial** lies along the Tidal Basin amid the cherry trees in the sacred area of other great presidents. The memorial is unique among presidential memorials in its extensive use of water and its use of four areas or rooms to denote his four terms, related also to the Four Freedoms mentioned in his speeches. Dedicated to the times in which he lived, it describes the early years of the crashing Depression with a single waterfall, multiple stair drops describes the public works such as the Tennessee Valley Authority, chaotic falls at varying angles denotes the chaos of World War II, and a still pool his death. Only after some controversy, Roosevelt is shown using a wheelchair, never seen by the public during his time in office.[20]

Washington as a *City*

An AIA exhibit at its meeting in 1939 originally designed to extol the McMillan Plan was described by a group of rebels from the Washington chapter as "a white city for tourists" that ignored the needs of the inhabitants for housing, health, recreation, and traffic control. The increase in population with mobilization for war made the housing crisis even worse while still perpetuating the segregated nature of the city. Some public housing had been built expressly for Negroes, but far less than the number of units needed. The gentrification of **Georgetown and Foggy Bottom** disrupted well-established Negro neighborhoods. One plan, not accomplished until post-World War II, was the destruction of the entire existing neighborhood of **Southwest** with its alley dwellings.

Building the City

An example of the permanent changes that occurred was the development of housing for the government workers who came during this era. The development of small detached houses throughout Arlington County and "garden-type" apartments such as **Buckingham Gardens** were coupled with the grander high-rise apartment houses along Connecticut Avenue in the district. The genteel **Kennedy-Warren Apartment Building** on Connecticut Avenue just north of the National Zoo was famous as the wartime home of the wives of army and navy officers stationed overseas. Started in 1930 with an addition in 1935, it remains the finest example of an art deco building ever built in Washington. Even more recently, it underwent the long-planned completion of the original design with the additional of a south wing.

Illustrative of the growth of the city during the 1930s and 1940s was the career of the leading builder of this era. Morris Cafritz, born in Lithuania, came at age eleven with his four siblings to Washington in 1898. The family was one of the few white-alley dwellers on Glick Alley that stretched from S Street to Rhode Island Avenue NW between Sixth and Seventh streets with an outside spigot and privy. The family, like so many other Jewish immigrants, ran a small grocery store. They soon moved to Georgetown where their house at 2706 N Street NW still had outdoor plumbing. Their neighbors were mostly unskilled Negroes.

Cafritz hawked newspapers on the corner of Fifteenth Street near the Treasury. At age nineteen, he ran a small grocery store on P Street on the eastern edge of Georgetown and took courses at National Law School before deciding his life was not law but business. He bought a coal company, a saloon near the Navy Yard in SE, and, with Prohibition looming, a bowling alley and then another. He began building two-story six-room row houses in 1916. He started Cafritz Construction Company in 1922 and began to buy and sell real estate. The **Argyle Golf Club** moved to Chevy Chase to become **the Columbia Country Club**. Its old property in Petworth near Georgia Avenue was available. Cafritz built three thousand Petworth row houses each with six rooms, a porch, and a bathroom. Many Jews formerly living on Seventh Street moved uptown to **Petworth**.

The Greek-pillared **Jewish Community Center** opened on Sixteenth Street and Q Street NW in 1925, with Cafritz in charge of its building fund. President Calvin Coolidge spoke at its dedication. Rabbi Abram Simon of the **Washington Hebrew Congregation** (WHC) blessed the foundation with oil. Renewed, it is once again the **Jewish Community Center** with the Morris Cafritz Center for the Arts and Cafritz Center for Community Service.

The WHC is the largest Jewish congregation in Washington and the first founded in 1852 by Act of Congress. Its location has followed the movement of the Jewish community from its original area around Eighth Street NW near I Street (now the New Hope Baptist Church) to Macomb and Massachusetts avenues NW in the 1950s on land contributed by Cafritz with an additional suburban campus in Potomac, Maryland, in the 1970s. It became identified with Reform Judaism in the nineteenth century. The bastion of "Classical Reform" derived from German Jewish roots, it has adapted to a more middle-of-the-road set of rituals, greater use of Hebrew, as well as support for the State of Israel mirroring the incorporation of the descendants of Eastern European immigration of the early twentieth century.

On the basis of the commitment to "reform," the Adas Israel conservative synagogue split from the WHC to build its own synagogue in the 1870s, now refurbished as the headquarters of the Jewish Historical Society. It also moved in the 1950s to the uptown Cleveland Park area, but its 1910 building has recently been restored as the **Historic Synagogue** at Sixth and I streets NW.

The **Mayflower Hotel** was the best in Washington at Connecticut Avenue and N Street NW. Built in 1924, it was designed by Warren and Wetmore, the architects of Grand Central Terminal in New York City. The Coolidge inaugural ball in 1926 took place there. It was also there in 1929 Rabbi Simon married Cafritz to the much younger and more sophisticated Gwendolyn. Cafritz built his art deco mansion on **Foxhall Road** in Northwest Washington, where in the post-WW II era, Gwendolyn Cafritz inherited the mantle of Washington's leading hostess.[21] The Gwendolyn and Morris Cafritz Foundation lives on after them, carrying out community projects such as the **Sculpture Garden of the National Gallery of Art** that contains a range of modern American sculptures.

The response to the Depression and World War II under Roosevelt brought more people to live in Washington. One lasting response to the housing shortage was the wartime development of **McLean Gardens** in Northwest Washington, formerly "Friendship," the country estate of the wealthy **Edward and Evelyn Walsh McLean.** The McLean's **Friendship** property was sold in 1942 to the Defense Homes Corporation to provide housing for defense workers. Both dormitories and garden-type apartments were built. The administration building provided amenities such as barber and beauty shops, cafeteria, laundry services, and a lounge. Day care was later provided. After the war, the property was sold to a private company. During the 1960s, the "whites only" policy was attacked and finally overturned with the passage of the Civil Rights Act of 1968.

During the 1970s, it underwent conversion to condominium apartments while maintaining its essential character.

The McLeans were active in the social life of Washington with both the mansion on Massachusetts Avenue and their uptown estate of "Friendship" complete with golf course. The downtown overblown fifty-room mansion (now the **Embassy of Indonesia**) at Twenty-first and Massachusetts avenues was built by her father in 1902 explicitly to be the most expensive residence in Washington.

The feisty daughter of an Irish immigrant who struck it rich in a Colorado gold mine, Evelyn Walsh was married to the socialite Edward "Ned" Beale McLean, the owner of the *Cincinnati Enquirer* **and the** *Washington Post* as well as heir to the founder of the Old Dominion Railroad in Northern Virginia (with the town of McLean one of its stops). The owner of the Hope diamond, Evelyn Walsh McLean, wore it as a plaything before selling it to Harry Winston who donated it to the **Museum of Natural History**. Lavish hospitality depleted their joint fortunes, and the *Washington Post*, one of the lesser of the Washington newspapers at that time, became the property of **Eugene Meyer** and then of his daughter **Katherine Graham**.

Cultural Life

The city also began to augment its cultural resources. One of the beauties of Washington is the degree to which its natural beauty has been preserved and enhanced. **Dumbarton Oaks** at Thirty-second Street NW at the Heights of Georgetown was first constructed in 1801. The name Dumbarton refers to a height called the Rock of Dumbarton on the Clyde River near Glasgow. The first owner of the property was Ninian Beall, a Scotsman. Transported to Maryland as a prisoner, he eventually became a large landowner. For a time, the property was the home of John C. Calhoun, vice president under John Quincy Adams and Andrew Jackson.

It gained its present appearance when owned by **Mr. and Mrs. Robert Woods Bliss** starting in 1920. Mrs. Bliss was an heiress to a patent medicine fortune and interested for many years in Byzantine art. Also, under her direction, the magnificent garden was created in cooperation with the landscape gardener Beatrix Farrand. Beatrix Farrand, wellborn relative of Edith Wharton, was famous for her work as a "landscape gardener" for the rich. She was noted for her concept of designing gardens in which there were "rooms," so evident in the garden she designed for Mrs. Bliss.

Mr. Bliss, a member of the Foreign Service, was a collector of pre-Columbian art. A small museum at Dumbarton Oaks designed in the minimalist style by Phillip Johnson documents that interest. Dumbarton Oaks was opened in 1940, even before the National Gallery of Art, as Harvard University's Byzantine Research Center. The main music room in the house was the site for the Dumbarton Oaks Conference during the summer and autumn of 1944 that identified the plan for an international organization following WWII.

Opened in the spring of 1941, the name of the *National* **Gallery of Art (NGA)** was chosen by its donor **Andrew Mellon** to enable others to augment the collection he himself had amassed and also to emulate London's National Gallery. In the tradition of W. W. Corcoran, wealthy Americans had amassed large art collections starting in the late nineteenth century in the tradition of the great patrons of the Renaissance. These collections became the basis for the expansion of public museums in the twentieth century. New York was the leader with the Morgan Library and the Frick Museum as well as the Metropolitan Museum, but Washington strove to compete.

The beginnings of the collection Mellon gave to the gallery were those paintings bought from the Hermitage in Leningrad sold by the Soviet government in the early 1930s. Among others, the Soviets sold him van Eyk's *Annunciation* and Raphael's *Alba Madonna*. He bought from Lord Duveen the Renaissance sculpture and paintings such as the fifteenth-century Florentine Botticelli's *The Adoration of the Magi* that eventually ended in the National Gallery along with a number of Rembrandts. The story is told that Duveen filled an apartment in the **McCormick Apartments** at Eighteenth and Massachusetts avenues (one of many Beaux-Arts buildings by Jules Henri deSibour and now the home of the National Trust for Historic Preservation) below that of Mellon, enabling the latter to visit it at will. Mellon ended up buying almost the entire lot of Italian Renaissance paintings and sculpture for the National Gallery.[22]

Despite the quality of the Mellon collection, there needed to be far more art to fill the new large building. At the dedication of the

NGA, President Roosevelt announced the donation of two other major collections. **Samuel H. Kress** and his brother Rush had built a chain of variety stores coast-to-coast in the smaller cities of the country with concern about the quality of the architectural design of their stores. In accordance with his business practices, he was also interested in buying art wholesale, particularly Italian Renaissance painting. Kress eventually gave the bulk of a very large collection to the National Gallery, including the Venetian Giorgione's late fifteenth-century *Allendale Nativity* (*The Adoration of the Shepherds*) as well as the great French nineteenth-century works, David's *Napoleon in His Study* and Ingres's *Madame Moitessier.*

The other early acquisition was the collection of the **Widener** family. The family had started out as meat packers in Philadelphia with their first fortune acquired during the Civil War by supplying meat to the Union Army. Their subsequent wealth came from monopolies in providing streetcar services. P. A. B. Widener built a huge mansion in Elkins Park near Philadelphia together with a gallery displaying Old Master paintings. His son Joseph continued to collect such works as the *Cowper Madonna* by Raphael and *The Mill* by Rembrandt, both now in the National Gallery. The extent of the collection containing furniture, porcelains, and tapestries, as well as paintings and sculpture, required a change in the National Gallery's early policy to collect only "fine art."

Lessing Rosenwald, the son of Julius Rosenwald of Sears, Roebuck, and Company collected prints and rare books. One of the early donors, he continued to develop what became the largest collection of fine prints for the National Gallery and gave his rare book collection to the Library of Congress.

By the end of the 1950s, the National Gallery of Art had become a world-class museum commensurate with Washington becoming a world-class capital alongside Paris and London. Unlike those cities, Washington emerged from World War II at the head of the Grand Alliance untouched by the war that had devastated Europe. It was now the international capital of the Free World. Map 5.1 shows the completion of portions of the Parks Commission Plan including the Lincoln Memorial and its reflecting pool, the Tidal Basin, Union Station, and the Library of Congress, as well as the entire Federal Triangle including the Apex Building, Jefferson Memorial, and expanded Departments of Agriculture and Interior.

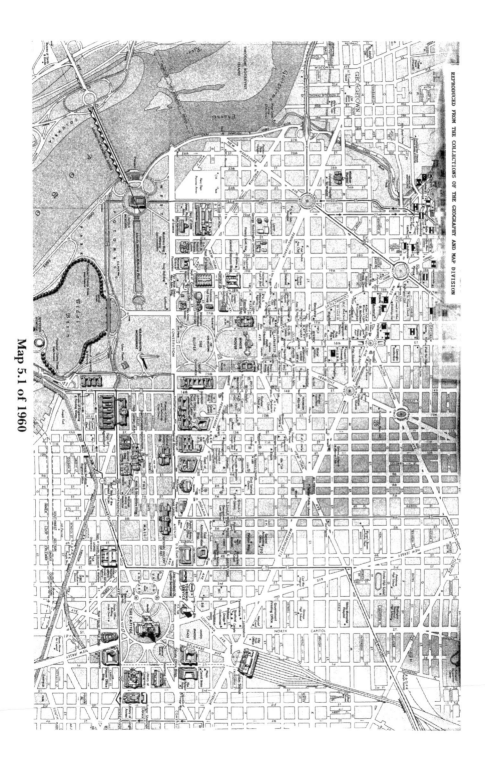

Map 5.1 of 1960

CHAPTER 6
THE PAX AMERICANA /
THE WORLD CAPITAL CITY (1960-2000)

Introduction

The District of Columbia reached its apogee in 1950 with a population of eight hundred thousand. Its always substantial African American percentage became a majority in the 1960s. The percentage of Negro students in what had still been a dual school system had risen to 57 percent in 1953. By 1957, the percentage rose to 71 percent and continued to rise to over 90 percent in the wake of desegregation. The population of the center city has since fallen while the population of the surrounding area has continued to rise. The riots around the Easter week of 1968 destroyed several entire areas of the city and, with transportation enhanced by the Beltway, shifted businesses and population to the suburbs.

The population of the Washington metropolitan area rose to eighth place in the country in 1990 with the District containing less than a third of the total. When one speaks of Washington, the boundaries are no longer those of the District of Columbia or even its adjacent counties in Maryland and Arlington counties in Virginia. It has become a regional city with government installations also widespread. There was a comparable reduction in the role of the District as the commercial and business center. The entire area had become the center for coordination of the worldwide economic, political, and military alliances. What had developed as a domestic information center had now become international. In its newest incarnation, it still retains the different layers of its previous history embodied in its buildings and monuments.

There was relatively little growth in population and government employment in the postwar era until the 1960s. That decade saw a 38 percent rise in the number of government jobs reflecting the continuation of war but now also the rise in the scope of federal activity.[1] The percentage of federal jobs has remained about 20 percent of the total as jobs have continued to increase. Next to New York and Los Angeles, Washington has the largest number of persons engaged in high-level services such as law and accounting. Washington office space increased to be filled with the three As of attorneys, accountants, and associations.

In the aftermath of the victory of the grand coalition in World War II, the United States was the world's greatest economic and military power straddling both major oceans. Its center was clearly Washington, now an international capital of what was described as the Free World. The city reflected both the fruits and the costs of such hegemony. Its architecture became more variegated, reflecting a greater pluralism, and inclusive of the international style while retaining its monumental nature. A number of war memorials further attest to the costs of such hegemony. The character of the city itself became a reflection of its role as an international capital. It was no longer possible to maintain a segregated city in the context of America's world role.

Washington as an *International Capital*

The first of the many "think tanks" that proliferated in the post-WWII era and still among the most important is the **Brookings Institution** whose building sits on Massachusetts Avenue between Sixteenth and Seventeenth streets NW. It traces its origins to the Institute for Governmental Research (IGR) founded in 1916 to bring science to the study of government. Robert Brookings, a successful St. Louis businessman, moved to Washington in 1917 to work on the War Industries Board. He helped found the IGR and later an institute of economics and a graduate school. All these were consolidated into the Brookings Institution in 1927. Among its other activities, it helped craft the legislation responsible for the Bureau of the Budget, the creation of the Congressional Budget Office (CBO), as well as the Marshall Plan and a number of tax reform initiatives.

The range of organizations headquartered in Washington is illustrated by those immediately adjacent to the White House that also vary in their design. The first is Chamber of Commerce Building representing businessmen. Facing Lafayette Park on H Street NW, it was built by Cass Gilbert in pre-Depression 1929 with Corinthian columns as part of his design for a monumental area in tune with the Department of the Treasury. The other is the post-World War II headquarters of the AF of L-CIO on Sixteenth Street, the headquarters of America's largest labor union organization. Built in 1954 when labor unions were still powerful, it lacks columns and has a contemporary style flat front illustrating lack of classicism appropriate with their constituency and their time.

In recognition of the international nature of Washington, the 1945 Bretton Woods Conference established a full range of financial institutions designed to maintain international economic order. They have had their headquarters along Pennsylvania Avenue just west of the White House. It is noteworthy that the choice for headquarters was Washington rather than New York City, otherwise the financial capital of the world. The array contains the World Bank Group consisting of the International Bank of Reconstruction and Development (IBRD), the International Finance Corporation (IFC), the International Monetary Fund (IMF), and the other various development banks scattered nearby.

Embassy Row

The monumental core extended beyond the original circles and squares designed by L'Enfant to the other sites defined by the diagonal streets crossing the grid. Recently, they also contain political figures emblematic of the international policies of the United States, particularly in the context of the competition with Soviet Russia in the Cold War. These include **Thomas Masryk,** the Czech patriot, adjacent to **Taras Shevchenko,** the Ukrainian nationalist and poet, both near Massachusetts Avenue and P Street NW. They joined **Robert Emmet**, a martyr of Irish nationalism, at Massachusetts Avenue and Twenty-fourth Street, **Mahatma Gandhi** fronting the Embassy of India at Massachusetts Avenue and Q Street NW, as well as **Winston Churchill** on Massachusetts Avenue in front of the British Embassy. These figures could be taken to represent freedom and independence compatible with American principles as well as special political interest groups.

Particularly related to American republican principles and long-standing political priorities are monuments representing leaders in Latin American political independence. They are clustered mainly in the vicinity of the **Organization of American States Building,** at Seventeenth Street and Constitution Avenue itself since 1910 (originally the Pan-American Union), an embodiment of American leadership in the Western Hemisphere since the Monroe Doctrine of 1825. The building itself by Albert Kelsey and Paul Philippe Cret draws from both French Beaux-Arts and Latin American influences. *North America* by Gutzon Borglum of Mount Rushmore fame north of the entrance is represented by a woman and child. The sculpture to the south of the entrance represents *South America* by Isidore Konti, an Austrian-born Jewish American sculptor. In relief above each of the sculptures is, respectively, *George Washington's Farewell to His Generals* by Gutzon Borglum and *The Meeting of Bolivar and San Martin* by Isidore Konti.

Monuments nearby, in addition to **Isabella of Spain** in 1966 (queen of Castile who united with Ferdinand of Aragon to form modern Spain), include in 1950 **General Gervasio Artigas,** national hero of Uruguay at Eighteenth Street and Constitution Avenue, contributed by Uruguayan schoolchildren. He is portrayed as a "gaucho" with his hat in hand. Felix W. de Weldon, the sculptor of the Iwo Jima Memorial, was responsible for the tall equestrian statue in 1959 of **General Simon Bolivar** is at Eighteenth Street and Virginia Avenue. Originally from Venezuela, Bolivar was the liberator of much of Spanish-speaking South America other than Chile and Argentina. **Benito Juarez of Mexico** is at Virginia and New Hampshire avenues since 1969. He was the first full-blooded Indian president of Mexico who was also the leader of opposition to the rule of the Austrian emperor Maximilian. The latter was placed in power with support of Napoleon III during the Civil War when the United States was unable to act. This recognition of the leaders of the Latin American countries in Washington may be a reflection of the emphasis given the "good neighbor" policy instituted by Cordell Hull, whose bust also is in the garden of the OAS. As Roosevelt's Secretary of State, he is credited with bringing about a more equal and cooperative relationship between the United States and the other American republics.

The multiplication of independent countries in the post-World War II era is reflected in Washington by the phalanx of mansions along **Embassy Row** that joined some of the earlier countries. They stretch along Massachusetts Avenue from Dupont Circle northwestward to the National Cathedral. Most noteworthy architecturally are **the Egyptian Embassy** on R Street near Sheridan Circle at 2301 Massachusetts Avenue by Glenn Brown. Built for Joseph Beale (a coal magnate from Pennsylvania and congressman), it has a neo-Italian Renaissance façade complete with a loggia framed by a Palladian window. The neo-Renaissance French château of the **Embassy and Chancery of Cameroon** was built in 1906-1907 as the Christian Hauge Residence at 2349 Massachusetts Avenue. Hauge was the first Norwegian minister to the United States appointed soon after the country gained its independence from Sweden. He died in an accident without having seen the completion of the mansion where his American-born wife continued to live until her death in 1927. The **Embassy of Japan** neo-Georgian complex was one of the few designed specifically as an embassy in 1931 by William Adams Delano of the firm Delano & Aldrich. In its courtyard, the staff was busily burning papers on the morning of December 7, 1941, as the Japanese bombers attacked Pearl Harbor.

The Islamic Center was built in 1949-1957 to reflect its Islamic architectural origins with a minaret and horseshoe arches. When built, it was the only Islamic religious site in the area. Now, with the increased Muslim population, it is one of many but is still one of the busiest on Fridays. Beyond is the **Naval Observatory** and its grounds, the official home of the vice president since 1974. Built in 1890, it was the successor of the first Naval Observatory founded in 1830 as one of the first U.S. governmental activities of a scientific nature. It is on the heights just beyond the fusing of English baroque and eighteenth century in the neo-Georgian **British Embassy** designed by Sir Edwin Lutyens in the 1920s. He was also responsible for the design of the imperial British capital of New Delhi during that same era.

The War Memorials

The price of international hegemony was paid in the series of wars. In the intervening generation of the "Cold War," two somewhat unsatisfactory wars were fought at great cost and at great distance at the periphery of

American power in Korea and Vietnam. The ambiguity of the results of these wars was reflected in the character of their memorials in the sacred precincts of Washington.

The Vietnam Veterans Memorial by Maya Lin in 1982 most clearly reflected the ambiguity of the post-World War II world of American hegemony for it listed the names of persons rather than the names of battles. Selected from over 1,400 entries in the largest architectural competition in history, the "wall" was funerary rather than triumphant or heroic. The American defense of South Vietnam against a guerilla insurgency from its Communist North failed. It was the first war that the United States lost. Moreover, there had been disunion over its morality and its value. Veterans returning from what was a very difficult war fought against guerrillas were not welcomed home. Military service was for some a mark of shame rather than the glory that had met the veterans of World War II.

A group of Vietnam veterans led by Jan Scruggs, a former enlisted man, created the Vietnam Veterans Memorial on the Mall to redress these issues, to encourage national healing and reconciliation. Scruggs determined that all names be there and not distinguished by their rank. Controversy over its design and its placement reflected the controversy over the war itself. One learns nothing about the war's cause or purpose because the cause and purpose were unclear. On entering the valley of the dead that the Vietnam Memorial Wall represents, the inscription is "1959 in honor of the men and women of the Armed Forces of the United States who served in the Vietnam War. The names of those who gave their lives and those who remain missing are inscribed in the order they were taken from us." The names and dates are inscribed on polished black granite that further contributes to the power of reflection that it creates. It ends with "1975—our nation honors the courage, service, and devotion to duty and country of its Vietnam veterans . . ." The sentiment behind it is neither patriotic nor unpatriotic, but an honoring of the boundary between the living and the dead that invites contemplation and participation from the visitor.[2]

Tom Carhart, originally a member of the Vietnam Memorial Commission, broke with colleagues over the choice of Lin's design, calling it a "deep gash of shame." He and others demanded something more that indicated patriotism and reverence for the country. He led a group that commissioned Frederick Hart's *The Three Infantrymen* just to the right of a high flagpole with the American flag placed at a slight distance from the wall. One of the infantrymen is white, another African American, and the third Hispanic to represent the racial diversity of the military. In addition, in 1994, the Vietnam Women's Memorial by Glenna Goodacre was added to honor the eight thousand nurses who served in Vietnam. It shows three nurses with one holding a soldier receiving help like the Madonna in the tradition of the Pieta. It is suggested that this amalgam of images has served to bring about the reconciliation that the memorial sought to achieve by incorporating the commemorative wishes of several different segments of those interested.[3]

The Korean War had taken place many years before. However, **the Korean War Veterans Memorial** was not completed until 1995.[4] Unlike World War II, there was no clear end point but merely a truce with a continued presence along the thirty-eighth parallel, nor were there any welcoming parades as individual soldiers returned home in the 1950s. The "police action" to protect South Korea from its neighboring Communist North Korea that took over fifty thousand American lives seemed to fade into obscurity, to be "a forgotten war." In the meantime, the Vietnam War had taken place between 1965 and 1973 with a great deal of conflict in the country. The dedication of the Vietnam Veterans Memorial in 1982 renewed interest in recognizing the veterans of the earlier war.

Although there were several similarities including a dark wall but on which there were faces of soldiers rather than names, there was a need to provide some of the realism that the symbolic Vietnam Wall had initially avoided. Bronze soldiers as though on a night patrol celebrate the infantryman, the simple soldier. Their number of nineteen (with their shadows on the wall) are symbolic of the thirty-eighth parallel that divided Korea. They form a triangle leading to a pool of water, as does the peninsula of Korea jutting into the sea. Unlike its neighbor, it did not need to bring about reconciliation. The Korean War did not divide the country. The United States fought as part of an international coalition under United Nations auspices.

The Korean War Veterans Memorial placed in a grove of trees in the shadow of the Lincoln Memorial and across the reflecting pool from the Vietnam Veterans Memorial together create a sacred triangle of memorials in the west end of the Mall.

The Completion of the Monumental Core

The National Museum of American History (initially called the Museum of History and Technology) was designed by the successor to the firm of McKim, Mead, and White in the 1950s. It was the first of the new post-World War II Smithsonian museums on the Mall between Twelfth and Fourteenth streets. The building was conceived as a modernized version of the temple format of the Lincoln Memorial. Regularly spaced slabs of concrete replicate the more traditional columns. The collection in this museum replicates the eclectic character of the earliest National Museum in the Patent Office in its range from the ruby red shoes worn by Judy Garland in the *Wizard of Oz* to the Woolworth lunch counter in Greensboro, North Carolina, where the first sit-in took place in 1960.

The political climate toward modernism in this post-World War II era remained hostile. The chairman of the House Committee on Public Buildings considered the "-isms" (surrealism, Dadaism, cubism) of modern art as foreign imports that represented depravity and destruction.[5] The continuing battle to place modern, more abstract art within the monumental core was seen as a battle between conservative and more experimental, even iconoclastic, political philosophies as well as lifestyles. An abstract sculpture called *Infinity* was placed in 1967 in front of the building of the **Museum of American History,** the first abstract sculpture commissioned by the federal government in Washington. Alexander Calder's stabile called *Gwenfritz*, in honor of its donor Gwendolyn Cafritz, was placed near the west front of that same building. The **sculpture gardens attached to the Hirschhorn and the Sculpture Garden of the National Gallery of Art** (the latter also donated by the Cafritz Foundation) now display a range of modern art.

There had long been interest in contemporary art to be displayed on the Mall. A design by the Saarinens in 1939 for an American art museum had never been built, at least partially because it deviated from the accepted standard for governmental architecture of that time. There was particular opposition from the Commission of Fine Arts. By the 1960s, there was no longer the original commitment to the neoclassical Beaux-Arts tradition established by the McMillan Commission and carried out by the Commission of Fine Arts. In the post-World War II era, the modern prewar design by Eliel and Eero Saarinen (father and son) for an American art museum on the Mall was reconsidered and indeed approved by a far different Commission of Fine Arts. However, with the move to the Patent Office in the offing, nothing was done. The elder Saarinen was a Finnish architect noted for his work in the United States starting in the 1920s at the Cranbrook School of Art in Bloomfield, Michigan, in the model of the Bauhaus. The son Eero went on in the post-World War II era to build the Gateway Arch in St. Louis as well as the **Dulles International Airport** in Northern Virginia.

The completion of the ensemble of museums along the Mall now diverged from roots in classical Europe. Instead of making the federal city worthy of the nation, the commitment was now to be worthy of the world. A site on the south side of the Mall was made open by the destruction of the redbrick Army Medical Museum designed by Adolf Cluss. Gordon Bunshaft, like Hirschhorn also of East European immigrant background, was one of the leading architects of the time, partner in the firm of Skidmore, Owings, and Merrill and a member of the Commission of Fine Arts. He had already been selected by President Lyndon Johnson to design the Johnson Library at the University of Texas.[6]

The Hirschhorn circular concrete design helped break up the line of the adjacent rectangular National Air and Space Museum to its east. Like a piece of modern sculpture, the **Hirschhorn Museum** at Eighth Street and Independence Avenue is aggressively modern in its appearance. It reflects the avant-garde art it houses but contrasts with the restrained character of the **Freer Gallery of Art** on the other side of the Smithsonian Castle. It is also in rebuttal to the principles behind the monumental **National Gallery of Art** opposite on the Mall.

The Hirschhorn contains the large art collection of Joseph Hirschhorn donated in 1966. A Jewish immigrant from Latvia, Hirschhorn was one of twelve children who came to New York in 1905. Desperately poor, the widowed mother worked in a sweatshop in the garment industry. Short and ambitious, Hirschhorn did well as a broker on Wall Street. In the 1930s, he parlayed his winnings into uranium mines in Canada. Interested in art since boyhood, after amassing his fortune, he began to collect contemporary art in large quantities. He would buy up whole studios of work from artists he liked. He acquired art to suit his personal taste in contrast to the more traditional art that the federal government tended to support and collect. Hirschhorn had been courted by President

Lyndon Johnson and Dillon Ripley, Secretary of the Smithsonian, to make Washington a cultural center equal to other capitals in the area of "art of our time" in which it was then lacking. It was to be Smithsonian's museum of modern and contemporary art. The collection was given to the country and the eponymous museum completed in 1974.[7]

The National Air and Space Museum was completed in 1976 on the south side of the Mall between Fourth and Seventh streets on the former site of the Armory dating from before the Civil War (and the Armory Hospital during that war). This site had earlier been considered for the Smithsonian American Art Museum to counter Mellon's National Gallery of Art, but the site was instead given to the more exciting issue of memorializing American air superiority that extended to the space race. An elegant airplane hangar, it echoes the neoclassic National Gallery of Art across the Mall in its use of the same Tennessee marble and by its jutting monolithic blocks that echoes the recesses and projections of the other. The most popular of the many Smithsonian museums along the Mall, it contains such planes as the *Spirit of St. Louis* piloted by Charles Lindbergh over the Atlantic in 1927 as well as space capsules.

So different from the original west gallery of the National Gallery of Art, **I. M. Pei's triangular East Gallery,** completed in 1978, is in the spirit of the aborted Saarinen design. Its design is derived from its triangular plot of land but also in the modern idiom to provide space appropriate for contemporary art. It consists of two triangles: an isosceles triangle (the museum) and a right triangle (the center for the advanced study in the visual arts). The museum portion is composed of two isosceles triangles coming to a focus in the center of the skylight, echoing the central dome of the original west building. It was made from the same quarry of Tennessee marble used earlier and does not face the Mall but is directed toward its elder brother. Despite the difference in idiom, the elegance and detail of the architecture shares that of the original as a sacred enclave dedicated to the creative achievement of individuals. The very large and well-lit interior atrium contains a huge Calder mobile; people move along stairways, escalators, and bridges. Pei, born in China, trained at MIT and Harvard. Walter Gropius, one of the founders of the Bauhaus in Germany in the 1920s, had fled to the United States and became the very influential head of the School of Architecture at Harvard. Pei built many buildings throughout the world in the style of Mies van der Rohe, another of the

Bauhaus pioneers. His most famous building is the pyramidal entrance to the Louvre.

The 1978 **East Gallery** was the gift of **Paul Mellon** and his sister **Alisa Mellon Bruce,** the children of Andrew Mellon. They also donated much of the museum's extensive collection of French impressionist art over the years since their father's initial donation. There were, however, other donors that helped create the extraordinary collection of nineteenth-century and twentieth-century art. One of the major donations was the **Chester Dale Collection. Chester Dale** started as a runner on Wall Street at age fifteen. He amassed a fortune in utility and railroad bonds. Married to an artist, he began to collect French art of the impressionists and postimpressionists from Manet to Monet to Matisse and Picasso. A shrewd businessman, he owned a share of a Parisian art gallery through which he bought art. He loaned many paintings to the National Gallery of Art while alive and donated the remainder after his death in 1962. The scope of his collection is illustrated by Monet's *The Houses of Parliament, Sunset,* one of his series paintings, and Picasso's *Family of Saltimbanques,* from his circus period in 1905.

The East Gallery was designed to permit the display of the large pieces characteristic of post-World War II art, mainly the American abstract expressionist and subsequent schools, no longer interdicted by the original ban on living artists. Many are part of the collection of **Robert and Jane Meyerhoff,** including works by Jasper John and Robert Rauschenberg among others. Meyerhoff is a major real estate investor from Baltimore. His donation to the *National* Gallery of Art rather than the art museum in his own city illustrates the attraction Washington now had. This contrasts with the nineteenth-century experience when philanthropists would endow institutions elsewhere.

The completion of the sites for museums clustered near and along the Mall during the subsequent decades provided an opportunity for a greater variety of styles and content to reflect a larger more inclusive image of the United States. **The Holocaust Memorial Museum** in the shadow of the **Washington Monument** was initiated during the Carter administration, but completed in 1993. The architect was James Ingo Freed, a partner of I. M. Pei and a student of Mies van der Rohe at the Illinois Institute of Technology. The main entrance on Fourteenth Street is monumental limestone in recognition of the façades of the surrounding buildings;

the north side made of brick is compatible with the adjoining redbrick building, now used as offices for the museum. The interior is asymmetrical and designed to reflect the discontinuity in the lives of the Jews of Europe during the Nazi era. It recognizes the uniquely Jewish experience during the WWII in Europe but also that of other people's subject to genocide. It also recognizes the American role in the liberation of the death camps while also documenting the lack of American response to the prewar plight of refugees from Europe.

There is recognition of African culture in the **National Museum of African Art** while the **Sackler Gallery of Far Eastern Art** complements the collection in the adjoining Freer Gallery. Arthur Sackler was a physician and research scientist who was also the publisher of the *Medical Tribune.* He had an extensive collection of Far Eastern art that is housed at Harvard University as well as in Washington. Both these museums on the Mall are built underground adjoining the Smithsonian Castle separated by a garden in the Victorian mode. It was named after Enid A. Haupt, a donor of gardens elsewhere, including the New York Botanical Garden. She was one of eight children of Moses Annenberg, publisher of the *Daily Racing Form*, *TV Guide*, and a number of television stations and newspapers in the Philadelphia area.

Most recent but also most deviant from the past is the recognition on the Mall of Native American culture in the **National Museum of the American Indian**. It is juxtaposed to and seemingly antithetical to the appearance and the nineteenth-century "Manifest Destiny" message of the decoration of the U.S. Capitol.

The Mall itself as the "national square" became the site for civil rights and antiwar demonstrations among others. Perhaps most illustrative of its new role as a national space was the recurrent displays, starting in 1992, of an AIDS quilt made up of panels celebrating the life of a person who died of AIDS. National public spaces such as the Mall became sites for peaceful assembly as an expression of "direct democracy" contrary to the principles that led to the original selection of the capital away from centers of population.[8]

The monumental core had been completed with the Mall as the center bordered by museums. One major effort of the recent years has been the improvement of the north side of Pennsylvania Avenue. In 1967-1972, the massive brutalist style **FBI Building** dedicated to its longtime director J.

Edgar Hoover arose on the north side of Pennsylvania Avenue between Ninth and Tenth streets. Hoover, born on Capitol Hill in Washington in the area of Eastern Market, joined the Department of Justice during World War I. He became head of the Enemy Alien Registration and helped organize the raids led by Attorney General Palmer deporting radical aliens in 1919. Appointed head of Bureau of Investigation in 1924 and of the Federal Bureau of Investigation (FBI) in 1935, Hoover became famous in pursuit of bank robbers during the 1930s. He directed the FBI to investigate possible subversion and civil rights organizations while the Mafia prospered during his time. In charge of counterintelligence, he used his power to collect possible incriminating information to remain director until his death in 1972.

To its credit, **the FBI Building** when built in the late 1960s was the first to adhere to the setbacks planned for the improvement of the north side of America's Main Street. Initiated by discussion of the participants during the course of the Kennedy inaugural parade cavalcade in 1961, improvements were particularly led by the Democratic Senator Moynihan of New York. One fruit of this effort was the **Freedom Square** placed from Twelfth to Fifteenth streets containing a heroic equestrian statue of Count Casimir Pulaski, a Polish patriot killed while fighting in the American Revolution. Another is the **Navy Memorial,** astride Pennsylvania Avenue between Seventh and Eighth streets opposite the National Archives as a postmodern 1980s version of the 1930s neoclassicism of the Federal Triangle that opens the vista to the neoclassicism of the 1830s Patent Office Building to the north.

The Executive Offices

The Seventh Street SW **Department of Housing and Urban Development (HUD) Robert Weaver Building** was designed by Marcel Breuer in 1968. Hungarian born, he trained at the Bauhaus in Germany before coming to the United States and Harvard under Walter Gropius. His buildings fulfill the 1962 directive of President Kennedy to improve the quality of federal architecture by an architect who epitomized modernity.

The HUD Building provided an unusually good home for what was a newly established department that was also emblematic of Breuer's own early work in the design of city dwellings. It is named after Washington-born Robert Weaver who was both the first secretary of the newly constituted Department of Housing and Urban Development and the first African American to become a cabinet member (in the Lyndon Johnson administration).

Breuer was also responsible in 1976 for the less attractive **Hubert Humphrey Building** between Second and Third streets and Independence Avenue SW for the Department of Health and Human Services. This building completes the post-World War II less innovative row of federal departments built along Independence Avenue. Hubert Humphrey was vice president from 1964 and 1968 under Lyndon Johnson. More relevant to the purpose of the building was his long-standing support for social legislation while in the Senate.

The influence of John Kennedy and that of Jacqueline Kennedy had its greatest impact on **Lafayette Square.** The Executive Office cluster near the White House was most innovative in offering an opportunity to house the burgeoning executive offices within the context of adaptive reuse while still basing itself on the 1962 directive to improve the quality of federal architecture.

David Finely was particularly influential in bringing about the result because of his strategic position in the various facets of the Washington establishment.[9] He had been special assistant to treasury secretary Andrew Mellon during the building of the Federal Triangle and then director of the Mellon-founded National Gallery of Art from 1938 to 1956. By the late 1950s, he was both chair of the Commission of Fine Arts and of the private National Trust for Historic Preservation (owner of the Decatur House) that he had helped found. Coincidently, he was a member of Jacqueline Kennedy's Fine Arts Committee for the White House committed to restoring the interior of the White House as a historic site. His personal connection to Lafayette Square was strengthened by his wife, a descendent of William Corcoran, who had been born at the old Corcoran mansion at the northeast corner of the square (now the site of the Chamber of Commerce Building).

The constraints included preservation on the west side of the square of the 1817 **Decatur House** at the northwest corner designed by Benjamin Latrobe for Stephen Decatur, the hero of the war against the Barbary pirates. Also at issue at its southwest corner was the historic **Blair-Lee**

House on Pennsylvania Avenue opposite the White House. Built in 1824, it is made up of several houses that now serve as the official guesthouse of the president. Its most salient historical association is with Montgomery Blair, Lincoln's postmaster general and confidante. Originally from Kentucky, he lived in St. Louis before moving to Maryland where his home on the border of the District in Silver Spring gives its name to that area.

The compromise appropriately first offered by Charles Glover, president of Riggs Bank, involved access to Jacqueline Kennedy though her mother Janet Auchincloss and was consistent with Finley's preference to maintain the nineteenth-century character of the square. He was supported by two other members of the Fine Arts Commission, namely, Peter Hurd, the New Mexican realist artist, and Felix de Weldon, the sculptor of the Iwo Jima Monument. The building of the **Court of Claims** housed in the Renwick-designed former Corcoran Gallery was also to be saved and replaced by a redbrick building on the east side of Lafayette Square.

John Carl Warnecke, a Bay Area architect, carried out Kennedy's 1962 directive very differently from Marcel Breuer in his HUD Building. The row of townhouses on the west side was preserved to serve as a façade to a high redbrick building reminiscent of Colonial Williamsburg housing the executive offices. The question remains whether "modernity" was served or rather a new trend of historic preservation that was respectful of its context reflecting at least initially the strong personal views of the first family.[10]

The White House

The influence of Jacqueline Kennedy was felt even more directly in the "restoration" of the furnishings of the state rooms of the White House, a salient part of cultural renaissance associated with that president and his "court." The issue of the interior furnishing had first arisen during the Coolidge administration. Starting in the 1920s, there had been increased interest in historical restoration with the installation of period rooms in places such as the American Wing of the Metropolitan Museum in New York and Colonial Williamsburg as the best-known examples. An advisory committee headed by Harriet Barnes Pratt, heiress to a Standard Oil fortune, was formed to purchase furniture but received no clear sanction. One result was the restoration of the Green Room with Hepplewhite antiques. During the Roosevelt administration, the Red Room was refurnished with new wall hangings but with mainly reproduction furniture and a small budget. As an illustration of the general approach of the past, after the rebuilding of the White House under Truman, the rooms were decorated by B. Altman in New York.

In 1961, under Mrs. Kennedy, a program of "historical restoration" began with ample funds raised from private sources with the assistance of collectors such as Henry Francis du Pont, of the munitions and chemicals family and the founder of Winterthur Museum in Delaware. The state rooms began to have a museum quality to be preserved and interpreted that has continued in subsequent administrations. An Office of the Curator of the White House has been established in recognition of its ongoing "museum" status.[11]

The *City* as the Capital of the Free World

In the Cold War, the battle was joined in terms of freedom versus tyranny. Just as the slave trade in the shadow of the Capitol building in the nineteenth century belied the claims of a nation based on freedom, so the racial segregation in the shadow of the Capitol belied the international stance of the United States in the twentieth century. Segregation in the District of Columbia was frequently the subject of international attention. The point had been made that "the District of Columbia should be a true symbol of American freedom and democracy for our own people and for the people of the world".[12]

The desegregation of the District of Columbia and of the federal establishment was theoretically under the control of the federal government but did not fully occur until a full century after the Emancipation Proclamation. The judiciary acted in the absence of action of the Congress controlled by Southern segregationists. In a unanimous opinion, the Supreme Court in 1953 upheld the laws initially written in 1872-1873 during Reconstruction and never repealed although "lost from the code." Public accommodation in restaurants was opened up in the *District of Columbia vs. Thompson Restaurant* case.

The schools remained segregated. The initial requirement for equality of funding for the Negro schools was not met in the years both prior and following WWII. The Negro population continually increased while the white population decreased due to moves to the suburbs. There were no new schools built, and severe overcrowding occurred in the Negro schools. The 1954 Supreme Court decision in *Brown vs. the Board of Education* repealed the "separate but equal" provision of 1896 *Plessy vs. Ferguson* that applied to public schools elsewhere. The Fourteenth Amendment "equal protection" clause used in *Brown* applied to "equality" and only to states, but not to the District of Columbia.

Noteworthy was the local nature of the initiatives to desegregate the public schools in the District of Columbia.[13] School desegregation in the District of Columbia was initiated in 1954 immediately after the Supreme Court issued a separate decision in *Bolling vs. Sharpe* (the latter, the president of the D.C. School Board). This case was brought by local citizens called the Consolidated Parent Group (CPG) dealing with the extraordinary nature of the District of Columbia and was brought under the Fifth "due process" Amendment rather than the issue of the schools "being separate but *un*equal." It thus applied the issue of "liberty" as being not quantifiable rather than the issue of "equality." It is noteworthy that *Bolling vs. Sharpe* was also brought under the human rights provision of the United Nations Charter invoking American racism as a matter of international concern.[14] Notable also was the participation of the faculty of the local Howard University Law School such as James M. Nabrit Jr. and Thurgood Marshall in the entire effort. Howard University had grown during the twentieth century in its prestige. Emblematic was its central quadrangle with neo-Georgian Founders Library by Louis E. Fry, a black architect, its most prominent building built during the 1930s in the style of Philadelphia's Independence Hall.

Julius Hobson and Black Politics

Just as the life of Frederick Douglass a century before, the life and career of Julius Hobson in the post-World War II era illustrates the development of the city in his time. Julius Hobson had grown up in segregated Birmingham, Alabama, in a house run by his grandmother, the daughter of a former slave. His mother, a teacher and then a principal, raised him without his father. He reached the rank of staff sergeant in the segregated WWII unit where he also earned two bronze stars for his reconnaissance missions in a Piper Cub. After the war, he had finished his undergraduate degree in electrical engineering at Tuskegee Institute in Alabama. Founded in 1881, the school was identified with its longtime president Booker T. Washington, who maintained it against heavy odds during the heyday of segregation in the South. He focused on economic improvement rather than political rights and sought white philanthropy on the basis of such "accommodation."

Hobson then enrolled at the graduate school of Howard University in economics. It brought him to Washington, but he was soon expelled for insulting his white professor. He was hired by the Legislative Reference Service at the Library of Congress at the level of GS-5 and raised to GS-7 but denied a raise, whereas whites were hired at GS-9. He continued to work at a variety of government jobs, but politics was his main job.

His son, "Hobby," was unable to go to the nearby school but was required to go to the Negro overcrowded school some distance away from their house in far Northeast. The father's application to transfer the nearby underutilized white school to division two (the Negro school system) was denied. It was his first effort of many subsequent efforts at improving educational conditions for Negro children. In 1954, the Supreme Court issued a unanimous decision in the school desegregation case in the District of Columbia, and his son started first grade at the nearby desegregated school.

Hobson felt that he had a mission in his life even to the detriment of his family. He became active in the Negro "civic associations" as distinct from the white "citizen associations." His research skills demonstrated the discrimination within the District police. In 1960, as president of the local chapter of Congress of Racial Equality (CORE), he began his picketing for hiring "blacks" at the local stores. Note the change in terminology that occurred in the 1960s from the earlier use of "Negro." Starting with Hecht's and Hahn's shoe stores by Christmas, the important Woodward and Lothrop department store agreed to hire black salesgirls. But it was 1962 before the Cosmos Club admitted the historian John Hope Franklin as its first black member.[15]

The March on Washington at the Lincoln Memorial

Julius Hobson was not the Washington leader of the **March on Washington for Jobs and Freedom** on August 1963. Hobson coordinated the marshals, but Rev. Walter Fauntroy, the minister who later defeated Julius Hobson in 1971 to be the first elected nonvoting delegate to the U.S. Congress, was head of the **Southern Christian Leadership Conference (SCLC)**. It was under their auspices that Rev. Martin Luther King Jr. spoke. Assembling on the hill around the Washington Monument, over two hundred thousand persons moved to the Lincoln Memorial. It became the most remembered protest in the history of the United States. It was an aim of its organizers that the demonstration would be acceptable to the general public. It was part of what had been local actions throughout the South that had combined "the rhetoric of Christian expectations and American democracy with tactics of Gandhi's nonviolent direct action".[16]

The use of the Lincoln Memorial for the 1963 March recognized the value of that site for the civil rights movement since the 1939 concert by Marian Anderson. The issue of reconciliation between the North and South was paramount when the memorial was conceived and built. Before 1939 and even since, efforts by Negroes were unsuccessful to modify that image by invoking Lincoln as emancipator. Now, for the first time since Reconstruction, the principle of racial justice could find support from whites as well as blacks. Despite Lincoln's actual vacillation on the issue, the period of nationalism engendered by the Depression and World War II could be united with the symbol of Lincoln to make civil rights for blacks part of being a true American.[17]

Pulling together a coalition of white and black organizations once again as in 1941 was A. Philip Randolph of the Brotherhood of Sleeping Car Porters, but now associated with Bayard Rustin. The latter, born in Pennsylvania, had strong Quaker roots. He had studied the elements of Gandhian nonviolent resistance and contributed to the activities of the Freedom Riders who acted to test the public accommodation limits in the South and the Montgomery Bus Boycott led by King. He had been an activist for a large number of causes throughout his life including the protection of the property of Japanese Americans interned during World War II and helped found CORE based as it was on nonviolent resistance. Imprisoned for his pacifist views during World War II, he was also a homosexual who often remained in the background of the civil rights movement to shield it from attack on that basis. Later in his life, he became identified with the Gay Liberation movement before his death in 1987.

Unlike the aborted 1941 March, the 1963 March had the cooperation of the Kennedy administration and invited the participation of white union and religious leaders. There was a civil rights bill awaiting action in Congress. There would indeed be a peaceful march without any note of civil disobedience. Huge numbers came. For example, as many as 450 busloads arrived from New York City. The success of this march in terms of numbers and the inspirational speech of Martin Luther King Jr. set the tone for many future protests. In the future, these would become even more prevalent as the Vietnam War proceeded and other liberation movements successively appeared for women and gays. The Civil Rights Bill was eventually passed under President Johnson in June 1964.

Martin Luther King went on to expand his ministry to the larger area of rights of the poor and the Vietnam War before his assassination in Easter 1968. In recognition of the broader range of American political life in 1986, he is the first of his race commemorated by a bust in the sacred precincts of the rotunda of the U.S. Capitol. (See Plate 6.1)

With the white flight to the suburbs, the majority of the city had become Negro, but the city was powerless to rule itself. Also under Lyndon Johnson, the District of Columbia regained at least some of its rights for self-government although not voting representation in the Congress. In 1968, Julius Hobson was the first official elected in the District of Columbia in ninety-four years, when he was elected at the first school board election. Once again, when the opportunity arose, Julius Hobson was one of those elected to the city council under the auspices of the Statehood Party he founded. But now, his most active role was for reducing physical

Plate 6.1
Bust of Martin Luther King, Jr
in the U.S. Capitol Rotunda

MARTIN LUTHER KING, JR.
1929–1968

barriers to the handicapped, for he was using a wheelchair because of the effects on his spine by multiple myeloma. It eventually caused his death in 1977. By that time, there was an elected black mayor as well as a majority on the city council. However, even the Voting Rights Act of 1964 still did not fully enfranchise the voters in the capital city. Self-rule instituted in stages since 1973 remains subject to fiscal oversight by the Congress and the District representative in the Congress has remained non-voting even until 2009.

Only in 1996 would there be a portrayal of blacks in relation to the Civil War in public sculpture in Washington.[18] The Grand Review of the Union Army in May 1865 down Pennsylvania Avenue had not included any representatives of the 178,000 colored fighting troops with their seven thousand white officers that served in the Union Army. Unlike the portrayal of the passive recipient of emancipation in Lincoln Square, they had fought for their own liberation. At the celebration of the unveiling of the **African American Civil War Memorial** in September 1996, three hundred blacks in Civil War Union uniforms marched down Pennsylvania Avenue in a reenactment of that 1865 Grand Review from which their ancestors had been excluded.

The film *Glory* in the early 1990s brought attention to the famous battle at Fort Wagner in Charleston Harbor in July 1863 in which Robert Gould Shaw and his colored Fifty-fourth Massachusetts Regiment had incurred heavy losses. Built at Tenth and U streets NW, the **African American Civil War Memorial** is in the midst of an African American neighborhood actually named after the local **Robert Gould Shaw High School**. "The Spirit of Freedom" hovers over figures of soldiers and a sailor. In the mode of postmodern monuments, it lists the names of the 185,000 persons involved in the Civil War. Incidentally, the original plaster cast of the famous **Robert Gould Shaw Memorial** by August Saint-Gaudens in Boston showing him as the white officer on horseback at the head of his colored troops is on display in the **National Gallery of Art**.

Religious Life

In keeping with the national, if not international, character of the city are its exemplary religious edifices. Ascending to the Piedmont atop one of the highest points in the district on Mount Alban at the end of Embassy Row is the **Washington National Cathedral**, officially the Cathedral of Saint Peter and Saint Paul. Most probably the last Gothic cathedral in the world to be built, it took nearly a century from 1906 to 1990. Built by the contributions of the laiety, one of its early supporters was J. P. Morgan, the leading financier of his time. The concept was inspired by the recommendation of L'Enfant to build a church "for national purposes," to be built where the Patent Office Building arose. The original neo-Renaissance design remains in **Hearst Hall** of the **National Cathedral School for Girls**. Charles McKim and then Daniel Burnham had suggested the cathedral should be in the classic design to conform to the other governmental buildings being planned.[19] However, Bishop Satterlee insisted on a neo-Gothic fourteenth-century English-Decorated style structure as more appropriate for an ecclesiastical landmark.

The polygonal east end is reminiscent of **Wells Cathedral**. The Gloria in Excelsis tower and nave is reminiscent of **Canterbury Cathedral**. By 1920, the sanctuary and choir had been finished. By 1971, all but the west front had been completed. Its richly carved west front is in the Decorated style of English Gothic although reminiscent of the west front of **Notre Dame** in Paris. The theme is *the creation of the universe*. Adam bisects the central door. The tympanum above the north Saint Peter tower denotes the *creation of day*; the equivalent on the south Saint Paul tower is the *creation of night*. The more recent additions such as some of the interior sculpture and stained glass were modern elements inserted into the more traditional mediaeval architectural structure.

As if to compete with the spires of the National Cathedral on the west, the spire of the **National Shrine of the Immaculate Conception** arises on the east side of Washington adjacent to the **Catholic University of America** and a large number of houses of the various Catholic orders along Harewood Road NE. It includes a lofty dome as well as an even loftier carillon. America's largest Catholic church, it is also the eleventh largest in the world. Its massiveness as well as its Byzantine-Romanesque style were designed to distinguish it from the neo-Gothic Episcopal National Cathedral started at the same time. All its symbols reflect its dedication to the Marian cult. Intertwined *A* and *M* stand for Ave Maria; the fleur-de-lis, Cedar of Lebanon, tower of ivory, and star of the sea are all emblems of Mary. The sculpture of the *Annunciation* is over the central portal. The figures on the doors are women of the Hebrew scriptures on the west and the Christian scriptures on the east. The curved almost solid walls are quite different from that of the National Cathedral where space is broken up. In keeping with its neo-Byzantine character, the interior is reminiscent of Saint Mark's Cathedral in Venice with the use of mosaic decoration. Gold, blue, and red colors associated with the Virgin Mary predominate.

Each of the several Protestant denominations expressed their national character in their names or in their architectural aims. Many are on or near Sixteenth Street, the Avenue of the Presidents. The **Universalist National Memorial Church,** at Sixteenth and S Street NW, was built in the 1920s in the Romanesque style with round arches. The **National Baptist Memorial Church** at Sixteenth Street and Columbia Road is reminiscent of Nash's All Souls Church in London's Langham Place but with a baroque bell tower. It is part of a religious complex at this intersection with the **All Souls Unitarian Church** replicating James Gibbs's 1721-1726 baroque Saint Martin-in-the-Fields in London. The exterior is the ideal temple with a full portico of columns rising from steps to pediment. Opposite is the former Mormon temple in the style of the Mormon temple in Salt Lake City, now the **Unification Church. The National City Christian Church** (Disciples of Christ) on Thomas Circle is another modification of Saint Martins-in-the-Fields, but by John Russell Pope. He used Ionic columns instead of the Corinthian in the original. More modern is the **National Presbyterian Center** with a high bell tower on Nebraska Avenue NW. On that same street adjacent to American University is **the Metropolitan Memorial United Methodist Church** by Harold Wagoner built in 1932 as an exemplary example of the mediaevalist architect Ralph Adams Cram neo-Gothic churches.

Cultural Life

The Kennedy Center for the Performing Arts was initially planned to be a national cultural center and was later named after the assassinated president whose bust by Robert Berks is in the center of the grand foyer. The work of Edward Durrell Stone, it was a much enlarged version of his highly acclaimed American Embassy in New Delhi. Its enlargement to encompass three separate auditoriums (concert hall, opera house, and theater) overwhelms the narrow bronze-painted exterior columns.

Stone essentially maintained the character of Washington buildings as "white buildings in a parklike setting" in this case facing the Potomac and adjacent to the famous **Watergate Apartments**.

The term "Watergate" was first used for the portion of the Rock Creek Parkway at the foot of the Lincoln Memorial that served mainly as a "band shell" in the 1930s. There were steps where an audience could hear the National Symphony Orchestra playing on an attached barge on the Potomac. The Watergate complex built in the 1960s of apartments, hotel, and office building (the last the site of the famous break-in) replaced the former lowland industrial area and brewery near the river that gave it the name of Foggy Bottom.

Furnishings and art for the Kennedy Center were gifts from the entire world illustrative of the young American president's impact. The chandeliers are Austrian, tapestries by Matisse from France, a sculpture by Barbara Hepworth from Britain, theater curtains from Japan, and sculpture of Cervantes from Spain. Most memorable are two sculptures by Jurgen Weber from Germany placed on the entrance plaza. One on the west depicts *America*, particularly New York, as a canyon between skyscrapers in which there are monster cars with huge teeth for grilles, the façade of St. Patrick is wedged between glass and steel, and the Statue of Liberty is engulfed in flames and smoke. Further east is another panel entitled *War or Peace*. On the left is the city smoldering surrounded by scenes of a person in an underground bunker while the city burns above. To the right is a scene of a family, nude couples kissing, and Louis Armstrong playing music. The Kennedy Center was not merely for the Washington area but was designed to have a national constituency to justify the federal contribution. It contains homage to President Kennedy as well as presenting a wide range of cultural events to fulfill its national and even international character.

Adding to the cultural life but under private auspices and built elsewhere on Foxhall Road in NW Washington is the **Kreeger Museum**. Designed by Phillip Johnson during 1996-1999, it houses the personal collection of Mr. and Mrs. Kreeger emphasizing nineteenth- and twentieth-century French art and sculpture. Phillip Johnson was one of the longtime leaders in modern minimalist international style architecture and one of the founders of the Museum of Modern Art in New York City. His work at Dumbarton Oaks housing pre-Columbian art is in his minimalist style.

His later work such as the Kreeger Museum was "postmodern." This building is made up of modules of varying height but otherwise similar proportions clothed in the travertine stone frequently associated with Roman buildings.

David Lloyd Kreeger was one of the many attracted to Washington during the New Deal. A lawyer for the Department of Agriculture, he left government employment to become CEO of the largest insurance company headquartered in the Washington area, Government Employees Insurance Company (GEICO). The fortune he amassed led to the enhancement of the cultural life of Washington, including the National Symphony and the Washington National Opera housed in the Kennedy Center as well as the Kreeger Theater in the Arena Stage in the renewed Southwest portion of the District.

Still another private collection open to the public is that of Marjorie Merriweather Post at **Hillwood** on Linnean Avenue NW in a neo-Georgian mansion expanded in the 1950s. The name of the street refers to the nineteenth-century extensive gardens built by Isaac Pierce near his mill on Rock Creek and given the name of Linneus, the great Swedish botanist. The heiress to the Post cereals fortune, Ms. Post collected eighteenth-century French furniture and Russian art, the latter particularly centered on the Russian royal family. Her ability to collect artifacts such as Faberge Russian art was helped by the disposal of the assets confiscated by the Soviet government being sold off in the 1930s. Ms. Post lived in Moscow in 1937-1938 as the wife of Joseph Davies, the American ambassador. The Russian motif is also carried out in the dacha built on the property. There is also a replica of Ms. Post's Appalachian mountain lodge.

Rebuilding the City

The Southwest quadrant of the city was laid out as part of the original L'Enfant Plan. The smallest of the four quadrants, it was isolated from the city during much of the nineteenth century by the City Canal running along the northern edge of the Mall uniting the Potomac and Anacostia rivers. Its housing stock deteriorated, and it became home to a large number of freed blacks and to Jewish and other immigrants in the post-Civil War era. Many of the row houses and tenements were without running water or indoor plumbing. A relatively large amount of low-cost federal housing was built during the 1930s to aid in slum clearance.

In the 1950s, in the first full flush of urban renewal, the entire "new" Southwest was to be a model for slum clearance. The Southwest Freeway was driven down the middle of the inhabited area, and all buildings, except only the existing federal housing, were removed. The goal was to build housing surrounded by greensward to be designed by a number of eminent architects in the modernist style of the times. I. M. Pei was responsible for the **Town Center** buildings, Chloethiel Woodward Smith for the **Capitol Park** apartments, and Donald Lethbridge of Keyes, Lethbridge, and Condon for their AIA prizewinning **Tiber Island and Carrollsburg Square**. Not incidentally, Carrollsburg was the name of the original eighteenth-century development planned for the area adjacent to the Anacostia River.

The **Arena Stage** was founded in 1950 but moved to its first permanent structure in Southwest in 1960 and was planned to be the cultural linchpin of the renewed area. Harry Weese of the leading firm of Skidmore, Owings, and Merrill was responsible for the design of the Arena Stage; Chicago-born Weese trained at MIT under Aalto and then at Cranbrook by the elder Saarinen and was also responsible for many buildings in Chicago echoing the modernist style. Led until 1990 by its founding artistic director Zelda Fichandler, the Arena Stage was one of the first not-for-profit theaters in the United States and a pioneer in the regional theater movement that spread throughout the country. It was the first regional theater to transfer a production to Broadway with *The Great White Hope* in 1967 starring Jane Alexander and James Earl Jones. It continues with a focus on plays by American playwrights. Despite the presence of the Arena Stage and a relatively diverse population in terms of race, the destruction of the poor housing stock has not been sufficient to overcome the close juxtaposition of the poor in the public housing with middle-class professionals.

Washington as a *Regional City*

The international gateway to the city had moved in the 1960s from National Airport along the Potomac far into Northern Virginia. The **Dulles International Airport** terminal was designed by Eliel Saarinen as a concrete building simulating flight. It was named after John Foster Dulles, secretary of state under Eisenhower. As a young man, Dulles was involved with the 1919 Versailles Peace Conference under his uncle Robert Lansing, then Secretary of State. An international lawyer, he maintained business ties with the German government even after Hitler's rise to power. As foreign policy advisor to the Republican Party post-World War II, under Eisenhower, he was the architect of many of the Cold War diplomatic initiatives including the partition of Vietnam after the French defeat.

The District of Columbia had become part of a far larger metropolitan area. Major government agencies developed in the suburbs such as the Bureau of Standards and Atomic Energy Commission even farther out in Maryland than the pre-World War II National Naval Medical Center and the National Institutes of Health. The Central Intelligence Agency joined the earlier Pentagon in Northern Virginia. **The Washington Beltway,** completed in the 1960s, serves to connect the region aside from the central city. Shopping centers appeared at its interchanges. "Inside the Beltway" has also come to represent the deracination of the capital city area from the remainder of the country. Each of the recent national presidential elections has had a candidate that runs against those "inside the Beltway." Thus, the differing visions of the republic and its capital as expressed in the Compromise of 1790 still remain part of national politics.

The major public works project of the postwar era was the building of the regional. **Washington Metro system** also designed by Harry Weese. Although extending far into Maryland and Virginia, the principle of the design of the national capital as the central city of the region remained intact. Even as late as 2009, there was still no Metro line that connects the suburbs to each other. First opened in 1976 at the time of the bicentennial, the original plan of the Metro was finally completed in 1991. It has become the busiest subway in the country, second only to New York.

"The nation's capital, a center for government, commerce and the arts, a mecca for visitor's domestic and foreign, had to have a transit system reflecting its special status." The Commission of Fine Arts insisted on maintaining a consistent pattern throughout the system. In light of its national importance, it was designed to be monumental. Indeed, its use of barrel vaulting and coffered ceiling was reminiscent of its predecessor neoclassical Union Station. Although the connection between the two structures was not necessarily clearly in the mind of the architects of the new, their concern about monumental character of the design led to a somewhat similar set of decisions.

The issues surrounding the founding of the District of Columbia and its history remain even as the capital becomes a region in its own right and is closely connected with the world. There is the tension between sectional and national interests inherent in the federal system and the degree to which these tensions are acted out on the battleground of the national capital where South still meets North and a *city* meets the *capital.* Map 6.1 of 2000 shows the superimposition of the Metro on the downtown section, the completion of the executive offices surrounding Lafayette Square near the White House, the FBI Building, and the transformation of remainder of the north side of Pennsylvania Avenue, the addition of the museums along the Mall as well as the changed street system of Southwest.

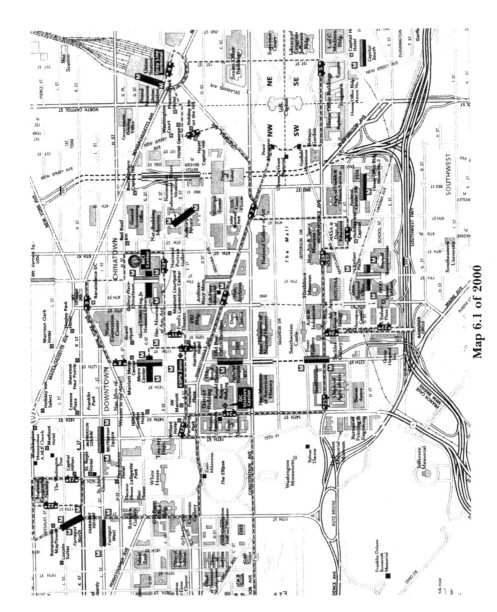

Map 6.1 of 2000

LIST OF CREDITS

List of Maps

Map 1.1-4.1 Courtesy Map Division Library of Congress
Map 5.1 Courtesy Esso Standard Oil Co
Map 6.1 Courtesy Gray Lines Washington, D.C.

Plates

Plates 1.1-1.6; 2.3-2.16; 5.2; 6.1 Courtesy Architect of the Capitol
Plates 2.1-2.2; 3.1-5.1 Courtesy Prints and Photographs Division
    Library of Congress
Plates 2.17-2.18 Courtesy of U.S. Capitol Historical Society

NOTES

Chapter 1

[1]   Federal Writers Project. *Washington:City and Capital.* 1937, Washington, D.C, 3-4

[2]   Kenneth Bowling. "A Capital before a Capitol," In Donald R. Kennon, Ed. *A Republic for the Ages. The United States Capitol and the Political Culture of the Early Republic.* Charlottesville, 1999.

[3]   Allen Clark, *Origins of the Federal City,* Washington, 1935, 7

[4]   William diGiacomantonio, "To Sell their Birthright for a Mess of Pottage" *Washington History* 122: 2000-2001, 31

[5]   Kenneth Bowling, *The Creation of Washington, D.C. The Idea and the Location of the United States Capital.* Fairfax, VA, 1991

[6]   Melvin Yazawa, "Republican Expectations: Revolutionary Ideology." In Donald R. Kennon, Ed. *A Republic for the Ages. The United States Capitol and the Political Culture of the Early Republic.* Charlottesville 1999

[7]   James Banner Jr, In Donald R. Kennon, Ed. *A Republic for the Ages. The United States Capitol and the Political Culture of the Early Republic.* Charlottesville 1999

[8]   Carl Abbott, *Political Terrain. Washington, D.C. From Tidewater Town to Global Metropolis.* Chapel Hill, NC. 1999 p30-32

[9]   Joel Achenbach. *The Grand Idea.: George Washington's Potomac and the race to the west.* New York, 2004, passim

[10] Kenneth Bowling, 1991, op cit, 208 et seq.

[11] Silvio Bedini, "Benjamin Banneker and the Survey of the District of Columbia" *Records of the Columbia Historical Society (RCHS)* 1969-1970, 7

[12] Kenneth Bowling, 1991 op cit, 219

[13] Pamela Scott, "Power, Civic Virtue, Wisdom, Liberty and the Constitution: Early American Symbols and the United States Capitol." In Donald R. Kennon, Ed. *A Republic for the Ages. The United States Capitol and the Political Culture of the Early Republic.* Charlottesville 1999

[14] Scott Berg, *Grand Avenues. The Story of the Grand Visionary who designed Washington, D.C.* New York, 2007, 36-72

15   Kenneth Bowling, "From 'Federal Town' to 'National Capital'" *Washington History*, 14: 2002,8

16   Stanley Elkins and Eric McKittrick. *The Age of Federalism*. New York, 1993,163-208

17   Richard Stephenson, *A Plan Wholly New* Washington, D.C., 1993, 22; Pamela Scott, "This Vast Empire: Iconography of the Mall" In Richard Longstreth *The Mall in Washington 1701-1991*. Washington, D.C. 1991

18   Richard Stephenson 1993, op cit, 23-24

19   Pamela Scott, 1991, op cit

20   William C. Allen, *History of the United States Capitol*, 2001, Washington, D.C.,10

21   Elbert Peets, "The Background of L'Enfant's Plan" In Paul Spreiregen *On the Art of Designing Cities. Selected Essays of Elbert Peets*, Cambridge, MA,1968, 3

22   Pamela Scott, *Capital Engineers. The U.S. Corps of Engineers in the Development of Washington, D.C.* Alexandria, VA, 2005,12

23   Kenneth Bowling, 1991 op cit., 224

24   Claudia Bushman, *America Discovers Columbus*, Hanover NH, 1992, 41-59 passim

25   Allen Clark, 1935 op cit, 70

26   Elbert Peets, 1968, op cit, 3-18

27   C. M. Harris, "Washington's Gamble, L'Enfant's Dream: Politics, Design and the Founding of the National Capital." *William and Mary Quarterly* 3rd Series, 56: July 1999

28   Pamela Scott, 1991, op cit

29   Michael Bednar, *L'Enfant's Legacy. Public Open Spaces in Washington, D.C.* Baltimore, 2006

30   Bob Arnebeck, *Through a Fiery Trial*. Building Washington, D.C. 1790-1800. Lanham, MD, 1991

31   C. M. Harris, 1999, op cit.

32   Pamela Scott, 1991, op cit; William Seale, *The President's House: A History*, Washington, D.C. 1986, 17-19

33   Damie Stillman, "From the Ancient Roman Republic to the New American One," In Donald R. Kennon, Ed. *A Republic for the Ages. The United States Capitol and the Political Culture of the Early Republic*. Charlottesville 1999

34   C.M. Harris, 1999 op cit

35   Rubil Morales-Vasquez, "George Washington, the President' House and the Projection of Executive Power." *Washington History*, 16: 2004, 36

[36] Pamela Scott, Temple of Liberty. *Building the Capitol for the New Nation.* New York, 1995,5

[37] C.M. Harris, 1999, op cit.

[38] James S. Young, *Governmental Community, 1900-1928.* New York, 1966, 21-37

[39] Charles E. Brownell, 'Thomas Jefferson's Architectural Models and the United States Capitol." In Donald R. Kennon, Ed. *A Republic for the Ages. The United States Capitol and the Political Culture of the Early Republic.* Charlottesville 1999

[40] Talbot Hamlin, *Greek Revival Architecture in America.* New York, 1964, 30

[41] Pamela Scott, in Donald Kennon 1999, op cit

[42] Pamela Scott, 1995, op cit, passim

[43] Glenn Brown, *History of the United States Capitol.* 1970, New York, 65

[44] Pamela Scott, 1999, op cit

[45] Talbot Hamlin, 1964 op cit, 27-45 passim

Chapter 2

[1] William S. Young, 1966 op cit, 21-37

[2] Joseph Crook, *The Greek Revival. Neo-Classical Attitudes in British Architecture.* London, 1972,16-36

[3] ibid, 77

[4] Vivien Fryd, *Art and Empire. The Politics of Ethnicity in the United States Capitol 1815-1860.* Athens, OH, 2001, 61

[5] Pamela Scott, "Robert Mills and American Monuments." In John Bryan Ed., *Robert Mills, Architect,* Washington, D.C. 1989

[6] William C. Allen, 2000, op cit

[7] John C. Bryan, *Robert Mills. America's First Architect.* New York, 2001 p291

[8] William S. Young, 1966 op cit, 31

[9] Charles J. Robertson, *Temple of Invention. History of a National Landmark.* Washington, D.C. 2006

[10] A.A. Luce and T.E. Jessop, Eds, *The Works of George Berkeley, Bishop of Cloyne* v. VII, London, 1955, 369-373

[11] Joseph Ellis, *After the Revolution. Profiles of Early American Culture.* New York, 1979,3-21

[12] Lois Marie Fink, *A History of the Smithsonian American Art Museum,* Amherst, 2007, passim

[13] Joseph Ellis, 1979, op cit, 11

14   Stacey Jones, *The Patent Office*, 1979, New York, passim

15   Douglas Evelyn, *"The Washington Years: The Patent Office."* In John Bryan, 1989 op cit.1989

16   Barbara Wolanin, *Constantino Brumidi. Artist of the Capitol*. Washington, D.C. 1998, 125-139

17   John Bryan, 2001op cit, 256-267

18   Pamela Scott, 1993 op cit

19   Lois Marie Fink, 2007 op cit

20   Daniel Walker Howe, *What Hath God Wrought. The Transformation of America. 1815-1848*. New York, 2007, 703

21   Vivien Fryd, 2001op cit, 19-37 passim

22   ibid, 39-41

23   Claudia Bushman, 1992 op cit, 132-145

24   Carl Abbott, 1999 op cit, 61

25   James S. McGregor, *Washington From the Ground Up*. 2007 Cambridge, MA, 73

26   ibid, 79

27   Claudia Bushman, 1992 op cit, 139 quoting the art critic Kenneth Lindsay

28   Vivien Fryd, 2001 op cit, 42-60 passim

29   Claudia Bushman, 1992 op cit, 144

30   Vivien Fryd, 2001 op cit, 89-105

31   James S. McGregor, 2007, op cit, 89-90

32   Francis W. O'Connor, "Symbolism in the Rotunda," In Barbara Wolanin, Ed., 1998, op cit, 149-154

33   Frederick Merk, *Manifest Destiny and Mission*. New York, 1963, 188; Vivien Fryd, 2001 op cit, 142-151

34   James M. Goode, "Thomas U. Walter and the Search for Propriety." In Donald Kennon, Ed. *The United States Capitol. Designing and Decorating a National Icon.* Athens, OH, 2000

35   Barbara Wolanin, "Meigs the Art Patron" In William C. Dickinson, Dean A Herren and Donald Kennon, Eds., *Montgomery Meigs and the Building of the United States Capitol*. Athens, OH, 2001

36   Pamela Scott and Antoinette Lee, *Buildings of the District of Columbia*. New York, 1993,135

37   Kathryn A. Jacob, *Testament to Union. Civil War Monuments in Washington*, D.C. Baltimore, MD, 1998, 30

38   Russell Weigley, 'Captain Meigs and the Artists of the Capitol. Federal Patronage of Art in the 1850s." *RCHS*, 1969-1970, 285

[39] Vivien Fryd, 2001, op cit, 111-124

[40] ibid, 190-200

[41] ibid, 209-211

[42] Joseph Ellis, 1979 op cit, 47

[43] Nina Burleigh, *The Stranger and the Statesman: James Smithson and John Quincy Adams and the Making of America's Greatest Museum.* New York, 2003, 168

[44] Lois Marie Fink, 2007, op cit, passim

[45] Todd Timmons, *Science and Technology in the Nineteenth Century.* Westport, CT, 2000, 171-173

[46] Daniel Reiff, *Washington Architecture. 1791-1861. Problems in Development.* Washington, D.C. 1971, 93

[47] Michael F. Conlin, *Science Under Siege; Joseph Henry's Smithsonian 1846-1865.* Ph.d Dissertation University of Illinois Urbana-Champlain 1999

[48] Kenneth Hafertepe, *America's Castle: The evolution of the Smithsonian building and its Institution.* Washington, D.C., 1984

[49] Paul Oehser, *Sons of Science. The Story of the Smithsonian Institution and its leaders.* New York, 1968, 60-70

[50] Cynthia Field, "A Rich Repast of Classicism: Meigs and Classical Sources." In William C. Dickinson, Dean A Herren and Donald Kennon, Eds., op cit. 2001

[51] David R. Goldfield, "Antebellum Washington in Context: The Pursuit of Prosperity and Identity," In Howard Gillette, Ed., *Southern City, National Ambitions.* Washington, D.C. 1985

[52] Carl Abbot, 1999, op cit, 61-67

[53] Howard Gillette, vide supra, 1995

[54] Mary Beth Corrigan, "Imaginary Cruelties? A History of the Slave Trade in the District of Columbia," *Washington History* 13: 2001/2002, 4

[55] Daniel Reiff, 1971, op cit, 26-36

Chapter 3

[1] Donald B. Myer. *Bridges and the City of Washington.* Washington, D.C.

[2] Vincent Lee-Thorp, *Washington Engineered,* Baltimore, 2006, 71

[3] Lonny Johnson, *The Lincoln White House,* MA Dissertation, California State University, Fresno, CA.1998

[4] O'Gorman

5   Ernest Furgurson, *Freedom Rising, Washington in the Civil War.* New York, 2004. 179; Kathryn Jacob, 1998 op cit, 29-33

6   James M. Goode, *The Outdoor Sculpture of Washington, D.C.* Washington, D.C.,1974. 131-132

7   Kathryn Jacob, 1998 op cit, 81-84

8   Kenneth Bowling, 2002, op cit

9   Linda Lyons, "The Pension Building. Form and Function." In William C. Dickinson, Dean A Herren and Donald Kennon, Eds. op cit 2001

10   Pamela Scott and Antoinette Lee, 1993 op cit, 183-186

11   Thomas Y. Cole, "A Struggle for a structure. Ainsworth Rand Spofford and a new building for the Library of Congress." In John Y. Cole and Henry Hope Reed, Ed., *The Library of Congress. Art and Architecture of the Thomas Jefferson Building,* New York, 1997

12   Frances Brousseau, *The Library of Congress 1873-1897: The Building, its architects and the politics of the nineteenth century.* Ph.D. Dissertation University of Delaware, 1998

13   James M. McGregor, 2007, op cit, 120

14   Herbert Small, "Handbook of the New Library of Congress" In John Y. Cole and Henry Hope Reed, Ed., op cit

15   Ernest Furgurson, 2004, op cit, 331

16   Vincent Lee-Thorp, 2006, op cit, 96

17   Henry C. Ways, 'Montgomery Meigs and the Washington Aqueduct." In William C. Dickinson, Dean A Herren and Donald Kennon, Eds. op cit 2001

18   Ed Hatcher, Washington's Nineteenth Century 'Citizens Associations' and the Senate Park Commission Plan." *Washington History* 14: 71,2002

19   Donlad Roe, "The Dual School System in the District of Columbia 1862-1954: Origins, problems, Protests," *Washington History* 16: 2004-200517

20   Constance McLaughlin Greene, *Washington. A History of the Capital,* Princeton. 1962 p313-362 passim; Howard Gillette, 1985, op cit, 48-68

21   Tanya Beauchamp, "Adolph Cluss: An Architect in Washington in Civil War and Reconstruction" *RCHS* 48: 3381971-1972

22   Vincent Lee-Thorp, op cit, 2006

23   Louise Hutchinson, *The Anacostia Story 1608-1930.* Washington, D.C. 1977 passim

24   Louise Hutchinson, *The Anacostia Story 1608-1930.* Washington, D.C. 1977 passim

[25] Carl Abbott, 1999, op cit, 112

[26] Michael Harrison, "The Evil of the Misfit Subdivisions." *Washington History* 14: 27, 2002

[27] Henry Glassie, "Victorian Homes." *RCHS* 1963-1965, 310

[28] Susan Myers, "Capitol Hill 1870-1900. The People and their Homes." *RCHS* 1973-1974, 276

[29] Sue Kohler, *Sixteenth Street Architecture v 2.* Washington, D.C.,1988

[30] Pamela Scott and Antoinette Lee, 1993, op cit, 319

Chapter 4

[1] Carl Abbott, 1991 op cit, 101

[2] Jon A. Peterson "The Senate Park Commission. A New Vision for the Capital and the Nation." In Sue Kohler and Pamela Scott. *Designing the Nation's Capital. The 1901 Plan for Washington, D.C.* Washington, D.C. 2006

[3] Tony P. Wrenn, "The American Institute of Architecture Convention of 1900. Its Influence on the Senate Park Commission Plan." In Sue Kohler and Pamela Scott., op cit, 2006

[4] Charles Moore, *Daniel H. Burnham. Architect. Planner of Cities.* Boston, 1921, 137

[5] Alan Lessoff, *The Nation and the City.* Baltimore, 1994, 253-258

[6] Pamela Scott, "A City Designed as a Work of Art" In Sue Kohler and Pamela Scott., op cit,2006

[7] Howard Gillette *Between Justice and Beauty.* Philadelphia, 2006, 88-100

[8] Peterson, 2007

[9] Charles Moore, 1921 op cit, 155

[10] Ulysses Grant III, "The L'Enfant Plan and its Evolution" *RCHS* 1932 33-34, 1

[11] William Anthony Tobin, *In the Shadow of the Capitol: The Transformation of Washington, D.C. and the elaboration of the modern United States nation-state.* Ph.D. Dissertation, Stanford University, 1994

[12] Sue Kohler *The Commission of Fine Arts: A Brief History 1910-1976.* Washington, D.C. 1977 p1

[13] Charles Moore., 1921 op cit, 232,255

[14] Sue Kohler, 1977op cit, 51

[15] Sally Tompkins, *A Quest for Grandeur. Charles Moore and the Federal Triangle.* Washington, D.C.1993

16   James M. McGregor, 2007 op cit, 204
17   William H. Wilson. *The City Beautiful Movement.* Baltimore,.1989,75-95
18   Alan Lessoff, 1994 op cit, 264-267
19   Dennis R. Montagna, *Henry Merwin Shrady's Ulysses S. Grant Memorial in Washington, D.C.* Ph.D. Dissertation University of Delaware, 1987
20   Christopher Thomas, *The Lincoln Memorial in American Life*, Princeton, 2002, 9-13
21   Alan Lessoff, "Washington Insider. The Early Career of Charles Moore." *Washington History* 6:1994-1995, 64
22   Charles Moore, "Personalities in Washington Architecture" *RCHS* 1937-1938. 1-16
23   Christopher Thomas, 2002 op cit, 152-158
24   Kirk Savage, *Standing Soldiers, Kneeling Slaves.* Princeton 1997, 115-125
25   William Seale, 1986 op cit, 649-669
26   Timothy Davis, "Beyond the Mall." In Sue Kohler and Pamela Scott., op cit,2006
27   Gail Spilsbury, *Rock Creek Park.* Baltimore, 2003
28   J. Fitzgerald Flack. "Scientific Societies in Gilded Age Washington." *RCHS* 1972-1973, 430
29   George H. Daniels, *Science in American Society*, New York, 1971passim
30   McKenna, 1951
31   Holly Tank, "Dedicated to Art: William Corcoran and the founding of his Gallery." *Washington History* 17: 2005, 27
32   James Borchet, "The Rise and Fall of Washington's Inhabited alleys, 1852-1972" *RCHS* 48: 1971-1972, 267
33   Sandra Fitzpatrick and Maria Goodwin. *The Guide to Black Washington*, New York, 1999
34   Michael A. Fitzpatrick "A Great Agitation for Business. Black Economic Development in Shaw." *Washington History* 2: 1990-1991, 43
35   Carl Abbott, 1999, op cit, 104

Chapter 5

1   Carl Abbott, 1999 op cit, 85
2   Lucy G. Barber, *Marching on Washington. The Forging of an American Political Tradition.* Berkeley, 2002, 75-107
3   Michael J. Rawl *Anacostia Flats*, Baltimore, 2006, 28-40 and passim
4   William Seale, 1986 op cit, 939-949

[5]   ibid, 982

[6]   ibid, 1007

[7]   Lucy Barber, 2002 op cit, 71-74

[8]   Jeanne Houck, *Historical Memory and the Mall 1865-1945*. Ph.D. Dissertation Stanford University 1993

[9]   Merrill Peterson, *The Jefferson Image in the American Mind*. New York, 1960,378

[10] Jeanne Houck, 1993 op cit, 309-312

[11] Sally Tompkins, 1993 op cit

[12] Sue Kohler, 1977 op cit, 45

[13] James McGregor, 2007 op cit, 53

[14] Bernard Schwartz, *A History of the Supreme Court*. New York, 1993, 40-41

[15] Katherine F. Taylor, "First Appearances: The Material Setting and Culture of the Early Supreme Court." In Christopher Tomlins, Ed., *The United States Supreme Court The Pursuit of Justice*. Boston, 2005

[16] Bernard Schwartz, 1993 op cit,230-243

[17] Scott Sandage, "A Marble House Divided: The Lincoln Memorial, the Civil Rights Movement and the Politics of Memory. 1939-1963" *The Journal of American History*, 80: 135, 1993

[18] Lucy Barber, 2002 op cit., 108-140

[19] James H. Goode, "Flying High. The Origins and Design of the Washington National Airport." *Washington History* 1989 20: 4

[20] William Seale, 1986 op cit., 916

[21] Burt Solomon, *The Washington Century* New York, 2004, 1-35

[22] Meryle Secrest, Duveen. *A Life in Art*. New York, 2004,344-46 and passim

Chapter 6

[1]   Carl Abbott, 1999, op cit., 101

[2]   Richard Hyde, *American Acropolis. The West End of the Washington Mall*. Ph.D. Dissertation. Graduate Theological Union, 1998

[3]   Liam van Beek, *Heroes in any other Conflict. The Viet Nam Veterans Memorial and Revisionism in the 1980s*. Masters Thesis Dalhousie University, 2005; Roderick Urquidi, Master Thesis, California State University, 2004

[4]   Brent Ashabranner, *Remembering Korea*. Brookfield, CT, 2001

[5]   Richard G. Wilson, "High Noon on the Mall. Modernism versus Traditionalism, 1910-1970." In Richard Longstreth, 2002 op cit.

6   Carol Krinsky, *Gordon Bunshaft of Skidmore, Owings and Merrill.* Cambridge, MA, 1988

7   Leslie Rabinovitz, Master Thesis *The Institutional History of the Hirschhorn Museum and Sculpture Garden, Smithsonian Institution, Washington, D.C. 1965-1974.* Master thesis University of Southern California, 1996

8   Lucy Barber op cit, 2002

9   Kurt Helfrich, "Modernism for Washington? The Kennedys and the Redesign of Lafayette Square." *Washington History* 8; 17,1996

10 ibid

11 Elaine Rice, *Furnishing Camelot. The Restoration of the White House Interiors 1961-1963 and the Role of H. F. DuPont.* Ph.D. Dissertation University of Delaware, 1993; William Seale, 1986 op cit., 1053-1057

12 Mary Dudziak, *Cold War Civil Rights.* Princeton, 2000, 99

13 Donald Roe, op cit, 2004-2005

14 Lisa Crooms, "Race, Education and the District of Columbia. The meaning and Legacy of Bolling vs Sharpe'" *Washington History.* 13: 4, 2004-2005

15 Burt Solomon, 2004 op cit, passim

16 Lucy Barber2002, op cit., 142

17 Scott Sandage, 1993 op cit

18 Kathryn Jacob, 1998 op cit., 145-148

19 Charles Moore, 1921 op cit v2, 47-69

BIBLIOGRAPHY

Books

Abbott, Carl. *Political Terrain. Washington, D.C. From Tidewater Town to Global Metropolis.* Chapel Hill, NC: University of North Carolina Press, 1999.

Achenbach, Joel. *The Grand Idea: George Washington's Potomac and the race to the west.* New York: Simon & Schuster 2004.

Allen, William C. *The Washington Monument.* New York: Discovery Books, 2000.

_____. *History of the United States Capitol.* Washington, DC: U.S. Government Printing Office, 2001.

Arnebeck, Bob. *Through a Fiery Trial. Building Washington 1790-1800.* Lanham, MD: Madison Books, 1991.

Ashabranner, Brent. *Remembering Korea.* Brookfield, CT: 21st Century Books, 2001.

Banner, James Jr. "The Capital and the State. Washington, D.C. and the Nature of American Government." In Donald Kennon, Ed. *A Republic for the Ages. The United States Capitol and the Political Culture of the Early Republic.* Charlottesville: University Press of Virginia, 1999.

Barber, Lucy G. *Marching on Washington the forging of an American political tradition.* Berkeley: University of California Press, 2002.

Bednar, Michael. *L'Enfant's Legacy. Public Open Places in Washington, D.C.* Baltimore: John Hopkins University Press, 2006.

Berg, Scott W. *Grand Avenues. The Story of the French Visionary who designed Washington, D.C.* New York: Pantheon Press, 2007.

Boime, Albert *The Art of Exclusion.* Washington, DC: The Smithsonian Institution Press, 1990.

Bowling, Kenneth. *The Creation of Washington, D.C. The Idea and Location of the American Capital.* Fairfax, VA: George Mason University Press, 1991.

_____. "A Capital before a Capitol," In Donald R. Kennon, Ed. *A Republic for the Ages. The United States Capitol and the Political Culture of the Early Republic.* Charlottesville: The University Press of Virginia, 1999.

Brown, Glenn. *History of the United States Capitol.* New York: Da Capo Press, 1970. (originally published in 1900 and 1903),

Brownell, Charles. E. "Thomas Jefferson's Architectural Models and the United States Capitol." In Donald Kennon, Ed. *A Republic for the Ages. The United States Capitol and the Political Culture of the Early Republic.* Charlottesville: University Press of Virginia, 1999.

Bryan, John M. *Robert Mills, America's First Architect.* New York: Princeton Architectural Press, 2001.

Burleigh, Nina. *The Stranger and the Statesman: James Smithson, John Quincy Adams and the Making of America's greatest museum, the Smithsonian.* New York: HarperCollins, 2003.

Bushman, Claudia. *America Discovers Columbus.* Hanover, NH: University Press of New England, 1992.

Carmichael, Leonard and J.C. Long. *James Smithson and the Smithsonian Story.* New York: G.P. Putnam's Sons, 1965.

Clark, Allen. "Origins of the Federal City". Reprinted from Records of the Columbia Historical Society v. 35-36 1935.

Cole, Thomas Y. "A Struggle for a Structure. Ainsworth Rand Spofford and a New Building for the Library of Congress." In John Y. Cole and Henry Hope Reed, Eds. *The Library of Congress. The Art and Architecture of the Thoman Jefferson Building.* New York: W.W. Norton & Company, 1997.

Crook, Joseph Mordaunt. *The Greek Revival. Neo-Classical Attitudes in British Architecture 1760-1870.* London: John Murray, 1972.

Daniels, George H. *Science in American Society.* New York: Alfred A. Knopf, 1971

Davis, Timothy. "Beyond the Mall; The Senate Park Commission's Plans for Washington's Park System," In Sue Kohler and Pamela Scott, Eds. *Designing the Nation's Capital. The 1901 Plan for Washington, D.C.* Washington: U.S, Commission for the Fine Arts, 2006.

Dudziak, Mary. *Cold War Civil Rights.* Princeton: Princeton University Press, 2000.

Elkins, Stanley and Eric McKitrick. *The Age of Federalism.* New York: Oxford University Press, 1993.

Ellis, Joseph J. *After the Revolution. Profiles of Early American Culture.* New York: W. W. Norton, 1979.

Evelyn, Douglas. "The Washington Years: The Patent Office. In John Bryan, Ed. *Robert Mills, Architect.* Washington, D.C.: American Institute of Architects, 1989.

Federal Writers" Project. *Washington:City and Capital.* Washington: U.S. Government Printing Office, 1937.

Field, Cynthia. "A Rich Repast of Classicism: Meigs and Classical Sources." In William C. Dickinson, Dean A. Herren and Donald R. Kennon, Eds, *Montgomery Meigs and the Building of the Nation's Capital.* Athens, OH: Ohio University Press, 2001.

Fink, Lois Marie. *A History of the Smithsonian American Art Museum.* Amherst: University of Massachusetts Press, 2007.

Fitzpatrick, Sandra and Maria Goodwin. *The Guide to* **BLACK WASHINGTON.** New York: Hippocrene Books, 1999.

Fryd, Vivien. *Art and Empire. The Politics of Ethnicity in the United States Capitol 1815-1860.* Athens, OH: Ohio University Press, 2001.

Furgurson, Ernest. *Freedom Rising. Washington in the Civil War.* New York: Alfred A. Knopf, 2004.

Gill, Brendan. "The Thomas Jefferson Building." In John Y. Cole and Henry Hope Reed, Eds. *The Library of Congress. The Art and Architecture of the Thoman Jefferson Building.* New York: W.W. Norton & Company, 1997

Gillette, Howard, Ed. *Southern City, National Ambition.* Washington, D.C.: George Washington University. Center for Washington Area Studies, 1985.

_____. *Between Justice and Beauty.* Philadelphia: University of Pennsylvania Press, 2006.

Goldfield, David R. "AnteBellum Washington in Context. The Pursuit of Prosperity and Identity." In Howard Gillette, Ed. *Southern City, National Ambition.* Washington, D.C.: George Washington University. Center for Washington Area Studies, 1985

Goode, James M. *The Outdoor Sculpture of Washington, D.C.* Washington: Smithsonian Institution Press, 1974.

_____. "Thomas U. Walter and the Search for Propriety." In Donald Kennon Ed. *The United States Capitol. Designing and Decorating a National Icon.* Athens, OH: Ohio University Press, 2000 p85-109.

_____. *Capital Losses.* 2nd Ed. Washington: Smithsonian Books, 2003

Green, Constance McLaughlin. *Washington. A History of the Capital.* Princeton: Princeton University Press, 1962.

Hafertepe, Kenneth. *America's Castle: the evolution of the Smithsonian Building and its institution.* Washington, D.C.: Smithsonian Institution Press, 1984.

Hamlin, Talbot. *Greek Revival Architecture in America.* New York: Dover Publications, 1964.

Howe, Daniel Walker. *What Hath God Wrought. The Transformation of America, 1815-1848.* New York: Oxford University Press, 2007.

Hutchinson, Louise. *The Anacostia Story 1608-1930.* Washington, DC: Smithsonian Institution Press, 1977.

Jacob, Kathryn A. *Testament to Union: Civil War Monuments in Washington, D.C.* Baltimore: Johns Hopkins University Press, 1998.

Jones, Stacey, *The Patent Office.* New York: Praeger Publishers, 1971.

Kite, Elizabeth. *L'Enfant and Washington 1791-1792.* Baltimore: Johns Hopkins Press, 1929.

Kohler, Sue *The Commission of Fine Arts. A Brief History 1910-1976.* Washington, DC: Commission of Fine Arts, 1977.

———. *Sixteenth Street Architecture, Volume 2.* Washington D.C.: The Commission of Fine Arts/U.S. Government Printing Office, 1988

Krinsky, Carol. *Gordon Bunshaft of Skidmore, Owings & Merrill.* Cambridge, MA: MIT Press, 21988.

Lee-Thorp, Vincent. *Washington Engineered.* Baltimore, MD: Noble House, 2006.

Lessoff, Alan. *The Nation and City.* Baltimore: Johns Hopkins Press, 1994.

Luce, A. A. and T. E. Jessop, Eds. *The Works of George Berkeley Bishop of Cloyne.* v. VII London: Nelson, 1955 p369-373.

Luria, Sarah. *Capital Speculations. Writing and Building Washington, D.C.* Durham, NH: University of New Hampshire Press, 2006.

Lyons, Linda B. "The Pension Building. Form and Function." In William C. Dickinson, Dean A. Herren and Donald R. Kennon, Eds, *Montgomery Meigs and the Building of the Nation's Capital.* Athens, OH: Ohio University Press, 2001.

McGregor, James H. S. *Washington from the ground up.* Cambridge, MA: Harvard University Press, 2007.

Merk, Frederick. *Manifest Destiny and Mission.* New York: Vintage Books, 1963.

Moore, Charles. *Daniel H. Burnham. Architect. Planner of Cities.* Boston: Houghton Mifflin Company, 1921.

Murray, Freeman. *Emancipation and the Freed in American Sculpture.* Washington, DC: published by the author, 1916.

O'Connor, Francis W. "Symbolism in the Rotunda." In Barbara Wolanin Ed. *Constantino Brumidi; Artist of the Capitol.* Washington, D.C.: U.S. Government Printing Office 1998. p141-156.

Oehser, Paul. *Sons of Science. The Story of the Smithsonian Institution and its Leaders.* New York: Greenwood Press, 1968.

Ostrowski, Carl. *Books, Maps and Politics. Cultural History of the Library of Congress. 1783-1861* Amherst, MA: University of Massachusetts Press, 2004.

Peets, Elbert. "The Background of L'Enfant's Plan." In Paul Spreiregen Ed. *On the Art Of Designing Cities. Selected Essays of Elbert Peets.* Cambridge, MA: MIT Press, 1968 p3-18.

_____. "Critique of L'Enfant's Plan." In Paul Spreiregen Ed. *On the Art Of Designing Cities. Selected Essays of Elbert Peets.* Cambridge, MA: MIT Press, 1968. p37-58.

Penczer, Peter. *The Washington National Mall.* Washington, DC: Oneonta Press, 2007

Peterson, Jon A. "The Senate Park Commission Plan for Washington, D.C. A New Vision for the Capital and the Nation," In Sue Kohler and Pamela Scott, Eds. *Designing the Nation's Capital. The 1901 Plan for Washington, D.C.* Washington: U.S, Commission of Fine Arts, 2006.

Peterson, Merrill. *The Jefferson Image in the American Mind.* New York: Oxford University Press, 1960.

Rawl, Michael J. *Anacostia Flats,* Baltimore: Publish America, 2006

Reed, Henry Hope. "The Decorators." In John Y. Cole and Henry Hope Reed, Eds. *The Library of Congress. The Art and Architecture of the Thomas Jefferson Building.* New York: W.W. Norton & Company, 1997

Reiff, Daniel. *Washington Architecture, 1791-1861 Problems in Development.* Washington, DC: U.S. Commission of Fine Arts, 1971.

Robertson, Charles J. *Temple of Invention. History of a National Landmark.* London: Scale Publications, 2006.

Savage, Kirk. *Standing Soldiers, Kneeling Slaves.* Princeton: University Press, 1997.

Schwartz, Bernard. *A History of the Supreme Court.* New York: Oxford University Press, 1993.

Scott, Pamela and Lee, Antoinette. *Buildings of the District of Columbia.* New York: Oxford University Press, 1993.

Scott, Pamela. "Robert Mills and American Monuments." In John Bryan, Ed. *Robert Mills, Architect.* Washington, D.C.: American Institute of Architects, 1989.

_____. "This Vast Empire": Iconography of the Mall, 1791-1848. In Richard Longstreth, Ed. *The Mall in Washington, 1791-1991.* Washington, DC: National Gallery of Art, 1991.

_____. *Temple of Liberty. Building the Capitol for the New Nation.* New York: Oxford University Press, 1995.

_____. "Power, Civic Virtue, Wisdom, Liberty and the Constitution: Early American Symbols and the United States Capitol." In Donald R. Kennon, Ed. *A Republic for the Ages. The United States Capitol and the Political Culture of the Early Republic.* Charlottesville: The University Press of Virginia, 1999.

_____*Capital Engineers. The U.S. Army Corps of Engineers in the Development of Washington, D.C. 1790-2004.* Alexandria, VA: Office of History, Headquarters, U.S. Army Corps of Engineers, 2005.

_____. "A City designed as a Work of Art": The Emergence of the Senate Park Commission's Monumental Core." In Sue Kohler and Pamela Scott, Eds. *Designing the Nation's Capital. The 1901 Plan for Washington, D.C.* Washington: U.S. Commission of Fine Arts, 2006.

Myer, Daniel. *Bridges and the City of Washington.* Washington, DC: Commission of Fine Arts, 1974

Seale, William. *The President's House: A History.* Washington, DC: The White House Historical Association, 1986.

Secrest, Meryle. *Duveen. A Life in Art.* New York: Knopf, 2004.

Small, Herbert. "Handbook of the New Library of Congress." In John Y. Cole and Henry Hope Reed, Eds. *The Library of Congress. The Art and Architecture of the Thoman Jefferson Building.* New York: W.W. Norton & Company, 1997

Solomon, Burt. T*he Washington Century. Three Families and the Shaping of the Nation's Capital.* New York: William Morrow, 2004.,

Spilsbury, Gail. *Rock Creek Park*. Baltimore: Johns Hopkins Press. 2003.

Spreiregen, Paul. *On the Art of Designing Cities. Selected Essays of Elbert Peets*. Cambridge, MA: MIT Press, 1968.

Stephenson, Richard. *A Plan Wholly New* Washington, D.C.: Library of Congress, 1993.

Stillman, Damie. "From the Ancient Roman Republic to the New American One." In Donald R. Kennon, Ed. *A Republic for the Ages. The United States Capitol and the Political Culture of the Early Republic*. Charlottesville: The University Press of Virginia, 1999.

Taylor, Katherine F. "First Appearances: the Material Setting and Culture of the Early Supreme Court." In Christopher Tomlins Ed., *The United States Supreme Court, The Pursuit of Justice*. Boston: Houghton Mifflin Company, 2005.

Thomas, Christopher. *The Lincoln Memorial in American Life*. Princeton: University Press, 2002.

Timmons, Todd. *Science and Technology in Nineteenth Century America*. Westport, CN: Greenwood Press, 2005.

Tompkins, Sally. *A Quest for Grandeur. Charles Moore and the Federal Triangle*. Washington, DC: Smithsonian Press, 1993.

Ways, Henry C. "Montgomery Meigs and the Washington Aqueduct." In William C. Dickinson, Dean A. Herren and Donald R. Kennon, Eds, *Montgomery Meigs and the Building of the Nation's Capital*. Athens, OH: Ohio University Press, 2001.

Wilson, Richard G. "High Noon on the Mall: Modernism versus Traditionalism, 1910-1970." In Richard Longstreth, Ed, *The Mall in Washington, 1791-1991*. New Haven: Yale University Press 2nd ed., 2002.

Wilson, William H. *The City Beautiful Movement*. Baltimore: Johns Hopkins Press, 1989)

Wolanin, Barbara. "Meigs the Art Patron." In William C. Dickinson, Dean A. Herren and Donald R. Kennon, Eds, *Montgomery Meigs and the Building of the Nation's Capital*. Athens, OH: Ohio University Press, 2001.

_____. *Constantino Brumidi; Artist of the Capitol*. Washington, D.C.: U.S. Government Printing Office 1998.

Wrenn, Tony P. "The American Institute of Architecture convention of 1900; Its Influence on the Senate Park Commission Plan." In Sue Kohler and Pamela Scott, Eds. *Designing the Nation's Capital. The 1901 Plan for Washington, D.C.* Washington: U.S. Commission of Fine Arts, 2006.

Yazawa, Melvin. "Republican Expectations: Revolutionary Ideology." In Donald Kennon, Ed. *A Republic for the Ages. The United States Capitol and the Political Culture of the Early Republic*. Charlottesville: University Press of Virginia, 1999.

Young, James Sterling. *Governmental Community, 1800-1828*. New York: Columbia University Press, 1966.

Dissertations and Articles

Beauchamp, Tanya. "Adolph Cluss: An Architect in Washington during Civil War and Reconstruction" *Records of the Columbia Historical Society.*48:1971-1972 338-357.

Bedini, Silvio. "Benjamin Banneker and the Survey of the District of Columbia." *Records of the Columbia Historical Society* (1969-1970) 7-29.

Borchet, James. "The Rise and Fall of Washington's Inhabited Alleys: 1852-1972." *Records of the Columbia Historical Society*. 48: 1971-1972, pp267-288.

Bowling, Kenneth. "From "Federal Town" to "National Capital"." *Washington History* 14: Spring/Summer 2002 8-25.

Brousseau, Frances. *The Library of Congress, 1873-1897: thee building, its architects, and the politics of nineteenth-century architectural practice.* Ph.D Dissertation University of Delaware, 1998.

Conlin, Michael F. *Science Under Siege: Joseph Henry's Smithsonian, 1846-1865.* Ph.D Dissertation at University of Illinois at Urbana-Champaign, 1999.

Corrigan, Mary Beth. "Imaginary Cruelties? A History of the Slave Trade in the District of Columbia." *Washington History* 13: Fall/Winter 2001-2002 4-27.

Crooms, Lisa. "Race, Education and the District of Columbia: The Meaning and Legacy of "Bolling vs Sharpe." *Washington History* 16: Fall/Winter 2004-2005. 15-23.

diGiacomantonio, William. ""To Sell Their Birthright For a Mess of Potage" The Origins of D.C. Governance and the Organic Act of 1801." *Washington History* 12:2-000-2001. 31-47.

Epstein, Ellen Robinson. "The East and West Wings of the White House," *Records of the Columbia Historical Society.* 49:1971-1972 596-917.

Flack, J. Fitzpatrick. 'Scientific Societies in Gilded Age Washington," *Records of the Columbia Historical Society* (1972-1973) 430-442.

Fitzzpatrick, Michael A. ""A Great Agitation for Business" Black Economic Development in Shaw." *Washington History* 2: Fall/Winter 1990-1991 49-73.

Glassie, Henry. "Victorian Houses." *Records of the Columbia Historical Society* (!963-1964) 310-365.

Goode, James M. "Flying High. The Origin and Design of Washington National Airport." *Washington History* (1989) 1 (20: 4-25.

Grant, Ulysses S. III. "The L'Enfant Plan and its Evolution." *Records of the Columbia Historical Society* (1932) 33-34: 1-24.

Harris, C.M. "Washington's Gamble, L'Enfant's Dream: Politics, Design and the Founding of the National Capital." In *William and Mary Quarterly*, 3rd series, 56: July 1999.

Harrison, Michael. "The "Evil of the Misfit Subdivisions"". *Washington History* 14: Spring/Summer 2002. 27-55.

Hatcher, Ed. "Washington's Nineteenth-Century Citizens" Associations and the Senate Park Commission Plan". *Washington History* 14: Fall/Winter 2002. 71-95.

Helfrich, Kurt. "Modernism for Washington? The Kennedys and the Redesign of Lafayette Square." *Washington History* 8: Spring Summer 1996, 17-37.

Houck, Jeanne B. *Historical Memory and the Mall in Washington, D.C. 1865-1945*. Ph.D. Dissertation. Stanford University, 1993.

Hyde, Richard. *American Acropolis: The west end of the Washington Mall*. Ph.D Disssertation. Graduate Theological Union, 1998.

Johnson, Lonny. *The Lincoln White House*. MA Dissertation, California State University Fresno, 1998.

Lessoff, Alan. "Washington Insider. The Early Career of Charles Moore." *Washington History* 6: Fall/Winter 1994-1995 64-80

Montagna, Dennis Robert. *Henry Merwin Shrady's Ulysses S. Grant Memorial in Washington, D.C.* Ph.D Dissertation. University of Delaware, 1987.

Moore, Charles. "Personalities in Washington Architecture" *Records of the Columbia Historical Society* (1937-1938) 1-16.

Morales-Vasquez, Rubil. "George Washington, the President's House and the Projection of Executive Power." *Washington History*. 16: 36-63, Spring/Summer 2004

Myers, Susan. "Capitol Hill, 1870-1900: The People and Their Homes." *Records of the Columbia Historical Society*(1973-1974) 276-299.

Rabinovitz, Leslie. *The Institutional History of the Hirschhorn Museum and Sculpture Garden, Smithsonian Institution, Washington D.C., 1965-1974.* Master's Thesis University of Southern California, 1996.

Rice, Elaine. *Furnishing Camelot: The restoration of the White House interiors, 1961-1963, and the role of H.F. du Pont.* Ph.D, Dissertation, University of Delaware, 1993

Roe, Donald. "The Dual School System in the District of Columbia, 1862-1954: Origins, Problems, Protests." *Washington History*, 16: Fall/Winter 2004-2005. 17-43.

Sandage, Scott. "A Marble House Divided: The Lincoln Memorial, the Civil Rights Movement, and the Politics of Memory, 1939-1963" *The Journal of American History* 1993.80: 135-167

Tank, Holly. "Dedicated to Art: William Corcoran and the Founding of his Gallery." *Washington History* 17: Fall/Winter 2005 27-51.

Tobin, William Anthony. *In the shadow of the capitol: The transformation of Washington, D.C. and the elaboration of the modern United States nation-state.* Ph.D. Dissertation, Stanford University, 1994.

Urquidi, Roderick. *Art of healing, salve of stone: The Vietnam Veterans Memorial and national reconciliation.* Master's Thesis California State University, 2004.

van Beek, Liam. *Heroes in any other conflict: The Vietnam Veterans Memorial and revisionism in 1980s America.* Masters Thesis Dalhousie University, 2005.

Weigley, Russell. "Captain Meigs and the Artists of the Capitol: Federal Patronage of Art in the 1850s." *Records of the Columbia Historical Society* (1969-1970) 285-305.

INDEX

17214116R00145

Made in the USA
Middletown, DE
12 January 2015